U27G58Y82

VELVET GLOVE

GLOVER MICHAEL

The Velvet Glove

By the same author

Rorke's Drift: A Victorian Epic
Wellington's Army in the Peninsula
The Napoleonic Wars
Warfare from Waterloo to Mons
Warfare in the Age of Bonaparte

The Velvet Glove

The Decline and Fall of Moderation in War

Michael Glover

*'You will observe the Rules of Battle, of course?' the White
Knight remarked, putting on his helmet too.
'I always do,' said the Red Knight, and they began banging
away at each other with such fury that Alice got behind a tree
to be out of the way of the blows.
'I wonder, now, what the Rules of Battle are,' she said to
herself . . .*

Through the Looking Glass, and What
Alice Found There, Lewis Carroll

HODDER AND STOUGHTON
LONDON SYDNEY AUCKLAND TORONTO

British Library Cataloguing in Publication Data

Glover, Michael, *1922–*
   The velvet glove : the decline and fall of
   moderation in war.
   1. War
   I. Title
   355'.02   U27
   ISBN 0-340-26643-0

For
Stephanie and John

Foreword

It is obvious that the only way to do away with the violence and brutality of war is to do away with war itself. Since human wisdom has, from time out of mind, shown itself incapable of achieving this infinitely desirable objective, efforts have always been made to minimise the horrors of war, to make it as tolerable as possible. My intention in this book has been to outline the history of the 'customs and usages of war' as they evolved in Europe and spread to other parts of the world. I have tried to relate the customs and usages to what happens on the battlefield, or wherever else the operations of war have been carried on, rather than to present them as a facet of international law.

I have done my best to avoid moral judgments, partly because I believe them to be out of place in works of history but mainly because I find it impossible to quantify the degrees of turpitude involved in the use of different means of waging war. Who can say that it is more or less ethical to kill with a sword than with a machine gun? It could be said that the machine gun is less moral since it is likely to kill more people but if that line of argument is pursued it must be remembered that the operation which dropped an atomic bomb on Hiroshima was not, in terms of deaths caused or damage done, the most devastating air raid in history. That had been carried out five months earlier using 'conventional' weapons. It resulted, among other things, in women and children being slowly boiled in a river. By comparison the instant incandescence of Hiroshima appears merciful.

Michael Glover
June 1982

Acknowledgments

In writing this book I have had valuable assistance from many people, but I would like particularly to thank Patrick Back, Ronnie Coubrough, David and Joy Curnow, Adrian Digby, Adrian Liddell Hart and Elliott Viney.

As always, I am indebted to the staffs of the London Library and of the Ministry of Defence Whitehall Library and, in particular, to Stephanie Glover.

Most of all, I am grateful for the help and comfort provided by my wife who thought of the original idea and nursed it through to its completion with patience, accuracy, advice and inspiration.

Contents

Prologue

The Pursuit of Moderation

Good faith is essential in war, for without it hostilities could not be terminated with any degree of safety short of the total destruction of one of the contending parties.

Should it be found impossible to count on the loyalty of the adversary there is a great danger of war degenerating into excess and indiscriminate violence.

The Manual of Military Law, 1914 edn

For at least a thousand years mankind has struggled to mitigate the hardships and savagery of war and in the efforts to do so two parallel lines of approach – the practical and the theoretical – have always been discernible. It was the practical line that first became apparent, the line followed by the soldiers and sailors, the actual combatants. In the tenth century a Byzantine general issued an order that,

No plighted troth or armistice must be broken, no ambassador or *parlementaire* harmed, no female captive mishandled; no slaughter of non-combatants is permitted; no cruel or ignominious terms may be imposed on a brave enemy.

The men who did the fighting have always recognised that theirs was a brutal trade and they have been concerned to make it as tolerable as possible. Carnot's dictum that 'War is a violent condition' is undeniable and the duty of fighting men has always been to fight and, if possible, win battles but, provided that 'the loyalty of the adversary can be relied upon, there are many ways in which the discomforts of campaigning can be alleviated without neglecting the main objective – to win the war. Obvious examples are the rescue of shipwrecked sailors and the humane treatment of sick, wounded and prisoners of war. If one side does its best for such unfortunates, it is highly likely that the other will do the same. No sailor can be certain that his ship will not sink and no soldier can be sure that he will not be taken prisoner and, in either eventuality, it is comforting to know that the enemy will do his best for the sufferer. Moreover war, especially before the twentieth century, was a very discontinuous business. Weeks and months could pass

11

without a shot being exchanged and in these intervals of quiet there was no point in disturbing the enemy if he was prepared to leave one's own troops in peace. Why snipe at the enemy's sentries when one's own are equally vulnerable? Why fight a daily skirmish for access to a stream at which cavalry horses can be watered? It is simpler to agree a timetable with the enemy so that both sides can use it in turn. To do so would not affect the outcome of the war and would certainly contribute to the convenience of all concerned. All that was required was a degree of trust between fellow-professionals – 'the loyalty of the adversary'.

There are usually sound military reasons for keeping the level of violence as low as possible. Its indiscriminate use has always been anathema to commanders since excess is the negation of the discipline on which any successful military body must depend. Economy of force, a concept recently much bandied about by politicians, has long been recognised as a military virtue. In any form of human activity it is wasteful to use a steam hammer to crack a nut and nowhere is this more true than in operations of war when it is likely to be both difficult and dangerous to move the steam hammer into position to perform its otiose task. Tactically and logistically it is unsound to use heavy artillery in a situation where small arms will suffice and excess in this form will bring its own punishment. In 1944 thousands of tons of bombs and shells were rained on to the town of Cassino – the bombardment of the abbey raises different questions – and it was reduced to 'a chaotic and almost impassable maze of ruins, rubble and craters'. Unpleasant as this torrent of high explosive must have been to the garrison, it failed to affect their morale and greatly improved their defensive positions. The Commonwealth troops assaulting them found themselves committed to what the *Official History* describes as 'a struggle in a lunatic giant's rubbish heap'. In fact the excessive use of force greatly hindered them and increased their casualties. As with so many factors which tend to mitigate the violence of war, economy of force is primarily dictated by the self-interest of the user.

The theoretical strand in the tradition came from lawyers, clerics and academics who sought to codify the practical set of usages which the combatants were evolving. Although this school of thought was given to quoting precedents from classical antiquity, the theoretical tradition may be said to have emerged with the publication in 1387 of *The Tree of Battles*, the work of a Provençal abbot, Honoré Bonet, who set about bringing together the rules of chivalry in war, a code of conduct which was by then little more than an idealised memory. The most illustrious of his successors was Hugo Grotius whose book, *The Laws of War and Peace*, first appeared in 1625. Grotius, a Dutch jurist and diplomat, described, as he understood them, rules of war which, as was inevitable at the time when the Thirty Years War was getting into its deplorable stride, were far harsher than those outlined by Bonet. Grotius had a flood of followers among whom the most readable, if not the most profound, was the Swiss, Eméric Vattel, who also combined the law with diplomacy. His book, *The Law of Nations* (1758), gave, like Bonet's, an idealised picture even though he was writing at a time when, in practical terms, the customs of war were at their most gentle. One characteristic was shared by all the writers of this theoretical school – none of them had ever seen active service and none of them could comprehend the complications, to say nothing of the confusions, involved in making war. Their attempts to establish a set of dogmatic laws for what is essentially a pragmatic business resemble rules for chess written by men whose only experience lay in playing draughts or checkers.

In the middle of the nineteenth century the two strands in the tradition came momentarily together. When the war between the American states broke out the government in Washington found itself faced with an increasingly bitter civil struggle being fought by armies composed almost wholly of amateurs. It was decided that the customs of civilised warfare should be codified and promulgated and the task was entrusted to an *émigré* Prussian lawyer, Francis Lieber, who as a boy had lived through, and possibly taken part in, the last Napoleonic campaign in Germany. He produced a remarkable synthesis of the usages as they had been recognised over the past hundred years and his conclusions were issued to the Union Army on April 24th, 1863, as *General Order Nº 100*.

As a reconciliation of the dogmatic and pragmatic approaches to controlling war Lieber's code was very successful and from it stemmed the long and continuing series of declarations and conventions which has emerged from Brussels, St Petersburg and, above all, Geneva and The Hague. Many of these agreements, in particular the *Regulations respecting the Laws and Customs of War* which were evolved at The Hague in 1899 and 1907, drew heavily on Lieber's work but the divergence between the two ancestral strains was very apparent. It was inevitably so since *General Order Nº 100* was a practical set of rules which could be enforced, while The Hague Rules were a set of aspirations that had to gain the concurrence of the nations of the world. Their drafting was a triumph for the committees which undertook the task but it was a triumph bought at the price of many compromises and evasions.

Two evasions stand out in The Hague Rules. The first was the

13

omission of any statement on what should be done if the enemy broke the rules. If, for example, the enemy takes to shooting prisoners of war, what redress is open to the innocent belligerent? In practice the only course is to threaten to kill an equal number of prisoners and, if the enemy does not stop the practice and punish the perpetrators, to carry the threat into effect. No lawyer or politician would hesitate to agree that the cold-blooded murder of prisoners should be prohibited but few of them would publicly assert that reprisals in kind should be taken. Such a subject was unsuitable for international agreements and was glossed over. Lieber, who was writing an order which had to be acted upon, could not afford to avoid the issue. His Article 27 laid down that,

> The law of war can no more wholly dispense with retaliation than can the law of nations of which it is a branch . . . A reckless enemy often leaves his opponent no other means of securing himself against the repetition of barbarous outrages.

Equally absent from The Hague Rules was any acknowledgment of the demands of military necessity. To those who took the pragmatic view none of the customs of war could be absolute. If a commander was faced with the choice of breaking the rules or of suffering decisive defeat it was the rules that would have to be disregarded. No commander would be forgiven for sacrificing his country's cause to a nice regard for punctilio. The fact is that commanders are usually under pressure from their political masters to use all means, legal or illegal, to bring war to a speedy victory. Civilians are the last to have much sympathy with the combatants' desire to limit the horrors of war. It was a politician, John Hampden, who enunciated the doctrine that 'The essence of war is violence and moderation in war is imbecility'. Lazare Carnot had abandoned soldiering for politics when he declared, 'One should make war *à l'outrance* or go home.'

Dr Lieber laid down unambiguously that 'To save the country is paramount to all other considerations', and he amplified this by writing,

> Military necessity . . . admits of all direct destruction of life and limb of *armed* enemies, and of other persons whose destruction is incidentally *unavoidable* in the armed contests of war. [Italics as in the original.]

Given that no nation enters a war without intending to win, Lieber's assertion is incontrovertible but it was not to be expected that such realism could be included in an international agreement.

These divergences between *General Order N° 100* and The Hague Rules demonstrate the chasm which lies between the two schools of thought. The dogmatic school believed that they could lay down laws for war as absolute as the Ten Commandments or the *Code Napoléon*. The pragmatists, those who had to do the fighting, knew that this was impossible and, after the emergence of The Hague Rules, every major power found it necessary to issue to its armed forces an explanatory statement which tried to reconcile the Rules to the demands of actual warfare. A comparison between the German *Kriegsbrauch im Landkriege*, the usages of war on land, and its British equivalent, 'The Laws and Usages of War on Land', which was included in the *Manual of Military Law*, shows how wide a variation of interpretation was possible.

Nevertheless the dogmatists believed that they had achieved a great triumph. They had succeeded in taming war and in 1908 the Chichele Professor of International Law and Diplomacy at Oxford, a prolific writer on the subject, declared that,

> The conduct of war is governed by certain rules commonly spoken of as 'the laws of war', which are recognized as binding by all civilized nations.

A decade later such confident optimism appeared absurd. The First World War left The Hague Rules in tatters and there was no belligerent nation which could honestly assert that it had not infringed many of them. A new crop of agreements concluded before 1939 fared no better in the Second World War.

This book sets out to look at the way in which the pursuit of moderation in war originated, flourished, declined and finally perished in the fireball above Hiroshima, the epitome of indiscriminate violence. It aims to treat the subject *de bas en haut*, to look at the laws and customs of war from the point of view of the men and women on the battlefield, the people who, in the last analysis, decide how much moderation there shall be in war.

PART ONE

TO START A WAR

There's no point in going to war if we're not going to win it.
Anthony Powell, *The Kindly Ones*

1

Declaration

War is a detestable business and no one but a psychopath would indulge in it without the most urgent necessity. What constitutes a sufficient degree of necessity has been a subject of controversy over the centuries but it is indisputable that, in all periods of history, humane and responsible men and women (and others who were neither humane nor responsible) have seen no alternative to committing their countries to war.

Even given the necessity for war the civilised conscience requires some way in which it can reconcile the licensing of mass slaughter with the Christian ethic. Somehow a church which preaches the virtue of turning the other cheek has to find a way of sanctioning the use of regulated violence, to say at the same time, 'Peace and goodwill towards men' and 'It is lawful for Christian men, at the command of the magistrates, to wear swords, and serve in the wars'.

It did not take long for ingenious jurists to go back to classical precedents and to conjure up the concept of 'just war'. In the Roman republic no hostilities could be undertaken unless the *Collegium Fetiale* had resolved that the projected war was just. This, according to Cicero, meant that it had been formally declared and that there was some good reason for fighting. The good reasons he suggested were repelling an invader, avenging a wrong or recovering something that had been unlawfully seized.

The idea of a just war was seized upon by the medieval church, which added its own extension that any war against infidels or heretics was by definition just. St Thomas Aquinas allowed any war to be just if the intentions of the participants were good and added to Cicero's permissible reasons the intention to encourage the right and to avert evil. A century later Abbot Bonet was making war sound virtuous by pointing out that the Almighty had commanded Joshua to do battle with his enemies. He added, 'The aim of war is to wrest peace, tranquillity and reasonableness from him who refuses to acknowledge his wrongdoing.'

Ethical sanction was not the only advantage accruing to those whose wars were just. The justice of one's cause gave the right to plunder the enemy since, by definition, the enemy's cause must be

19

unjust and the unjust had no right to property. Naturally no belligerent would admit that he was fighting unjustly and no state was so devoid of propagandists that some justification could not be adduced for their aggression. Thus all wars, provided that they were formally declared, were, at least in theory, fought to encourage the right and to avert evil. Machiavelli, always a realist, summed up the position in the early sixteenth century by asserting that 'War is just when it is necessary'.

A hundred years later Hugo Grotius said much the same thing in more cumbrous language, 'The consent of nations admits that all wars declared by sovereign authority on both sides are to be judged lawful in their external effects.'

By the eighteenth century Vattel reduced the whole concept to absurdity by laying down that 'Regular war . . . is to be accounted just on both sides.' Since among the reasons he believed permissible to undertake war was the averting of a danger which seems to threaten – such as the Polish attack on Germany in 1939 – it is clear that he would have agreed with Hitler who, on August 22nd, 1939, remarked, 'In starting . . . war, it is not right that matters but victory.'

Vattel did not even consider a formal declaration essential, particularly if the adversary was not one of the 'polished nations of Europe'.

If the nation on whom we have determined to make war will not admit any minister or herald to declare it – whatever the custom may otherwise be, we may content ourselves with publishing the declaration within our own territories or on the frontier; and if that declaration does not come to the knowledge of that nation before hostilities, she can only blame herself. The Turks imprison and maltreat even the ambassadors of those powers with whom they are determined to come to a rupture: it would be a perilous undertaking for a herald to go and declare war against them in their own country. Their savage disposition therefore supersedes the necessity of sending one.

For him a declaration of war was the last action in the diplomatic struggle to preserve peace, 'as a further effort to terminate the difference without the effusion of blood, by making use of the principle of fear to bring the enemy to more equitable sentiments'. If that effort was unsuccessful he saw no need to 'give the enemy time to prepare for an unjust defence'.

The declaration need not be made until the army has reached the frontiers; it is even lawful to delay it until we have entered the enemy territories, and there possessed ourselves of an advantageous post; it must, however, precede the commission of any act of hostility.

Vattel's view was a long way from the law which, according to Froissart, obtained in the Holy Roman Empire whereby three days' notice had to be given before a declaration became effective. The eighteenth century seems to have agreed with him and in 1788 the German jurist von Martens summarised the position as being that,

> The universal law of nations acknowledges no general obligation of making a declaration of war to the enemy previous to a commencement of hostilities. Many of the ancient nations looked on such a declaration as essential, and it was practised in Europe until the seventeenth century: but nowadays, nations content themselves with publishing a declaration of war through their dominions, and explaining their motives to other powers in writing.

Five years after this was written the young French republic followed the line that von Martens had suggested. In February 1793 the National Convention debated and passed a long motion which set out twelve complaints against Britain and Holland. Some of the complaints were untrue, others, such as the assertion that Parliament had forbidden the circulation of *assignats*, the worthless French banknotes, in England, were merely irrelevant. The motion, however, ended,

> The National Assembly declares in the name of the French Nation that, considering the multiple acts of hostility and aggression of the above-mentioned powers, the French Nation is at war with the King of England and the Stadtholder of the United Provinces.

Since the British ambassador and his staff had already left Paris, the only way in which Britain could learn that they were at war with France was from the French newspapers when, in the fullness of time, they percolated across the Channel.

Such declarations *in pectore* frequently make it difficult to know when any given war actually began. This was certainly the case with the war which broke out between France and Britain in 1803, an uncertainty which, as will be seen (pp. 34–36), caused much inconvenience to many people. Another case is that of the Franco–Prussian War. Many historians assert that it started on July 15th, 1870 but it was not until the following day that the Minister for Foreign Affairs in Paris wrote to the *chargé d'affaires* in Berlin that,

> At this moment, when hostilities between Prussia and ourselves are imminent, I have to send you the last instructions of the Imperial Government. You should send to the Cabinet in Berlin a declaration conforming to the enclosed draft [an explanation of the French view of the Hohenzollern candidature, which was being circulated to all French diplomatic missions], by which you will notify them that we consider ourselves at war with their country. You will ask for your passports.

This declaration was not handed to the Prussian government until July 19th.

Some declarations had more formality than substance. When Sweden, under pressure from France and Russia, declared war on Britain in 1809 the written declaration was accompanied by a confidential note saying that 'it was by no means the intention of the Swedish government to follow up its declaration by any act of hostility'. The reverse was true of the letter sent by the Austrian commander, the Archduke Charles, in the same year to Marshal Lefebvre, commanding the Bavarian army.

> In conformity with the declaration made by His Imperial Majesty to the Emperor Napoleon [which could scarcely have reached Paris], I hereby apprise the General in Chief of the French army that I have orders to advance with my troops and treat as enemies all who oppose me.

When Louis XIII of France declared war on Spain in May 1635, he sent a herald to proclaim the fact in the Grand'Place of Brussels, then a Spanish possession. The words used by the herald have been lost but when, thirty-seven years later, Louis XIV went to war with Holland his proclamation, which seems to have been designed for home consumption, read,

> His Majesty hath declared, as he does now declare, that he has determined and resolved to make war against the States General of the United Provinces, both by sea and land; and so consequently commands all his servants to fall upon the Hollanders,

and forbids them for the future to have any commerce, communication or correspondence with them upon pain of death.

This form of words does not greatly differ from that used two centuries later by Japan when she made war on China in 1895.

> We, by the Grace of Heaven, Emperor of Japan, seated on a throne occupied by the same dynasty from time immemorial, do hereby make proclamation to all our loyal and brave subjects, as follows.
>
> We hereby declare war against China, and we command each and all our competent authorities, in obedience to our wish and with a view to the attainment of our national aims, to carry on hostilities by sea and on land, with all the means at their disposal, consistently with the Law of Nations.

Despite the ritual obeisance to international law, this is scarcely a convincing document since the only stated cause of the war is the attainment of undefined national aims. The Chinese counter-declaration is far more impressive both in the richness of its language and in its propaganda value.

> As Japan has violated the treaties and not observed international law, and is running rampant with her false and treacherous actions, commencing hostilities herself and laying herself open to condemnation by the various Powers at large, we therefore desire to make it known to the world that we have always followed the path of philanthropy throughout the whole complications while the Wojên [Japanese], on the other hand, have broken all the laws of nations and treaties, which it passes our patience to bear with. Hence we command Li-Hung Chang to give strict orders to our armies to hasten with all speed to root the Wojên out of their lairs. He is to send successive armies of valiant men to Korea in order to save the Koreans from the dust of bondage. We also command the Manchu generals, viceroys and governors of maritime provinces, as well as the commanders in chief of the various armies, to prepare for war and to make every effort to fire on the Wojên ships if they come to our ports, and utterly destroy them. We exhort our generals to refrain from the least laxity in obeying our commands in order to avoid severe punishment at our hands.
>
> Let all know this edict as if addressed to themselves individually. Respect this!

Next time Japan went to war she dispensed with the formality of a declaration and in February 1904, within a few hours of the breaking off of diplomatic relations at St Petersburg, torpedo boats tore out of the darkness into the harbour of Port Arthur where the unsuspecting Russian Pacific fleet lay, fully illuminated, at anchor. The attack was not as devastating as Admiral Togo had planned but two battleships and a cruiser were disabled and the Russians never regained the initiative that they had lost that night.

Such an unheralded attack was not unprecedented. There was the action of Sweden which, in 1634, had attacked Denmark and overran the whole country. It was not until a year later that the Swedes condescended to supply so much as an explanation. Japan's behaviour, however, shocked the polite nations and led to The Hague *Convention relative to the Opening of Hostilities* (1909).

I. The Contracting Powers recognize that hostilities between them must not commence without a previous and explicit warning in the form of either a declaration of war, giving reasons, or an ultimatum with a conditional declaration of war.
II. The existence of a state of war must be notified to the neutral Powers without delay, and shall not be held to affect them until after the receipt of notification, which may, however, be given by telegraph. Nevertheless neutral Powers may not rely on the absence of notification if it be established beyond doubt that they were in fact aware of the existence of a state of war.

Japan signed this Convention, although Bulgaria, Greece, Italy, Romania, Serbia, Spain and Turkey refused to do so, and in 1914 Japan went through the formality of declaring war on Germany, possibly because there were insufficient German forces in her vicinity to make a surprise attack worthwhile. In 1931, when she invaded Manchuria, and in 1937, when she invaded China proper Japan neither declared war nor notified the neutrals. Climactically on December 7th, 1941 she struck simultaneously at Hawaii, Malaya, Hong Kong and the Philippines. The attack at Pearl Harbour, a modernised version of the assault on Port Arthur, achieved a success beyond the wildest dreams of Admiral Togo and shattered the American Pacific Fleet.

Joseph C. Grew, the U.S. ambassador to Tokyo, recorded in his diary for December 8th (the dates are confusing because Tokyo and Hawaii are on different sides on the International Date Line).

At 7 a.m. I was awakened by a telephone call from Kase [interpreter at the Foreign Ministry], who asked me to come and see the Minister as soon as possible . . . I hurriedly dressed and got to the official residence at about 7.30 . . . Tojo [was] grim and formal. He made a brief statement and then handed me a memorandum of thirteen paragraphs, dated December 8, which he said had been communicated by Admiral Nomura [Japanese ambassador at Washington] to the Secretary of State today, breaking off the conversations. The final paragraph read,

'The Japanese Government regrets having to notify hereby the American Government that, in view of their attitude, it cannot but consider that it is impossible to reach an agreement through further negotiations.'

Tojo said that he had seen the Emperor (at 3 a.m., I understand) and that the memorandum constituted the reply to the President's message. He made me a little speech thanking me for my cooperation during the conversations and came downstairs to see me off at the door. Not a word was said about Pearl Harbor [where the attack had started some four hours earlier]. On returning to the Embassy I shaved and breakfasted and then sent off my report to the [State Department] but it probably did not get through. Shortly afterwards we heard that Imperial Headquarters had announced that Japan was in armed conflict with the United States and Great Britain. This was contained in a Yomiuro [news agency] statement issued early that morning. At first it was difficult to believe, although it had all the markings of officialdom and later in the morning Ohno of the Foreign Office called on [the First Secretary] and read to him, his hands trembling, the official announcement that armed conflict had commenced. Soon afterwards the Embassy gates were closed.

It is fair to add that Grew believed that Tojo 'had no prior knowledge that an act of war was to be committed' and that the Japanese had prepared a handsome declaration of war against both the U.S.A. and Britain. This had been written on heavy paper which bore the sixteen-petalled chrysanthemum and was embossed with the imperial seal before being signed by the emperor and all his cabinet. This exquisite document declared that, 'It has been truly unavoidable, and far from Our Wishes that Our Empire has been brought to cross swords with America and Britain.' It was never delivered but the text was read over the radio after the initial attacks had been launched.

The Americans, however, continued to be legally at peace until Congress had voted for war and the British insisted on the old-fashioned formalities. On December 8th a letter on Foreign Office

25

writing paper was delivered to the Japanese ambassador in London.

> Sir,
> On the evening of December 7th His Majesty's Government in the United Kingdom learned that Japanese forces without previous warning either in the form of a declaration of war or an ultimatum with a conditional declaration of war had attempted a landing on the coast of Malaya and had bombed Singapore and Hong Kong. In view of these wanton acts of unprovoked aggression committed in flagrant violation of International Law and particularly of Article I of the Third Hague Convention relative to the opening of hostilities, to which both Japan and the United Kingdom are parties, His Majesty's Ambassador at Tokyo has been instructed to inform the Imperial Japanese Government in the name of His Majesty's Government in the United Kingdom that a state of war exists between our two countries. I have the honour to be, with high consideration,
> Sir,
>> Your obedient servant,
>> Winston S. Churchill.

This was, in the words of The Hague Convention a 'declaration of war, giving reasons'. On the two occasions that Britain has declared war on Germany she proceeded by the alternative method of 'an ultimatum with a conditional declaration'. In 1914 the ultimatum was delivered in two stages. At 9.30 a.m. on August 4th the Foreign Secretary cabled instructing the ambassador at Berlin to protest against the German demand to march through Belgium.

> His Majesty's Government are bound to protest against this violation of a treaty to which Germany is a party in common with themselves, and must request an assurance that the demand made upon Belgium will not be proceeded with, and that her neutrality will be respected by Germany. You should ask for an immediate reply.

Four and a half hours later, at 2 p.m., no reply having been received, a second cable was sent.

> We hear that Germany has addressed note to Belgian Minister for Foreign Affairs stating that German Government will be compelled to carry out, if necessary by force of arms, the

measures considered indispensable. We are also informed that Belgian territory has been violated at Gemmenich. In these circumstances, and in view of the fact that Germany declined to give the same assurance respecting Belgium as France gave last week in reply to our request made simultaneously at Berlin and Paris, we must repeat this request, and ask that a satisfactory reply to it and to my telegram [of 9.30 a.m., see above] be received here by 12 o'clock tonight. If not you are instructed to ask for your passports and to say that His Majesty's Government feel bound to take all steps in their power to uphold the neutrality of Belgium and the observance of a Treaty to which Germany is as much a party as ourselves.

This second telegram was the actual ultimatum and it is noticeable that it uses neither the word 'war' nor any of its synonyms. While the ambassador was told to ask for his passports, the *Guide to Diplomatic Practice* specifically states that this step does not necessarily imply war. As to the threat that Britain would take 'all steps in their power', it might, according to precedent, mean nothing more than sending out invitations to a conference. Nor did the telegram make clear whether the ultimatum was due to expire at midnight by London time or by Berlin time, which was an hour earlier.

In the period of waiting for the time limit to expire a touch of black humour was added by a message from the Admiralty, who told the Foreign Office that they had intercepted a German wireless message to the effect that Germany had declared war on Britain. This caused a furious burst of activity when a new letter to the German ambassador had to be drafted and typed, beginning, 'The German Empire having declared war on Great Britain . . .' Scarcely had this, and the ambassador's passports, been delivered to the embassy by hand when the Admiralty reported that their previous information had been wrongly decyphered. The original letter was retyped and the junior Foreign Office clerk on duty, Harold Nicolson, was given the unenviable task of going to the embassy and substituting the correct letter. Fortunately the ambassador, who received Nicolson in pyjamas, had not bothered to read the original. The formal declaration was not made until a quarter past midnight on August 5th, when a statement was issued by the Foreign Office to the *London Gazette*.

Owing to the summary rejection by the German Government of the request made by His Majesty's Government for assurances that the neutrality of Belgium will be respected, His Majesty's

Government have declared to the German Government that a state of war exists between Great Britain and Germany as from 11 p.m. on the 4th of August.

Much the same procedure was followed in 1939. On September 1st, a message 'not to be considered as an ultimatum' was sent to Berlin demanding that the Germans withdraw their troops from Poland. This produced no response and the government decided to instruct their ambassador to arrange a meeting with the German Foreign Minister at 9 a.m. on September 3rd, so that he could hand him a letter. Since the ambassador did not receive this telegram until 4 a.m. that morning he had great difficulty in arranging the meeting and eventually had to be content with giving the letter to the minister's interpreter. Unlike the ultimatum of 1914, that of 1939 was categorical in stating that,

Unless satisfactory assurances were received by His Majesty's Government before 11 a.m. of the suspension of all aggressive action against Poland and of the withdrawal of German forces from that country, a state of war would exist between our two countries from that hour.

To make matters simpler the existence of British Summer Time meant that 11 a.m. was at the same time in London and Berlin. In the event no German answer was forthcoming but at 11.30 a.m. the ambassador was summoned to see von Ribbentrop who handed him a long memorandum outlining the German case against Poland. By that time the war had been in progress for half an hour and the air-raid sirens had sounded in London.

There is a curious sidelight on the British declaration in 1939. Printed letters had been prepared so that, as soon as hostilities commenced, all departments of state could be informed. The wording, with alternatives, began,

I am directed by the Prime Minister to inform you
that His Majesty's Government have decided
that war has broken out between His Majesty's
to declare war against
Government and
. . . . . with effect from . . .

In the event both alternatives were struck out and replaced by the words 'that a state of war exists between the United Kingdom and Germany'. This may have been done to avoid the kind of misunderstanding that caused Harold Nicolson so much embarrassment in 1914.

The Italian Foreign Minister at the time, Mussolini's son-in-law Count Ciano, preferred issuing declarations of war in person. When he made the announcement to the British ambassador in June 1940,

> Sir Percy Lorraine was laconic and inscrutable. He received my communication without batting an eyelid or changing colour. He confined himself to writing the exact formula used by me and asked me if he was to consider it as advanced warning or as a general declaration. Learning that it was the latter, he withdrew with dignity and courtesy.

Shortly afterwards Mussolini, in a broadcast speech, 'formally' declared war on France and Britain from midnight that night.

Ciano had more difficulty a year later when he wished to declare war on the U.S.S.R., as he found that, at the crucial moment, the Russian ambassador had taken his whole staff bathing at Fregene. Later in 1941, on December 11th, he sent for the American *chargé d'affaires*, a 'somewhat timid' gentleman who arrived under the impression that Ciano wanted to discuss the forthcoming visit of some journalists. When a declaration of war was read to him he turned pale and said, 'This is very tragic.'

29

2

Clearing for Action

The occasion on which international law operates at its best is when, on the outbreak of war, diplomats have to be repatriated. Not only is there a strong element of reciprocity in the operation but it is one in which each ministry of foreign affairs is on trial before their *chers collègues ennemis*. It is the last sacrifice on the altar of protocol. Technically a belligerent is not obliged to arrange that the diplomats of his adversary have safe conduct beyond the frontier of the state to which they are accredited and if they should stray into the territory of another belligerent they do so at their own risk. In March 1744, soon after France declared war on Britain, the French ambassador to the Emperor at Frankfurt was posted to Berlin and on his way strayed into Hanoverian territory at Elbingerode. Perhaps because he was accompanied by his brother, Marshal Bellisle, both men were arrested and sent to England. The French claimed that they were prisoners of war and offered to ransom them. The British considered them as prisoners of state and detained them, in most agreeable circumstances, at Windsor Castle for five months before releasing them as an act of royal grace. To avoid any recurrence of such an incident the Americans, when they expelled the German ambassador in February 1917, went to considerable trouble to obtain from the British a safe-conduct for the ship in which he was sailing. The British readily agreed but took the precaution of taking the ship, the Danish liner *Frederick VIII*, into Halifax, Nova Scotia, and subjecting it to a search that lasted twelve days including, it was said, playing all the gramophone records in the baggage of the embassy staff in case they should contain messages in code. That done, Ambassador Bernsdorff was permitted to go home in peace.

It was only in the middle of the nineteenth century that it became the custom for all the embassy staff to be sent home. Usually a diplomatic agent remained to deal with immediate business. During the short period in which Prussia was at war with Britain in 1806–07, George Jackson stayed with the Prussian government as *chargé d'affaires* and throughout the war of 1812 there was an American diplomatic agent in London. Napoleon was considered to be particularly ill-mannered when he refused to allow a British diplomat to reside in Paris between 1803 and 1814; there had been an official agent there during most of the revolutionary war. When the Franco–Prussian War broke out the French were expecting to leave a staff at their embassy in Berlin. On July 19th, 1870 their *chargé d'affaires* called on Bismarck to inform him that whereas the French community in Prussia was being left under the protection of the British embassy it was proposed that each side should leave their head of chancery *en poste*. Bismarck refused, saying that only the caretaker, who was a Prussian, and the *huissier*, an Alsatian – *'Alors il est Allemand' s'écria M. de Bismarck'* – could remain. The Military Attaché was ordered to leave Berlin that very evening and the rest on the following day. As the *chargé* reported,

> I left Berlin on the evening of 20 July with all the embassy staff. Our departure gave rise to no hostile demonstrations since protective measures had already been taken and the President of Police, M. de Wurmb, came in person to supervise them.

1870 seems to have been the first occasion on which neutral powers were formally appointed to protect enemy nationals. While the French asked the British to undertake this task, the Prussians in France were cared for by the Americans. In the next major war such activities took up much American diplomatic time. In August 1914 the U.S. minister in Brussels took over the Austrian, British, German and Russian legations and their minister described the scene at the German legation:

> Herr von Below had a *procès-verbale* already prepared, but I preferred mine and we signed and sealed that. Then in that room of gloomy oak, the two white-haired German functionaries – old Gradowsky, *conseiller-aulique*, and another, bureaucratic and formal, bearing a tall white candle and a long stick of red sealing wax, proceeded slowly and solemnly round the room, sealing the oaken cupboards where the archives were. We stood in silence while this was being done. Then the strained farewells.

The Germans soon came to Brussels and reclaimed their archives but the British, French and Russian files remained safe. The Germans even respected the British archives in Belgrade when they had them in their power. When the Austrians had opened fire on the city in July 1914 the British legation was exposed to the shelling and was hit several times. The *chargé d'affaires* so little expected the storm that was soon to burst over Europe that he placed his archives for safety in the German legation. When frantic

31

telegrams from London ordered him to remove and burn them, the Germans happily let them go.

At much the same time Prince Lichnowsky, German ambassador at London, was setting off for home in considerable style.

> Our departure was put through in a thoroughly dignified way. The King had previously sent his equerry, Sir E. Ponsonby, to express his regret that I was leaving and that he could not see me himself . . . A special train took us to Harwich. There a guard of honour was drawn up for me. I was treated like a departing sovereign.

The British ambassador at Berlin was having a less pleasant time.

> The small force of police which had been sent to guard the embassy was soon overpowered, and the attitude of the mob became more threatening. We took no notice as long as it was confined to noise, but when the crash of glass and the landing of stones in the drawing room where we were all sitting warned us that the situation was getting unpleasant, I telephoned the Foreign Office an account of what was going on. Herr von Jagow [Minister of Foreign Affairs] at once informed the chief of police and an adequate force of mounted police, sent with great promptness, very soon cleared the street.
>
> After order had been restored, Herr von Jagow came to see me and expressed heartfelt regrets at what had occurred. He said that the behaviour of his countrymen had made him more ashamed than he had words to express. It was an indelible stain on the reputation of Berlin.
>
> On the following morning, the 5th of August, the Emperor sent one of his aides-de-camp to me with the following message. 'The Emperor has charged me to express his regret for the occurrences of last night, but to tell you at the same time that you will gather from these occurrences an idea of the feelings of his people respecting the action of Great Britain in joining with other nations against her old ally of Waterloo.'

There were no more demonstrations and the whole staff of the embassy were sent off in a special train to the Dutch frontier accompanied by a colonel of the Prussian Guard.

The French ambassador to Berlin at that time had a less comfortable journey, since the Germans insisted that he must go by way of Denmark on a train that also carried the staff of the Russian embassy.

I was accompanied by Major von Rheinbaden of the Alexandra Regiment of the Guard and by a police officer. In the neighbourhood of the Kiel Canal soldiers entered our carriages. The windows were shut and the curtains pulled down; each of us had to remain isolated in his compartment and was forbidden to get up or touch his baggage. A soldier stood in the corridor in front of the door of each compartment, which was kept open, revolver in hand and finger on the trigger. The Russian *chargé d'affaires*, the women and children and everyone was subjected to this treatment. At the last German station I thought that our troubles were over when Major von Rheinbaden came, rather embarrassed, to inform me that we could not proceed to the Danish frontier if I did not pay the cost of the train. I expressed my astonishment that I had not been forewarned of this. I offered to pay by cheque on one òf the largest Berlin banks. This facility was refused to me. With the help of my companions I was able to collect in gold the sum required at once, which amounted to 3,611 marks 75 pfennigs.

It can only be supposed that this unmannerly demand for payment in cash arose from some local misunderstanding since the amount was later refunded to the French Foreign Office through the Spanish ambassador in Paris.

There were no demonstrations when the British ambassador left Berlin in 1939. A small crowd gathered to see the embassy staff leave but 'it was an absolutely silent crowd, and if there was hatred or hostility in their hearts they gave no sign of it'. The only hitch occurred when the special train that had been provided stopped at the last station before the Dutch frontier. The Germans had suddenly developed suspicions that their staff in London might be detained and would not send the train on before the ship bearing their own ambassador had entered Dutch territorial waters. 'There was no discomfort or discourtesy about it, as there was fortunately a restaurant car attached to our train.'

While the diplomats expected to go home, other civilians would, until recent times, expect to stay in an enemy country if they normally resided there. The eighteenth-century view was that war was a business for professionals and it followed that non-combatants should get on with their usual occupations. The internment of civilians would have been regarded as a barbarous practice, although in 1746 the French arrested the entire British colony in Paris. This unusual act came shortly after the arrival of news of the Young Pretender's defeat at Culloden, two years after war had been declared between the two countries. The intention seems to have been to hold the prisoners as hostages for the Prince's life and, although this was never stated, all were released, with apologies, as soon as it was known that he was safe.

According to Eméric Vattel, writing twelve years after the Paris incident,

> The Sovereign declaring war can neither detain the persons nor the property of those subjects of the enemy who are within his dominions at the time of the declaration. They came to his country under the public faith. By permitting them to enter and reside in his territory, he tacitly promised them full liberty and security for their return. He is therefore bound to allow them a reasonable time for withdrawing with their effects.

A number of treaties existed which defined the time for which an 'enemy alien' could expect to remain undisturbed. Since 1667 it had been agreed that, if England and Holland should go to war, their respective nationals must be left in peace for six months, while a similar treaty between France and Holland set the period at nine months. In 1739 Britain and Russia agreed on a year and Denmark had treaties with both Sicily and Genoa allowing for a two-year period of grace. In each case, however, these were minimum periods and the custom, according to Martens, was 'to let the subjects of an enemy remain during the whole course of the war, or so long as they live peaceably and quietly'. It was not impossible for travellers to visit enemy countries. In 1762, when Britain and France had been at war for six years, Laurence Sterne, without even the formality of obtaining a passport, went to Paris where he was enthusiastically received not only in the *salons* of the capital but by the Duc de Choiseul, chief minister to Louis XV. At the end of the century John Cleaver Banks was authorised to study Sanskrit manuscripts at the *Bibliothèque Nationale* despite the long-running war.

This civilised limitation of the effects of war was dealt a severe blow by the French government on May 23rd, 1803.

> St Cloud, 2nd Prairial, Année XI
> All the English enrolled in the Militia from the age of 18 to 60, holding commissions from his Britannic Majesty, who are in France, shall be made Prisoners of War, to answer for the Citizens of the Republic who have been arrested by the vessels or subjects of his Britannic Majesty before the declaration of war.

The Ministers, each as far as concerns him, are charged with the execution of this present decree.
   Bonaparte, First Consul

On the face of it this decree was sufficiently plausible. It was not unreasonable, though in the past it would have been unusual, to detain those who held military or naval commissions and who, on their return, would take part in the fighting. What happened, however, was that every British male within the age limits (and some outside them) was taken into custody and of the eight hundred so detained only sixty had any kind of commission. Fourteen of them were naval or marine officers, four of them surgeons, and the remaining forty held military commissions of some kind in the regular army, the East India Company's forces or the militia. Scarcely half a dozen of them had active commissions (although two held unrevoked French commissions). One officer had been on half pay for twenty years and another, who had been given a commission in a regiment which was disbanded before it was formed, had never done a day's duty.

As for the rest, who held no commission, Bonaparte argued that, although there was no conscription for Britain's regular army, every British male was liable, between the ages of sixteen and sixty, to service in the militia. This was legally correct, though wrong in practice, but would have been more convincing if eighteen clergymen, who were specifically exempt from militia service, had not been detained. It may be added that no question arose of releasing those who reached the upper age limit of sixty.

Nor was the reason for this unprecedented arrest – the allegation that 'Citizens of the Republic . . . have been arrested by the ships of his Britannic Majesty before the declaration of war' – true. It is, as has been noted, very difficult to decide the exact date on which the Napoleonic War started but there can be no doubt that the act complained of by Bonaparte occurred when war was under way. On April 26th the British ambassador, Lord Wentworth, had presented a conditional ultimatum stating that, unless certain demands were agreed, he would set out for home in seven days. Bonaparte and Talleyrand succeeded in delaying him until May 12th, a week after, on their orders, the French ambassador in London had asked for his passports. On May 13th, the day after Wentworth left, Bonaparte issued an order to detain all British ships in Dutch, Genoese and Tuscan (but not French) ports. By May 16th Wentworth had reached England and Britain published an Order in Council authorising the issue of Letters of Marque under which French ships could be captured by privateers and also authorising the detention of all Batavian (Dutch) ships in British ports. It is generally held that the start of the war dates from this day, May 16th, but it is possible to argue that it did not start until May 18th, when George III sent down to Parliament a long message (which made no reference to war) explaining how the war had come about. This, however, is irrelevant since the declaration of war is an exercise of the Royal Prerogative and cannot be done by Parliament. Certainly no member of Parliament was by then in any doubt that the war was in progress.

The first act of the hostilities took place on that day when the 36-gun frigate *Doris* attacked and captured the smaller French warship *L'Affronteur* (14) off Ushant. Bonaparte, however, made no complaint about this action. He based his case on an incident on the following day, May 19th, when French coastal shipping was attacked off Brest. According to the French account,

> While it was still believed in Paris that negotiations were still in progress, it was learned by telegraph from the Maritime Prefect of Brest that the English had seized two merchant ships in the bay of Audierne.

If negotiations were still in progress it is hard to explain why the French ambassador in London had left thirteen days earlier and the British ambassador had been gone for a week. Even harder to explain would be why the French had ordered the seizure of British ships six days before the incident off Audierne. It is quite clear that Paris was fully aware that war had broken out and needed a pretext to carry out a planned operation against inoffensive civilians. It was at least sufficient to keep many hundreds of *détenus* penned up for eleven years. It should be added, however, that Bonaparte did not disregard all the established conventions about civilians. In 1807 the Napoleon Prize of the *Institut de France* was awarded to Sir Humphry Davy and five years later that distinguished natural philosopher was given a passport to cross France and study in French-dominated Italy.

The nineteenth century saw a return to pre-Napoleonic practices in this field. During the Crimean War Russian civilians were allowed to live undisturbed in Britain and France and, although some allied subjects were expelled from the naval bases of Kronstadt, Odessa and Sebastopol, most continued to reside in Russia. In the Franco–Prussian War the 2,000 Frenchmen living in Germany were allowed to remain in their homes and occupations and, when war was declared, the *Journal Officiel* announced that no action would be taken against German civilians in France. The situation changed when the war started to go badly for the French army and on August 12th, 1870 it was announced that, to protect them from the anger of the populace, any German who could not be vouched for by a respectable citizen would be deported. Little action seems to have been taken after this decision and, when Paris was about to be invested, the governor, General Trochu, decreed that all Germans must leave the *Département* of Seine. Many were unable to do so in the time available and 2,000 of them lived through the siege, being dependent on the U.S. embassy for their food.

Although U.S. citizens were deported from Cuba during the Spanish–American War, no other civilians were disturbed in either the United States or Spain and her colonies. Much the same practice was followed in the Russo–Japanese War of 1904 in which no action was taken against civilians except the expulsion of the Japanese who lived in the naval base of Vladivostock. When the South African War of 1899 broke out, both the Transvaal and the Orange Free State decreed the expulsion of all British nationals but only in Johannesburg was any action taken. Even there many *uitlanders* who had business interests to protect were allowed to stay until, in April 1900, a powder factory blew up. All the British were then expelled from the city.

When war came in 1914 both sides did their best to maintain the old traditions in their treatment of resident enemy aliens. The views of all the great powers could be summarised in the words of the 1914 *Manual of Military Law*.

It is a universally recognized rule of International Law that hostilities are restricted to the armed forces of the belligerents and that ordinary citizens of the contending States, who do not take up arms and who abstain from hostile acts, must be treated leniently, must not be injured in their lives or liberty, except for cause or after due trial. It is no longer considered admissible to detain as prisoners subjects of one of the hostile parties travelling or resident in the country of the other at the time of the outbreak of war . . . This immunity, however, cannot apply to persons known to be active or reserve officers, or reservists, of the hostile army.

Britain and France went further than this and allowed a period of grace for reservists to leave the country. Germany immediately interned all men of military age and, while leaving the remainder to live in peace, forbade them to leave the country. France and

Germany reached an agreement whereby 20,000 German civilians, women and men not of military age, were exchanged for a slightly smaller number of French civilians but Anglo–German negotiations for a similar exchange ran into trouble over the definition of military age and the fact that there were ten times as many Germans in Britain as there were British subjects in Germany. It was not until 1917 that Britain agreed to trade some 7,000 Germans for 700 British.

While attempts were being made to reach this agreement, feelings on both sides were exacerbated by a court case in England. Information was laid that the honorary German consul in Sunderland, Nicholas Emil Ahlers, had, on the instructions of the German embassy, provided tickets for three German reservists, thus enabling them to leave Britain on August 5th, less than twenty-four hours after war was declared in London. Ahlers, who was a naturalised British subject and had no desire to return to his native country, was necessarily charged with high treason. His defence, almost certainly true, was that he did not know that war had broken out and both the Solicitor-General, who was prosecuting, and the trial judge urged that his defence should be accepted. The jury, inflamed by war-fever, rejected this advice and insisted on finding him guilty and for high treason there was a mandatory sentence of death. When Ahlers appealed it took Lord Reading, the Lord Chief Justice, many hours of lucubration before he could find a technicality on which he could be released. Ahlers changed his name and his residence and settled down to a peaceful existence as a loyal British subject.

In the spring of 1915 there were more than 40,000 German and Austrian civilians at liberty in Britain, only 1,900 having been interned as being of military age or otherwise suspect. Then came the news of the sinking of the *Lusitania* (see p. 124) and a wave of mob violence swept the country and the Empire. In many places Alsatians, Dutch and Swiss, who spoke with a German accent, were attacked. In Liverpool and West Ham, in anti-German riots, 257 people, including 107 policemen, were injured. Following mob outbreaks in South Africa and Victoria, British Columbia, martial law had to be imposed. The government felt that it had no alternative to the internment of all enemy aliens and, by December 1915, 54,749 were behind barbed wire. Not unnaturally the Germans replied by interning all the British civilians in the country. Nevertheless in February 1917 a complaint was made in the House of Commons that 4,294 enemy aliens, including 287 of military age, were still at large.

It was not to be expected that the easy-going Hapsburg Empire

would follow such an uncivilised practice and an American diplomat passing through Budapest in 1915 wrote that,

> The populace has not molested enemy aliens, and their govern-
> ment has not indulged in wholesale internments of enemy
> subjects. In Hungary I found English horse trainers, English
> tutors and French governesses going tranquilly about their
> peaceful occupations. English tailors advertised their business in
> the Hungarian newspapers, and their clients went to them as
> readily as they would have gone in peace time. French chefs and
> servants were, as a matter of course, retained in the employ of
> noble families, and were treated with unvarying consideration
> and sympathy by their Hungarian fellow-servants.

When Portugal entered the war, she acted more forcibly. All
German residents were expelled within fifteen days except those of
military age, who were interned on the island of Terceira in the
Azores. By contrast Italy and Germany came to sensible arrangements in advance. Three days before Italy declared war an agreement was signed whereby the nationals of the two countries could,
apart from a few named localities, live and work as usual, retaining
the right to go home at any time. There was to be no sequestration
of property, patent rights would be preserved, contracts and debts
would remain enforceable and the pensions due to many Italian
workers from Germany would continue to be paid. With only a few
defections, this agreement was honoured throughout the war.

All these cases contained an element of reciprocity for good or
ill. There was, however, no reciprocity between Germany and
Japan. When the latter declared war on August 23rd, 1914 she took
no steps against German nationals. Their movements were not
restricted, German teachers and businessmen continued with their
work. Even Japanese–German trade was not restricted from
Tokyo. This, however, displeased the British who placed eighty-
six Japanese firms on a Black List so that their products could be
seized wherever they were found. It was the only case in the war of
1914–18 in which the products of any allied country were thus
declared contraband.

The Germans took a very different view and immediately interned all the Japanese in Germany. This, wrote the American
ambassador,

> was stated to be in order to save them from the fury of the
> population, and certainly the people seemed to be greatly

39

incensed against the Japanese. The members of the Siamese
Embassy, who in appearance greatly resemble the Japanese,
were often subjected to indignities, and for a long time did not
dare to move about freely in Berlin or even leave their homes.
When I finally obtained permission for the release [of the
Japanese] and for their departure from Germany, I had to send
someone with each party to the Swiss frontier to protect them
from injury . . . No restaurant in Berlin would sell them food
and arrangements had to be made to give them food in the [U.S.]
Embassy.

The First World War saw the breakdown of the immunity of
resident enemy nationals. Internment served no military purpose
and was for the most part merely the result of pressure from
non-combatants who were being taught, almost for the first time,
to hate their enemies. When the Second World War broke out
internment was accepted as an inevitable consequence. The Germans set about it immediately, the French interned all males
between seventeen and seventy years of age but allowed any who
were suitable to enlist in the Foreign Legion. The British allowed
all German nationals, a term which then included Austrians and
Czechs, six days (until September 9th) to leave the country. In both
Britain and France the problem was complicated by the presence
of large numbers of refugees, many of them Jewish, from 'Greater
Germany' who were passionately opposed to the Nazi regime.
Internment was, in the first instance, a very partial affair but, after
France fell and Britain was threatened with invasion, the government decided to make a clean sweep. All enemy aliens were
rounded up and imprisoned, the majority in the Isle of Man. The
whole operation was conducted at short notice and resulted in
administrative chaos and much suffering. Many historians have
castigated Britain for taking such draconian action but the government had not only to guard against the tiny majority of refugees
who might be enemy agents but the possibility that, if invasion or
even heavy air raids took place, the large number of enemy aliens
might well find themselves the objects of mob violence such as that
which had followed the sinking of the *Lusitania* in 1915. It is
scarcely disputable that, in the overheated circumstances of the
summer of 1940 only a tiny, if vociferous, minority of the British
public did not support internment. Certainly it was not an action of
which Britain could be proud and Churchill, as so often in 1940,
typified the feeling of the country when he wrote,

Naturally I feel distressed at having to be responsible for action so utterly at variance with all the fundamental principles of British liberty, *habeas corpus*, and the like. The public danger justifies the action taken.

No country is immune to the argument of military necessity.

PART TWO

PARTICIPANTS

We have to make war as we must, and not as we should like to.

Kitchener of Khartoum

3

A Business for Professionals?

There have always been two conflicting answers to the question of who should take part in a war and both views are set out in a single paragraph of the 1914 *Manual of Military Law*.

According to the British view, the first consequence of the existence of a condition of war between two States is that every subject of the one State becomes an enemy to every subject of the other. For it is impossible to sever the subjects from their State, and the outbreak of war between two States cannot but make their subjects enemies. It is, however, a universally recognized rule of International Law that hostilities are restricted to the armed forces of the belligerents, and that the ordinary citizens of the contending States, who do not take up arms and who abstain from hostile acts, must be treated leniently, must not be injured in their lives or liberty, except for cause or after due trial, and must not as a rule be deprived of their private property.

The authors do not attempt to conceal that the first two sentences of this paragraph contradict the third. The first two rule that there should be total war, the third contends that there should not.

When Hugo Grotius wrote in the course of one of the most 'total' wars of all history he was in no doubt that, once war had been declared every human being, every animal, every acre of land and every coin was totally engaged. Every subject of the enemy was liable to be killed and his property must be at the disposition of those who could lay their hands on it. To support this theory he quoted Cicero, 'If we have the right to kill a man, it cannot be improper to despoil him.' More than a hundred years later, when warfare had become more restrained, Vattel could not wholly reject the theory of total war – 'Nations have nothing to do with each other except in their quarrel as nations' – but he had reservations about how the quarrel should be conducted.

We have not the same rights against all classes of enemies . . .
There are enemies who make no resistance; and consequently

we have no right to maltreat their persons, or use any violence against them, much less to take away their lives.

In particular he was concerned with the position of women.

> Since women and children are subjects of the [enemy] state, they are to be ranked as enemies. But it does not thence follow that we are justifiable in treating them like men who bear arms . . . Although there be some women who are equal to men in strength and courage, yet such instances are not usual; and rules must necessarily be general, and derived from the ordinary course of things. Besides, women are necessary for other services in society; and, in short, the mixture of both sexes in the army would be attended by too many inconveniences.

Vattel expresses no opinion of the doings of Joan of Arc, who felt it her duty to direct armies, as opposed to lesser ladies such as Hannah Snell, who joined the army for non-military reasons. He was dead before the exploits of Agostina Zaragoza, who may have enlisted in the artillery to be near her lover but who earned her commission by repelling a French assault on her native city in 1808 but he might have approved of the actions of the Spanish priests in that war who led many of the guerrilla bands. Vattel was far from agreeing with the general view that clergymen should stand aside from war.

> To defend one's country is an action not unworthy of the most sacred hands. That article of canon law which forbids men to shed blood is a convenient device to exempt from personal danger those men who are often so zealous to fan the flames of discord and excite bloody war . . . An exemption from bearing arms should be allowed to such of the clergy as are really useful – to those who are employed in teaching religion, governing the church, and celebrating the public worship. But those multitudes of useless monks and friars – those drones, who under pretence of dedicating themselves to God, dedicate themselves in fact to sloth and effeminacy – by what right do they pretend to a prerogative that is ruinous to the state?

Combatant clergy have, in fact, a long and distinguished history. At the battle of Bouvines the Bishop of Beauvais went into action wielding a club, since to use a sword would break the canon law which forbade him to shed blood. At the battle of Crécy one of the English divisions was commanded by the Bishop of Durham and in the Thirty Years War the Cardinal Infant, second son of Philip II of Spain, was one of the more successful commanders on the Imperialist side. It was only the chances of war that ensured that he never fought a battle against his Brother in God, Cardinal de la Valette, Archbishop of Toulouse, who commanded a French army. When the deposed James II invaded Ireland the Rev. George Walker, Anglican vicar of Donaghmore, raised a regiment to oppose him, saying that to do so was 'not only excusable but necessary'. His conduct as joint-governor of Derry during the siege earned him nomination as bishop of the city but, before he could be installed, he was killed at the Battle of the Boyne. It was, perhaps, ungenerous of William III to remark, on hearing of his death, 'What took him there?'

Frederick, Duke of York, second son of George III and a great commander in chief of the British army had been created Bishop of Osnabruck at the age of one, but this was only a 'secular dignity'. The last of the battling bishops, Leonidas Polk, lieutenant-general in the Confederate army, fought with distinction at Shiloh and Chickamauga and his death in action at Pine Mountain in 1864 caused a vacancy in the see of Louisiana.

It was not only women and priests that the eighteenth century sought to exclude from war but everyone who did not belong to the regular forces of the nations. The Thirty Years War had shown how disastrous excess and indiscriminate violence could be but out of that struggle had emerged one useful feature for the future – a sure way of distinguishing soldier from civilian. Before the seventeenth century it was only the bodyguards of sovereigns who were uniformly dressed. In England the Yeomen of the Guard, dating from 1485, was the sole uniformed body before the Civil War. In most armies uniformity in the colour of dress within regiments increased as colonel-proprietors found it cheaper to buy cloth in bulk, but the first uniformly dressed army to go into battle did not appear until 1630 when the troops of Gustavus Adolphus astonished Europe not only by their skill at arms but by their blue and buff uniforms.

By the start of the eighteenth century, with all the main armies uniformly dressed, it became possible to be sure who was a soldier and who was a non-combatant. But war at that time was still restricted in scope. The armies of Louis XIV, of Frederick the Great and of Maria Theresa fought on a limited scale. Their objectives were comparatively small – a fortress, a frontier province, a sugar island – and their operations, correspondingly, confined in area. No one sought the total overthrow of his adversary or the occupation of all his territory. Armies could, therefore, carry the bulk of their supplies and could keep requisitions from the countryside to an acceptable minimum. The soldiers were long-term professionals under a severe discipline so that outrages, though they could never be wholly eradicated, were kept within bounds.

In any warring country the vast bulk of the population was un-affected except in so far as taxes were likely to be increased to pay for military expenditure. Only the minority who lived in the war zone felt the effects of campaigning and these were kept to a minimum. Apart from those who chose to live in fortress towns (for whom see pp. 128–37 below), the remainder were expected to carry on with their normal lives. If their locality was occupied by the enemy the local government was required to carry on even if under more or less strict military control. The usual taxes would be raised and passed to the occupier who would use them to pay for such requisitions as he was forced to make. The occupied zone would, in practice, be paying a temporary allegiance to the con-queror and, provided they did no more than their normal duty, neither the officials nor the people would be censured by their own government if or when they returned to their old allegiance. The concept of the collaborator (as opposed to the deliberate traitor) had not yet evolved. In return for quietly continuing his daily life, the non-combatant under occupation could expect that his life, property and livelihood would be secure except during fighting in the immediate neighbourhood and from the inconveniences in-separable when quartering a hostile (or even a friendly) army. In Vattel's words,

> At present war is carried on by regular troops: the people, the peasants, the citizens, take no part in it, and generally have nothing to fear from the sword of the enemy. Provided the inhabitants submit to him who is master of the country, pay the contributions imposed, and refrain from all hostilities, they live in as perfect tranquillity as if they were friends: they even continue in possession of what belongs to them; the country people come freely to the camp to sell their provisions, and are protected, as far as possible, from the calamities of war.

Vattel's description of conditions, in this as with most of his writings, shows a rosier picture than was usual at the time but it was the condition which those in charge of armies were trying to establish. It was to their advantage to do so. All countries were predominantly agricultural and it was to every commander's advantage to see that as much food was grown and harvested in the area he occupied as possible. Any supplies that could not be procured locally would have to be brought forward by the cumbrous and expensive supply train. In the fourteenth century Bonet had written,

> Ox-herds, and all husbandmen, and ploughmen with their oxen, when they are carrying on their business, and equally when they are going to it or returning from it, are secure, according to written law. And in truth that this should be so is not without good reason, because it is expedient and convenient for all sorts of people, since those who cultivate the soil work for all men and for everybody, and all manner of folk live of their labour. Therefore right reason does not permit that they should receive any ill or annoyance, seeing that they have no concern with war or with harming anybody.

Eighteenth-century soldiers needed to be fed as much as those of the fourteenth century since the transport arrangements were only marginally improved and the reasons for leaving the peasantry to get on with their jobs remained. All soldiers agreed that only regularly constituted combatants could take part in war. Anyone rash enough to intervene if he was not a professional was likely to get very short shrift.

This view was concisely summarised by General Ricardo Carillo, the Spanish commander of an abortive expedition which invaded France across the Pyrenees in 1793. To his French opponent he wrote,

> The rules of war not permitting peasants or bourgeois to have, use or carry arms – something neither you nor I would approve, since it would bring about the devastation and ruin of the land – I declare and I hope your Excellency's humanity will lead you to declare with me, that any peasant or bourgeois who is found to have arms upon his person or hidden in his premises, and above all, if he uses the same against my troops or any village which I have occupied, whether he calls himself a *miquelet* or anything else, and if he is not serving in some unit of which he is wearing the uniform, badges and equipment (or if he is an officer and is wearing anything other than his uniform and badges of rank) I shall hang him immediately, and I shall be justified in so doing. At the same time, my troops will refrain from murder and rape, will respect property, goods, and the life and liberty of all peaceful persons, irrespective of their political opinions, on

condition that they remain in their villages and houses and continue their normal occupations.

When that letter was written France was initiating the *levée-en-masse*, mobilising the whole strength of the nation and raising armies on an unprecedented scale. There were insufficient arms to put in their hands and no uniforms in which to dress them. If the ragged volunteers had to wait until they were properly dressed the new republic would be overwhelmed. Carillo's opponent, General Deflers, replied, 'The armed forces of the Republic consist of the whole population of France . . . All Frenchmen are soldiers.'

Fifteen years later the positions were reversed. The Spanish armies had been smashed and the defence of Spain was left to the type of person whom Carillo had felt justified in hanging. When Napoleon changed the scope of warfare he changed the rules. As the *Grande Armée* rampaged from one end of Europe to the other it was no longer a question of a few magistrates in border areas working temporarily under military control but of whole governments being put on leading strings or utterly dispossessed. Moreover France could not feed the vast armies she put in the field. They had to live off the countries they conquered and in the Iberian peninsula there was not enough food for both them and the inhabitants. The irruption of a quarter of a million hungry and rapacious Frenchmen into Spain meant that the Spaniards were faced with the alternatives of starving or of fighting for their food. They took their knives, their fowling-pieces and their pitchforks and set out to wage a *guerrilla*, a little war, intending to make the life of the invaders intolerable.

The emergence of guerrillas (strictly *guerrilleros*) poses extremely difficult problems for more orthodox soldiers. They wear no uniforms, their officers hold no commissions, they draw no pay or rations, they may be accountable to no one, they are not subject to military law and they have no bases. All these deficiencies bring consequences which are unlikely to endear them to their opponents or, on many occasions, to their friends. Without pay or rations they must live off the countryside, competing both with the enemy and the local population for the available supplies. Their lack of formal discipline means that their requisitioning is likely to be indistinguishable from looting and may well be accompanied by the working off of private or political grudges, usually under the guise of reprisals for real or imaginary collaboration with the enemy. The lack of bases means that it is very difficult to keep prisoners, even if it were possible to feed them. Since a guerrilla band can hardly move about the country with prisoners in tow, temptation to dispose of them in a summary manner is considerable.

Since guerrillas seldom conform to the usages of war, the natural reaction of regular troops is to treat them as bandits and to give no mercy. This view is not always unjustified. It is never safe to assume that all guerrillas, partisans or freedom fighters are necessarily paragons of patriotism or disinterested virtue. While the kind of breakdown in normality which conjures up guerrilla warfare will often stir the most worthy citizens to action, it also gives an opportunity to the least desirable elements in a population who see in it an opportunity to further their own interests – which may comprise pillage, rape or the propagation of some political creed – under the guise of fighting for their country. Not the least of the contributions made to his country by Epoz y Mina, the greatest of the Spanish guerrilla leaders, was his elimination of another such leader, Echavaria,

> who was the terror of the villages of Navarre, which he plundered and oppressed in a thousand ways, till they complained to me about him. I arrested him and caused him to be shot with three of his principal lieutenants.

Any disciplined soldier feels a particular horror against an undisclosed enemy, against the man, or woman, who appears to be a peaceable citizen but who may at any moment become 'a spy, a brigand, and assassin and a rebel'. There is little chance of bringing such people to battle and, all too often, the only form of retaliation seems to be punishment of the population at large. Such a course is rarely effective as, to their cost, the French learned in Spain. In December, 1811 their governor in Navarre, General Abbé, proclaimed that no quarter would be given to guerrillas and that their families would be held responsible for the deeds of those who could not be apprehended. Villages would be fined for the crimes of the inhabitants and, if these were ineffective, the villages would be burned. Navarre was Mina's home ground and he reacted by declaring 'a war of extermination against all Frenchmen, regardless of rank' in which he would execute four French for every hostage shot. Both sides implemented their threats and Navarre was swept by a wave of terror until, in March 1812, Abbé ordered the execution of three members of the Junta of Burgos who were held as hostages. On Mina's orders eighty French prisoners were shot, twelve in reprisal for the hostages and the remainder in the proportion of ten for every Spaniard killed in taking the prisoners. Abbé thereupon withdrew his proclamation and the war in Navarre relapsed into the usual brutal round of killings and counter-killings.

In Portugal, at the same time, the French were facing a different but equally intractable problem. Portuguese law, which had been designed to deal with recurrent Spanish invasions, made every male between sixteen and sixty (only excepting the clergy and the friars) liable to military service in defence of the country. The most active young men went into the regular army which was supported by a formally organised militia but every layman not conscripted by the regulars or the militia was required to serve in the *Ordenanza*, a kind of Home Guard formed into companies of 250 and commanded by the chief person of the neighbourhood under the title of Captain-Major. On the first occasion when the French invaded Portugal in 1807 the *Ordenanza* had done no training for decades and were totally ineffective. They had no uniforms and few muskets although 'those peasants who have no fire-arms have pikes, or a long pole with a bayonet fixed at one end'. On the surface they closely resembled the guerrillas of Spain but there was a fundamental difference because they were a long-recognised part of the Portuguese military establishment and the captains-major held commissions from the Portuguese Crown. In 1810 when the French under Massena made their third attempt to subdue the country the *Ordenanza* were called out by proclamation and ordered to,

> Do the enemy all the mischief in their power . . . not by assembling in large bodies, but by impeding his communications, by firing on him from the mountains and strong passes, and by annoying his foraging and other parties he may send out.

The French, who could see no difference between guerrillas and *Ordenanza*, treated them as if they were bandits and Massena issued his own proclamation stating that any Portuguese found bearing arms and without a uniform would be shot without trial. Wellington, as Marshal General of the Portuguese army, remonstrated against such harshness.

> Since the *Ordenanza* is part of the Portuguese army, since it is equally under military law, and since it has behaved fairly to the French soldiers who have fallen into its hands, I beg you will give orders that the officers and soldiers of the *Ordenanza* who become prisoners shall, with other troops of the Portuguese army, have the benefit of the laws and customs of war.
>
> Since I have commanded this army I have done all in my power, and I have succeeded, in waging war in a fair fashion, and

I have ensured that the customs established and recognised among civilised nations have been respected: but if the French army continues to shoot prisoners from the *Ordenanza* one cannot be certain that other soldiers from this body, as well as other Portuguese soldiers, will not retaliate on prisoners taken from the French army. It will be beyond my powers to protect them; and the orders you have given will cause misfortune to such soldiers who fall into the hands of the Portuguese troops.

Massena replied by asking how he 'could treat as soldiers those who only pretended to be such so that they could commit cowardly murders?' Wellington then wrote,

You seem to be under the impression that only those wearing a uniform can enjoy the rights of war: but you must remember that you yourself added to the glory of the French army while commanding soldiers without uniform.

He did not add that a reward in cash was paid to the *Ordenanza* for every French prisoner brought in alive.

It is an obvious paradox that Massena, the revolutionary general, found himself in the position taken up by General Carillo, the representative of the *ancien régime* in 1793 while Wellington, essentially a man of the eighteenth century, was using the same argument with which General Deflers had replied, defending the concept of a nation-in-arms. In truth every general who has penetrated into enemy territory will demand peace in his rear areas and will have to take stern measures to obtain it. Equally any general who is forced to retreat will encourage attacks on his opponent's communications. It was only three years before Wellington found himself in Massena's position. As soon as the Anglo–Portuguese army was over the Pyrenees, he issued a proclamation demanding that the non-combatants stay peacefully in their villages. When an isolated outbreak of anti-allied violence did break out, at Bidarry and Baygorry, he sent to the mayors of the two villages a message of which Carillo and Massena would not have disapproved,

I will act toward them as the French did towards the villages of Spain and France; that is I will totally destroy them and hang up all the people belonging to them that I find there.

As it happened the violence stopped and he never had to decide whether to implement the threat.

The example of popular resistance set by Spain and Portugal spread rapidly. In 1809 there was a rising in the Tyrol led, according to Napoleon, by an Austrian general of Belgian extraction who roused the peasantry to surprise and capture a detachment of 700 conscripts on their way to join their units. Having massacred all of them, he repeated the exploit with 1,800 Bavarians in the French service. Instructing Marshal Lefebvre to put down the rising, Napoleon left no doubt about his views on dealing with such situations: 'Make no ridiculous proclamations: be severe; disarm the countryside; take a large number of hostages and make examples to stop the affair spreading.'

Simultaneously the Duke of Brunswick, who was later to die at Quatre Bras, led a widespread revolt in North Germany. His chief supporter, Major von Schill, brought with him a regiment of Prussian hussars. Since Prussia was then at peace with France, Schill was fighting without the authority of his own government and Napoleon described him, in a *Bulletin de l'Armée d'Allemand*, as 'the brigand Schill, who has given himself, and with reason, the title of general in the British service, after having shamed the name of the King of Prussia'.

The hussars were eventually driven back to the shore of the Baltic where, after Schill had fallen in action, they surrendered. Napoleon decided to make an example of the twelve surviving officers – *'faire une justice éclatante de ces misérables'* – but a French court-martial ruled that they were prisoners of war. The emperor quashed this verdict, convened another court and had them all shot.

The most spectacular outbreak of irregular operation in the Napoleonic Wars was sparked off by the French invasion of Russia. General Davidov orchestrated a most effective guerrilla campaign against the French communications while they occupied Moscow but it was during the *Grande Armée*'s long retreat that the peasantry struck at them with a ferocity that not even the Spaniards matched. Sir Robert Wilson, who had attached himself to the Czar's army, wrote,

At Vyazma, fifty French were buried alive and [at another town] sixty dying naked men had their necks laid along a felled tree with Russian men and women with large faggot sticks, singing in chorus, with repeated blows struck out their brains in succession . . . Such is the inveteracy of the peasants that they buy prisoners from the Cossacks and put them to death.

When the French fell back into Germany the Prussians raised an irregular force, but under direct military control. Its constitution suggests that it would have been a type of *Ordenanza,* rather than a guerrilla, but its regulations were drawn so as to ensure that its members should not have the benefit of being treated as regular combatants. They were specifically enjoined not to conform to the customs of war.

7. When the *Landsturm* is called out, the war becomes a fight for national existence which sanctions any means that may be employed. The most severe and unrelenting measures are the best, because they are those most likely to bring the just cause to a successful result in the shortest time.

8. The aim of the *Landsturm* is to hold up the march of the enemy and to bar his retreat, to harass him incessantly, to capture his munitions, couriers and recruits, to surprise him by night, to break up his hospitals; in short to trouble and molest him in every conceivable way, and to destroy him singly and in detachments, whenever and wherever this is possible . . .

39. No special uniform or distinctive dress is permitted for the *Landsturm* since this would betray the wearer, and render him more likely to be pursued by the enemy.

It is clear that in drafting these regulations the Prussian government, whose army had scarcely distinguished itself since the death of Frederick the Great, was determined to reject the eighteenth-century distinction between soldiers and civilians. The early levies of the French republic, the guerrillas and the *Ordenanza*, fought without uniforms because no uniforms were to be had. The *Landsturm* rejected uniforms because they might hamper their clandestine operations. Among the 'most severe and unrelenting measures' prescribed for them was attacking enemy hospitals. It is hardly surprising that, when the French caught any of the members they executed them immediately although the contribution of the *Landsturm* was, in practice, very small. Fifty-seven years later the situation was reversed. The Prussians were deep into France and treating the French irregulars as the French had treated the *Landsturm* in 1813. One of the republican leaders pointed out that the *francs-tireurs* were only doing what the Prussians had done in the previous war. Bismarck (or, according to some accounts, von Moltke) replied, 'True, and we can still see the trees on which you hanged them.'

4

Partisans or Bandits

In 1813 Francis Lieber, who was then thirteen years old, may possibly have fought with the *Landsturm* but when in 1863 he drafted *General Order N° 100* for the U.S. Army he utterly rejected the thinking which lay behind the regulations for the *Landsturm*. His code is an unequivocal assertion that war is for regular combatants only.

> Men, or squads of men who commit hostilities, whether by fighting or by inroads for destruction or plunder, or by raids of any kind, without commission, without being part and portion of the hostile army, and without sharing continuously in the war, but who do so with intermitting returns to their homes and avocations, or with the occasional assumption of peaceful pursuits, divesting themselves of the character or appearance of soldiers – such men or squads of men, are not public enemies [i.e. are not regular combatants of the enemy], and therefore, if captured, are not entitled to the privileges of prisoners of war, but shall be treated summarily as highway robbers or pirates. (Article 82)
> Armed prowlers, by whatever names they may be called, or persons of the hostile territory, who steal into the lines of the hostile army, for the purpose of robbing, killing, or destroying bridges, roads or canals, of cutting the telegraph wires, are not entitled to the privileges of the prisoner of war. (Article 84)
> War rebels are persons within the occupied territory who rise in arms against the occupying or conquering army or against the authorities established by the same. If captured they may suffer death, whether they rise singly, in large or small bands, and whether called upon to do so by their own, but expelled, government or not. They are not prisoners of war: nor are they, if discovered and secured before their conspiracy has matured to an actual rising, or to armed violence. (Article 85)

The wholeheartedness with which Lieber embraced the eighteenth-century view, with its absolute prohibition of violence to all those not in uniform and the insistence that inhabitants of occupied territory owe allegiance and obedience to the occupiers, may be due to the circumstances in which he wrote. The Union army was engaged in a civil war and confidently expected to make deep inroads into rebel territory. Certainly his doctrine made an immediate appeal to his former compatriots when they invaded France in 1870. The Prussians clearly expected widespread guerrilla activity from the start and a week before Sedan the Prussian Crown Prince, who was commanding an army, wrote in his diary, 'The scheme being organised for the defence of the country (they talk of *francs-tireurs*) must be opposed with all possible earnestness.'

Four days later, having heard that the *sous-préfet* of Rheims had distributed six thousand rifles to the populace, he added,

> The arming of the inhabitants of this neighbourhood has already assumed great proportions, compelling us to take energetic steps to enforce the surrender of all weapons. Single shots are fired, generally in a cowardly, cunning fashion, at patrols, so that nothing is left to us to do but to adopt retaliatory measures by burning down the house from which the shots came, or else by the help of the lash or forced contributions. It is horrible but, to prevent greater mischief, unavoidable.

At the Battle of Sedan, fought in the same week that the Crown Prince wrote that comment, an incident occurred which so impressed the Germans that they were still quoting it forty years later. When, after a stiff fight, the Bavarians drove the French Marines out of the village of Bazeilles they found that the inhabitants had been assisting in the defence. According to their own account, every civilian found with a weapon was shot immediately. Even if the wholesale massacre of men, women and children – the French version of the story – is exaggerated, it is certain that many innocent non-combatants were burned in the cellars when the Germans fired the village.

It is probable that the Germans overestimated the amount of guerrilla warfare, of operations carried out by men and women who had no governmental authority, during the Franco–Prussian War. They had some excuse for exaggerating its scope when they came across documents such as the circular issued by the *Préfet* of Côte d'Or to his *sous-préfets* and *maires* on November 21st, 1870.

> France does not require that you should assemble *en masse* and openly oppose the enemy. It expects only that three or four determined men should leave each village every morning and

conceal themselves in such places as are indicated by nature and from which, without danger, they can shoot Prussians. Above all they should shoot mounted men whose horses they should deliver to the *arrondissement*. I will give a reward for the delivery of each horse and see that these heroic deeds are published in all the newspapers of the *département*, as well as in *Le Moniteur*.

Certainly the Germans showed no reluctance in instituting harsh reprisals for acts which they supposed to be committed by non-combatants. At Charmes they burned down the casino when shots were fired at some baggage waggons. When a railway bridge was burned down near Fontenoy, the village was razed to the ground and a fine of ten million francs was levied on the province of Lorraine.

It may be that the Germans deliberately enlarged the scope for such reprisals by introducing a semantic confusion. They referred to all irregular combatants as *francs-tireurs*, using the word as a synonym for brigand, whereas *francs-tireurs* were organised and authorised soldiers. They had their origins in the French Revolution when fifteen battalions with that name were raised in the Vosges. Although not part of the regular army they were subject to military discipline, their officers held commissions and, when it became available, all ranks wore uniforms and fought alongside regular troops. They were, therefore, more nearly regular troops than, for example, the *Ordenanza*. After 1814 the battalions fell into lethargy but the Second Empire reactivated them as rifle clubs and in 1870 they took the field under the same conditions as in 1793. They fought beside the regulars after the early débâcles of the war and it was a *franc-tireur* unit composed of newspaper men who took Le Bourget from the Prussian Guard during the siege of Paris. Far from being without uniform, some *franc-tireur* battalions had a high degree of sartorial fantastication. The *Francs-Tireurs de Nice* wore grey Tyrolean jackets and matching hats and an Algerian unit affected the burnous. Some returned emigrants from South America formed a *franc-tireur* unit which carried lassos and wore ponchos. Their commander was conspicuous in 'a *mousquetaire* coat and a plumed hat, with a light coloured moustache of extraordinary length'.

While there were, as there had been in Spain, a number of guerrilla bands whose object was to plunder friend and foe alike, the great majority of those whom the Germans described as *francs-tireurs* and treated as bandits, were authorised members of the French armed forces. The problem was identifying them. After the collapse of the Second Empire and the capture, at Sedan and Metz, of most of the regular troops, the new government had to improvise an army and, in the early days, uniforms were unobtainable. Large numbers of the *Garde Nationale Mobile* were sent into battle in the traditional blue blouse of the French working man with a red brassard or, in some cases, a red epaulette to show that they were soldiers. The Prussians complained, through the American minister, that,

> The blue blouse is the national costume, the brassard is distinguishable only at a short distance, and can be taken off or replaced instantly with the result that it is impossible for the Prussian troops to distinguish the individuals from whom they have to expect acts of hostility. In consequence, those not recognizable as soldiers on all occasions and at the necessary distance, who kill and wound Prussians, will be tried by martial law.

Considering the problems that the Germans were facing from people who were shooting at them in civilian clothes, the concession of trying them rather than shooting them out of hand was not ungenerous, provided that the German soldiers were prepared to arrest irregulars before they shot them. Before the end of 1870 they tightened up the procedure and issued a General Order which read,

> Every prisoner who claims to be treated as a prisoner of war must prove his status as a French soldier by the production of an order issued by a competent authority and addressed to himself showing that he has been summoned to the colours and is borne on the rolls of a military unit raised by the French Government.

This solved the problem of any French soldier dressed in less than complete uniform who was able to get close enough to his enemy to be able to show his papers.

The Brussels Conference of 1874 discussed exhaustively the question of who was an authorised combatant and who was not. The great military powers urged that fighting should be restricted to men in uniform. The German delegate admitted that in the past the raising of a whole population to resist an invader had been legitimate and laudable but urged that the spread of long-range weapons meant that a popular uprising would lead to the breakdown of public order. He was supported by the Russian delegate who claimed that,

> War has altered its character . . . It becomes necessary to regulate the inspiration of patriotism. Otherwise, in opposing irregular bodies of enthusiasts to regularly organised armies, the risk of compromising national defence and of rendering it more fatal to the country itself than to the invader would be incurred.

The smaller countries, who could not raise mass armies to resist invasion, argued that popular resistance was their only chance of effective defence. The Belgian delegate said that,

> If the citizens were to be sacrificed for having attempted to defend their country at the risk of their lives, they need not find inscribed on the post against which they were to be shot, the article of a treaty signed by their own Government which had, in advance, condemned them to death.

Since France, smarting from her recent defeat, sided with the smaller nations, there was no hope of a compromise and it was largely on this point that the conference broke up without having reached any substantial agreements. Things went better at The Hague in 1899 when, in Section 1 Chapter 1 of The Hague Rules, a definition of a legitimate belligerent was agreed.

> The laws, rights and duties of war apply not only to armies, but also to militia and volunteer corps fulfilling the following conditions:
> 1. To be commanded by a person responsible for his subordinates.
> 2. To have a fixed and distinctive emblem recognizable at a distance.
> 3. To carry arms openly: and
> 4. To conduct their operations in accordance with the laws and customs of war.
> In countries where militia or volunteer corps constitute the army, or form part of it, they are included in the definition of 'army'.

This definition, which was repeated unaltered in the revised Rules of 1907, did very little to simplify the real problem since Conditions 2 and 3 were both capable of very wide interpretation. In the war of 1904 the Japanese told the Russians that the 'fixed distinctive emblem' must be 'easily distinguishable by the naked eye' but they offered no objection when they were informed that the Russians had raised a volunteer corps on the island of Sakhalin which had no uniform although the members would wear in their caps a cross which might bear the letters M.P. (*Mandchuriski Polk*), while the greatcoats, for those who had greatcoats, would be piped in red. The members would also wear a red brassard with a width of two-thirds of an inch. On their side the Japanese raised volunteers to defend Ping-Yang and informed the Russians that the members would be recognisable because they wore European-style clothes (as distinct from the native inhabitants who dressed in the Chinese style) and would be identifiable by a flower embroidered in red on their jackets. Since they were also to wear a white sun helmet they might have fallen within the conditions laid down by the German *Kriegsbrauch* which insisted that the distinctive emblem must be 'recognisable at long (*weite*) ranges'.

In the 1914 *Manual of Military Law* the British did their best to elucidate The Hague definition.

> The . . . condition relative to the fixed distinctive sign recognisable at a distance, would be satisfied by the wearing of a military uniform, but less than a complete uniform will suffice. The distance at which the sign should be visible is left vague but it is reasonable to expect that the silhouette of an irregular combatant in a position of standing against the skyline should be at once recognisable from the outline of a peaceful inhabitant, and this by the naked eye of ordinary individuals, at a distance at which the form of an individual can be determined. As encounters now take place at ranges at which it is impossible to distinguish the colour or the cut of clothing, it would seem to be desirable to provide irregulars with a helmet, slouch hat or forage cap, as being completely different in outline from the ordinary civilian headdress. It may, however, be objected that a headdress does not legally fulfill the condition that the sign must be fixed. Something in the nature of a badge sewn on the clothing should therefore be worn in addition.
>
> It is not necessary to inform the enemy of the distinctive mark adopted to fulfill [this] condition, although to avoid misunderstandings it may be convenient to do so.

Leaving aside the final sentence which is a masterpiece of meiosis, the manual's exposition cannot be said to do much to amplify The Hague Rules. It first postulates that the irregular combatant would be seen against a skyline, a position which even the most incompetent irregular combatant would be likely to avoid if he valued his life. It goes on to advise the wearing of a distinctive hat, only to add that this would not meet the requirements laid down in the Rules.

Nevertheless the British had the most recent experience of fighting a war against an enemy without uniform. The Boer commandos went into action in their everyday clothes, yet no Boer captured in action had been treated other than as a prisoner of war.

Also of doubtful usefulness was the third Hague condition, that belligerents should 'carry arms openly'. It might have been valid in the days of the muzzle-loading musket when the firer had to stand to load his piece, but could it be held to include a sniper with a breech-loader firing from behind cover? Nor, as the *Manual of Military Law* pointed out, could it be relied upon in the case of a man carrying a pistol or a grenade, to say nothing of a dagger or a swordstick.

The fact was that The Hague definition of a belligerent was a compromise which was just definite and exclusive enough to satisfy Germany and Russia without giving too much objection to the smaller powers who, in a later section, were given some concession to the right of a civilian to defend his home against an invader.

> The inhabitants of a territory which has not been occupied, who, on the approach of an enemy, spontaneously take up arms to resist the invading troops without having time to organise themselves in accordance with Article I, shall be regarded as belligerents if they respect the laws and customs of war.

This was a very limited concession since it applied only to those who were actually under attack. Once the tide of war had swept past any given locality the right to rise against the invader lapsed, and the invader should not have to use troops to guard his communications. Guerrilla warfare, as it had been understood in Spain, the Tyrol, Russia and Prussia, had been outlawed and the sanguine Professor Holland could write comfortably in 1911,

> The separation of armies and peaceful inhabitants into two distinct classes is perhaps the greatest triumph of International Law. The effect in mitigating the evils of war has been incalculable.

Since the war of 1914–18, the first major conflict after the ratification of The Hague Rules, was not a war of movement there was little opportunity for irregular warfare. Only in Belgium was any substantial area of enemy territory overrun, at least on the western front, and Belgium is not a country ideally suited for guerrilla war. The Germans had started with the expectation that they would meet resistance, especially from the Walloon inhabitants, and were clear about how they would deal with it. The *Kriegsbrauch* laid down that,

> To protect oneself against attacks and injuries from the inhabitants and to employ ruthlessly the necessary means of attack and intimidation is clearly not only a right but a duty to the staff of the army.

They made their intentions clear from the moment that they invaded Belgium and, as each village and town was occupied, they put up posters threatening death to anyone who shot at German soldiers or who assisted the escape of Belgian or allied soldiers. Death was also the penalty for being found within two hundred metres of 'the landing grounds of aeroplanes or balloons'. Hostages would be taken to ensure the good behaviour of the population and 'villages where the inhabitants undertake acts of hostility against our troops will be burnt'. Such Belgian authorities as remained at their posts did what they could to stop the population taking the war into their own hands. Burgomasters urged the people to hand sporting guns and other weapons over to the police and posters and pamphlets were issued explaining The Hague Rules as they applied to civilians under occupation.

Some shots were, nevertheless, fired at the Germans and the Germans reacted with a policy of *schrecklichkeit*, of calculated ruthlessness designed to frighten the civilian population into quiescence. As early as August 23rd, 1914 the people of Namur were informed that the inhabitants of nearby Ardenne had attacked some Germans and that, as a reprisal, the town had been burned to the ground and 110 people (a number that seems to have been understated) had been shot. Next day 384 citizens of Tammines were shot on a similar pretext and, within the week, 612 people, including a child of three weeks, were executed at Dinant. It should be added that fuel had been added to the German ruthlessness by rumours of frightful stories of atrocities being committed against Germans by Belgian civilians. One tale, which received wide credence, told of a hospital in Aachen where the eyes of thirty wounded German officers were gouged out by Belgian women and girls. It was not true, but it was believed.

The climax came at Louvain. The city was occupied without incident but on the following day a German was wounded in the leg and the burgomaster, who had urged the people to hand in their weapons and to remain quiet, was seized as hostage and shot with two other worthies. The main trouble came on August 25th, when the Belgian garrison of Antwerp made a sortie which penetrated as far as Malines. Following a minor panic among the Germans there some soldiers were still in disorderly flight when they reached Louvain, fourteen miles away. In the streets a riderless horse charged into and upset a gun team, whereupon the Germans became convinced that they were under attack and, in the darkness, opened fire on their compatriots who, equally certain that they had met the enemy, fired back. When order was at length restored the Germans blamed all the trouble on the people of Louvain who, as far as can be ascertained, had been content to take cover and let the enemy fight it out with his own troops. A terrible reprisal was instituted. For six days the Germans set fire to the city, street by street, and did not spare the magnificent fourteenth-century Clothworkers' Guildhall with its irreplaceable library of 230,000 books and manuscripts. Two hundred hostages were shot.

Imperial Germany made no attempt to deny their ravages at Louvain. To have done so would be a denial of their policy of *schrecklichkeit* since exemplary punishment cannot be exemplary if it is not known. They went further and claimed that their policy had been successful since they were not greatly troubled thereafter by guerrilla operations in Belgium. What cannot be told is the amount of such operations that would have taken place had it not been for the punishment of Louvain.

If irregular combatants played little part in the fighting between 1914 and 1918, the same cannot be said of the Second World War. Although the Japanese set an example when they killed some 200,000 Chinese in and around Nanking in December 1937 on the grounds that they were harbouring bandits, it was inevitable that a war in which long-range bombers brought death and destruction to areas hundreds of miles from anything resembling a conventional battlefield should revise drastically the role of the civilian. Hitler's Germany showed how it meant to deal with irregulars on the first day of the war. On September 1st, 1939 when the Nazis were occupying the 'Free City' of Danzig they were held up by fifty-one armed post office workers who installed themselves in the Polish Post Office on Heveliusplatz. When the building was set on fire the thirty-five survivors were driven to surrender. All were shot by the S.S. although there could scarcely be a clearer case under The Hague Rules of 'inhabitants of a territory which has not been occupied who, on the approach of an enemy, spontaneously take up arms to resist the invading troops without having had time to organise themselves', than these Poles who resisted on the first half day of a war which had not even been declared. Two days later the German residents of Bydgoszcz attempted to seize the town and its important railway station. Two hundred and fifty of them were captured, tried by court-martial and shot by the Poles. Since these Germans were unquestionably Polish citizens there can be little doubt that the Poles were within their rights to execute them as armed rebels but the Germans took savage reprisals and, according to Polish accounts, shot 20,000 innocent Poles.

When Hitler overran Europe on a scale far surpassing Napoleon, he created conditions in which widespread guerrilla warfare was inevitable. When the populations of France, the Low Countries, Poland, the Balkans and much of Scandinavia were conquered they could see little hope of a peace treaty which would restore them to some approximation of the life they had known. Nor, with Britain and later Russia rocked back on their heels, could occupied Europe look for any immediate prospect of rescue. Irregular warfare was their only chance of salvation. By the time that Britain and Russia had recovered their balance and the United States had developed a capacity for waging land war in Europe, the resistance movements were established and were diverting large numbers of Axis troops to contain them. Naturally the allies did all they could to sustain and strengthen these valuable supporters and equally naturally no attention was drawn to the fact that, since all these underground movements had grown up after the countries concerned had been occupied, they were all in breach of The Hague Rules.

The only country that organised civilian resistance in advance was Britain. On May 14th, 1940, before the full extent of the French catastrophe was apparent, the Secretary of State for War broadcast an appeal for men to join the Local Defence Volunteers (later retitled Home Guard). He was careful to add that the new force would be issued with uniforms and that it would be under the orders of Commander in Chief, Home Forces. These two stipulations should have brought the Home Guard within The Hague Rules but the Germans refused to accept this and replied with a threatening broadcast.

The British Government is committing the worst crime of all. Evidently it permits open preparations for the formation of murder bands. The preparations which are being made all over England to arm the civilian population for guerrilla warfare are contrary to the rules of international law. German official quarters warn the misled British public and remind them of the fate of the Polish *francs-tireurs* and gangs of murderers. Civilians who take up arms against German soldiers are, under international law, no better than murderers, whether they are priests or bank clerks. British people you will do well to heed our warnings.

If the *Wehrmacht* had been able to invade Britain in the early weeks of the Home Guard's existence they would have found few of that force in uniform unless they had landed in the West Riding of Yorkshire where they would have found the Harrogate Home Guard smartly dressed in barathea battledress provided through the generosity of Sir Montague Burton. In the rest of the country the fate of captured Home Guards would have depended on the unlikely supposition that their captors would have agreed with the tentative definition given in the *Manual of Military Law* that a distinctive headdress and a fixed emblem would be sufficient to establish belligerent status. Brassards bearing the words Home Guard (or in some early cases L.D.V.) were soon issued and should have been sewn to the civilian clothes of the wearer and, as early as May 22nd, eight days after the appeal for volunteers, it was announced in the House of Commons that a quarter of a million forage caps had been issued to the Home Guard.

The most spectacular guerrilla effort of the Second World War was that of the Soviet Union. It was called into being by Stalin on July 1st, 1941, eight days after the German invasion. In a broadcast he called on the Soviet people 'to create intolerable conditions for the enemy, to pursue and annihilate them at every step, and to disrupt their every measure'.

The Russian 'Popular War' had the advantage over all previous resistance movements in that it could be orchestrated by the existing and all-pervasive organisation of the Communist Party. As early as June 28th, the party in Kiev started creating partisan detachments to operate in the German rear as soon as the area was overrun and three days later, the day of Stalin's broadcast, the Central Committee for Byelorussia ordered all Communists and Young Communist Leaguers who were fit enough to carry arms to stay behind in occupied territory. In addition to the existing framework provided by the party the detachments were linked by wireless, thus overcoming the great disadvantage of all previous guerrilla campaigns – the problem of co-ordinating action by scattered units.

There were, of course, early confusions but, in time, elaborate and widespread operations could be mounted. The most impressive was the 'rail war' arranged to coincide with the Soviet offensive at Kursk in 1943. A hundred and seventy detachments from the Ukraine, Byelorussia, Orel, Smolensk, Kalinin and Leningrad took part and,

On the first night of the operation, 3rd August, when two hundred radio sets received the order from Moscow, 42,000 rails

66

were destroyed and 6,000 German trains were either destroyed or brought to a halt by the damaged rails.

Between 1941 and 1944 a million partisans fought behind the German lines in the Soviet Union and they destroyed 9,644 bridges, 21,376 trains, 16,869 locomotives, 170,812 railway waggons and 4,538 armoured fighting vehicles.

Although they had a strong stiffening of Soviet soldiers who had been overrun in the initial German advance, there can be little doubt that this vast force was outside The Hague Rules for all that it had been called out by the government and acted on lawful military orders. To the Russians this illegality was more than offset by the effectiveness of the force which, they estimated, diverted one Axis division out of every ten in the country to the defence of their supply lines against partisan depredations. The Germans, as was to be expected, treated the partisans as bandits and resorted to all the classic forms of reprisal – mass executions, the taking of hostages and the devastation of towns and villages. Not only did they fail to contain the resistance, they actually succeeded in increasing it. So stupidly was the policy of *schrecklichkeit* applied by the S.S. and the Gestapo that they created formidable new partisan movements in areas of the U.S.S.R. in which, on their first arrival, the Germans had been greeted as liberators.

Only in one country did the German policy of terror pay an interim dividend but even there the final result was more costly than most of their failures. Two resistance movements arose in Yugoslavia. One was organised by the relics of the royal government, while the other came from the elements opposed to it, principally from the Communist Party. The royalists, the *chetniks*, could almost be considered as a regular army except that it had no base. It was led by General Mihailović, Minister of War in the exiled government, its officers held commissions, all ranks wore, at least at the outset, uniforms and its main strength came from officers and men of the pre-war army. It took its orders from the legal government which, even if it had been driven from the country, had never surrendered. It scored some early successes, but its leaders could not face the reprisals which followed. In the sparsely populated region of Ravna Gora the Germans executed 9,000 hostages, three hundred for every German the *chetniks* had killed. Mihailović lost his nerve and slid into a position scarcely distinguishable from collaboration with the enemy. His followers drifted away, many of them taking service with the more active partisans led by the Communist, Marshal Tito.

Tito made up his mind that, if his movement was to succeed, he and his followers must not be deterred by *schrecklichkeit*. It was an appalling decision to have to take but it was justified by events. By the end of 1942 thirty divisions of Axis troops – 120,000 Germans, 350,000 Italians and 80,000 Bulgarians, to say nothing of 300,000 local levies (mostly Croat *Ustachi*) – were required to hold the main centres and the railways through the country. At the end of the war the partisans claimed to hold 20,000 German prisoners. The cost, however, was desperately high. The war cost Yugoslavia the lives of 1,700,000 men, women and children, more than one in ten of the pre-war population.

The irregular combatant came into his and her own in the Second World War and no way of dealing with him or her was found. In France alone the Germans, apart from punishments to those accused of crimes, executed 29,660 hostages, innocent people held responsible for the actions of others. This had no substantial effect on the operations of the resistance. It is easy to accuse the Germans and their allies of using senseless brutality in their ineffectual attempt to contain the threat to their occupation forces. It was a threat that their opponents never had to face. If, when they occupied Italy and Germany, they had found active underground resistance it may well be that they would have been forced to use tactics different only in scale from those employed by the Germans. In 1943 when snipers behind the lines caused casualties among British troops, General Oliver Leese ordered hostages to be taken from every Sicilian village which his troops occupied. As it happened the sniping soon stopped (it had, in all probability, been carried out by German soldiers stranded behind the allied lines), but what would the general have done if it had continued? The *Manual of Military Law* laid down that, 'If hostages are taken at all, they suffer captivity and not death.'

Would the imprisonment of a number of prominent citizens have been sufficient to halt a determined guerrilla campaign? History suggests that such a move would have had little effect and some other form of pressure would have had to be devised.

The war of 1939–45 marks the obsequies of the doctrine that war was a business for professionals, that civilians, except those unfortunate enough to live in the path of the fighting, had no part in hostilities and must be protected by both sides. War had returned to the condition described by Grotius in the Thirty Years War, where all subjects of a belligerent state were liable to be killed and all their property was at the disposition of the enemy. There are no longer any non-combatants.

5

Privateers or Pirates

The oceans, being of vast size, make an ideal theatre for guerrilla operations. If in 1941 it was possible for the Royal Navy, aided by aircraft, wireless and radar, to lose touch with a battleship as large as the *Bismarck* how much easier it must have been, before the invention of those aids to searching, for a small ship to slip through the blockade of the world's most powerful navy and prey on merchant ships. A determined captain, bent on evasion, would be very unfortunate if he fell in with a hostile patrol as he made his break for the distant trade routes. Navies, moreover, are a recent development. The first ocean-going, purpose-built sailing warships did not take to the seas until the reign of Elizabeth I. Previously any state that required a fleet for a particular task merely requisitioned merchant ships and supplemented their crews with soldiers. All merchant ships would in any case be armed even in time of peace. Pirates remained an important menace even in European waters until the nineteenth century. As late as 1816 a Barbary pirate took a prize within sight of Dover.

Fleets were a wartime phenomenon and if in peace a single naval operation was required it could be left to civilians to execute. The civilians, however, had to be properly authorised to take violent action. If they did not have the correct documents they would have been pirates and every sailor's hand would have been against them. For the redress of legitimate grievance they had to have a Letter of Reprisal issued by a sovereign authority. Such documents had made their appearance as early as the thirteenth century and in 1295 Bernard Dongresilli, 'citizen and merchant of Bayonne' (then a possession of the English Crown) was returning from North Africa with his ship, *St Mary of Bayonne*, loaded with almonds and Malaga grapes, 'all of which he bought with his own money'. A storm forced him to put into Cascais where, according to his Letter of Reprisal issued by King Edward I,

> Certain sons of perdition, coming out of Lisbon, made for the ship in hostile fashion, and after spoiling the aforesaid merchant and others on board, of their ship, merchandise and other goods, carried off the whole to the city of Lisbon. And of all the goods

so spoiled and carried off, the King of Portugal received for his own use the tenth part: and the rest of the goods the robbers divided amongst themselves. And the said Bernard claims, by reason of the said spoil and robbery, he is damnified to the amount of £700 sterling.

Having no ships of war, all the King of England could do, although the case was one in which a foreign king was clearly implicated, was to give the aggrieved merchant authority to put things right by his own efforts. King Edward, therefore,

Now give and grant to him, Bernard, his heirs successors and posterity, liberty to make reprisals upon the people of the Realm of Portugal, and upon their goods, wheresoever he may find them [and] to retain and keep to himself, until he . . . shall be fully satisfied for his goods so spoiled, or their value as declared above, together with expenses reasonably incurred by him in that regard.

It is not known how successful Dongresilli was in recovering his £700 nor how he set about doing so. It seems unlikely that he operated on the scale of Ango, a Dieppe shipowner, who lost a ship to Lisbon pirates in 1525. Having obtained a Letter of Reprisal from the King of France, he equipped a squadron of seventeen armed ships and established a blockade of the Tagus, thus bringing the trade of Lisbon to a standstill. Unable to drive Ango's ships away, the Portuguese sent ambassadors to Paris to complain to Francis I, but he merely replied, *'Messieurs, ce n'est pas moi qui fais la guerre; allez trouvez Ango, et arrangez vous avec lui.'*

As a way of settling international commercial disputes without expense to the Treasury, Letters of Reprisal had no equal but they were indiscriminate in their effects since they authorised the aggrieved party to recompense himself on any national of the state to which the original robbers belonged. Bernard Dongresilli, for example, could set upon any Portuguese ship and recoup his loss and, unless he happened to meet the original 'sons of perdition' he would be robbing an innocent trader who would obtain his own Letter of Reprisal against any subject of the English Crown, and set a vicious circle in motion. Nevertheless the custom of issuing such letters continued for many centuries, although in 1713 the Treaty of Utrecht included a clause that they should only be issued following a denial of justice and after four months' notice had been given to the ambassador of the offending state.

From authorising private men to set right their own wrongs in peace, it was only a short step to making use of their services in war. Again it was important to ensure that such private warships should be distinguishable from pirates and for this purpose they were issued with a Letter of Marque. This authorised the holder to capture any enemy ship on which he could lay his hands but the business details were different. Letters of Reprisal authorised only the recouping of actual losses suffered and 'expenses reasonably incurred' but Letters of Marque allowed the holder to take part in a highly profitable business and it was only to be expected that the state would do its best to skim off some of the dividends. In two September days in 1690 Jean Bart, the great French privateer,* took eight Hanseatic ships valued at 79,500 *livres*, a handsome fortune. Of this Bart had to give one-tenth to the *Amiral de France* and one-fifth of the remaining nine-tenths to the King of France.

The percentages that had to be paid to the government varied with the state of the war at sea. The worse the overall situation, the less was demanded. In 1243 an English Letter of Marque issued to two shipowners laid down that 'they are to render to the King, in his Wardrobe, the half of all their gains'. In 1405 another consortium got a much better bargain since Henry IV agreed 'that whatsoever they, John and Philip, succeed in winning, gaining and having by capture, they may have and keep for their own proper use'.

There were many loopholes for the abuse of Letters of Marque. It was too easy for privateers to degenerate into pirates, working wholly for their own benefit, preying with equal ferocity on enemy, friendly and neutral shipping and continuing to do so when the war was over. It was to control the men of the Cinque Ports whose depredations in the Straits of Dover were notorious in peace and war that piracy was made high treason in 1413. Twelve years later Marcellus, Abbot of Canterbury, was found guilty of piracy in the Straits and only his benefit of clergy enabled him to escape with his life.

Letters of Marque were carefully drawn up so as to ensure that privateers behaved with credit, as well as profit, to their native land. In 1760 Birchman Pillans, master of the 170-ton ship *Tryal* was authorised to,

> Set forth in a warlike fashion . . . to attack, surprise, seize or take any place or fortress upon the land, or any ship or vessel, goods or ammunition, arms, stores of war, or merchandize, belonging

* The term privateer appears not to have been used before 1664 but since there is no useful synonym for it it has been used in this chapter for ships sailing under Letters of Marque or Reprisal in earlier periods.

to or possessed by any of his Majesty's enemies upon the land, or in any sea, haven or river, excepting only within the harbours or roads of any Princes or States in amity with his Majesty.

Moreover such captures as Pillans did make had to be brought before an Admiralty court which would establish whether or not they were lawful prize. To ensure that he kept within the rules he was required to deposit before sailing two sureties for £1,500. The other control on a privateer's conduct was the possibility of what might happen to them if its crew were captured. Supplied with a Letter of Marque they could count on being treated as prisoners of war, provided they acted in accordance with the customs of war at sea. If they did not they were likely to be hanged as pirates. Their authorisation, therefore, always included a paragraph setting out their duties. One of 1666 ran as follows:

> Noe person or persons taken or surprized in any ship or vessell, though known to be of the enemy's party, shall be in cold blood killed, maimed or wounded, or by other torture or cruelty treated contrary to the common usages and just provisions of warr; otherwise the said commissions to bee [sic] voyd to the taker to all intents and purposes.

A hundred and ten years later this wording had scarcely changed when the Congress of the United Colonies of America issued their own Instructions to Privateers.

> If you, or any of your Officers or Crew shall, in cold blood, kill or maim, or by Torture or otherwise, cruelly, inhumanly, and contrary to the common Usage and Practice of civilized Nations in War, treat any Person or Persons surprized in the Ship or Vessel you shall take, the offender shall be severely punished.

It is obvious that the greatest opportunities for successful privateering arose in countries which were not strong in conventional naval power. Dominant navies soon swept the seas of most of their enemies' merchant ships and left few pickings for privateers. Their opponents by contrast would find the oceans swarming with trading vessels. In the days of Spanish naval supremacy the English were the leaders in private warfare, although most of the Elizabethan sea-dogs operated without Letters of Marque. The Queen was too crafty to sanction their ravages in advance though she was ready enough to authorise their captures retrospectively when there was a share of the proceeds to be collected. It was, during the next reign, the unsuccessful attack on San Tomas in Guiana, that finally secured the execution of Sir Walter Raleigh. In the century that followed, dominance at sea gradually passed to the British and the lead in privateering was taken by France who made rich pickings from the British merchant marine. It was estimated that during the war of the League of Augsburg (1688–97) Britain lost 4,200 ships, valued at £30 million, to privateers, most of them French. Such activities were greatly strengthened after 1692 when Louis XIV, his ships of the line shattered at Barfleur, La Hogue and Vigo, decided that his remaining ships of war could best contribute by engaging in a *guerre de course*, a war against commerce. He rented frigates and other small warships to *armateurs*, magnates who were prepared to equip and man them at their own expense so as to reap rich dividends from the capture of British and Dutch shipping. As an inducement the king gave up his claim to a fifth of the proceeds in 1709, the *Amiral de France* following his example in 1748. With many officers and men of the French navy encouraged to take service aboard privateers the King began giving regular commissions to successful privateer commanders.

Some of them were very successful indeed. While Marlborough was winning his famous, if inconclusive, victories on land, the great figure at sea was René Duguay-Trouin, a commander of privateers from St Malo, who collected round himself a squadron strong enough to engage British convoys in the English Channel. On one occasion he captured sixty merchantmen, having sunk one and captured three warships of the escort. In 1711 he defeated a Portuguese naval squadron and later seized and held to ransom the city and port of Rio de Janeiro with all its shipping. Before he retired from privateering he had captured sixteen warships and more than three hundred merchant ships.

Under the Bourbons French privateers were very strictly controlled. They were forbidden to harass fishing boats and in 1779 they were ordered not to interfere with Captain James Cook while he was engaged in exploration. The early republican governments were not so scrupulous. In January 1793, before France was at war with Britain, the Minister of Marine was instructed to issue blank Letters of Marque, thus making the usual controls on them meaningless. One famous privateer, Richéry, attacked the Labrador fisheries, sinking eighty boats, an exploit which, with other attacks on neutral shipping, brought about an undeclared war with the United States, a conflict which reached its climax when U.S.S. *Constellation* (38) attacked and captured the French frigate *Insurgente* (36) off the Leeward Isles. Between February 1793 and December 1795 French privateers brought in 2,099 ships as prizes.

As under the *ancien régime* much of the French naval strength was allotted to their support and a return rendered by the French Admiralty in 1797 noted that twenty-six out of forty-six French frigates, sixteen out of nineteen corvettes, and two out of six brigs were '*confié à des armateurs pour faire la course*', that is to say they had been leased to private enterprise for privateering.

The United States was the other great home of privateers. When the Thirteen Colonies began their struggle for independence they had no fleet and they had to rely on private ships to make head against the most powerful navy in the world. Three hundred and forty-three ships were authorised by Congress to,

> By force of Arms, attack, subdue and take all Ships and other vessels belonging to the inhabitants of Great Britain, on the High Seas, or between high-water and low-water marks, except ships bringing persons who intend to settle and reside in the United Colonies, or bringing Arms, Ammunition or Warlike Stores to the said Colonies, for the use of such Inhabitants as are Friends to the American Cause, which you shall suffer to pass unmolested, the Commanders thereof permitting a peaceful search, and giving satisfactory Information of the Contents of the Ladings, and the Destination of the Voyages.

Led by the redoubtable Paul Jones, American privateers brought in a total of 1,151 prizes during the war, a figure surpassed in the war of 1812 when the 515 privateers commissioned captured 1,345 British merchant ships.

Before the Crimean War broke out in 1854 the British issued a declaration to the neutral powers that,

> Her Majesty declares that being anxious to lessen as much as possible the evils of war, and to restrict its operations to the regularly organised forces of the country, it is not her present intention to issue Letters of Marque for the Commissioning of Privateers.

When simultaneously Napoleon III made a similar declaration for France, privateering in European waters was a thing of the past. The joint renunciation was an act of policy rather than of principle. The Russian fleets were penned up in the Baltic and the Black Sea and their merchant fleet was too small to make privateering a paying proposition. Any attempt to make it so would arouse neutral opinion against the countries issuing the Letters of

Marque. The United States was shocked at any idea that the ban on privateering might be expected to apply to them in the event of any future war and, that December, President Pierce sent a message to Congress disassociating the country from any such proposal.

> When the honor and rights of our country require it to assume a hostile attitude, it confidently relies on the patriotism of its citizens, not ordinarily devoted to the military profession, to augment the army and navy . . . The proposition to enter into engagements to forego a resort to privateers, in case this country should be forced into war, is not entitled to more favorable consideration than would be a proposition to agree not to accept the services of volunteers for operations on land.

In view of this forthright declaration it surprised no one that when the Crimean War was over and, as an appendage to the peace treaty in 1856, the powers of Europe – Austria, Britain, France, Prussia, Russia, Sardinia and Turkey – signed the Declaration of Paris which agreed, amongst other provisions, that *La Course est et demeure abolie*, the United States refused to sign. To explain American obduracy on this point, the minister in London was instructed to call on the Foreign Secretary, Lord Clarendon.

> I admitted that the practice of privateering was subject to great abuses; but it did not seem to be possible, under existing circumstances, for the United States to agree to its suppression . . . Suppose, for example, we should again be engaged in a war with Great Britain, which I earnestly hoped might never be the case; to what situation must we be reduced if we should consent to abolish privateering.
> The navy of Great Britain was vastly superior to that of the United States in the number of vessels of war. They could send cruizers into every sea and capture our merchant vessels, whilst the number of our cruizers was comparatively so small as to render anything like equality in this respect impossible. The only means we would possess to counterbalance in some degree their far greater strength would be to convert our merchant vessels, cast out of their employment by the war, into privateers and endeavour, by their assistance, to inflict upon Britain such losses as they would be able to inflict on American commerce.

Money and sentiment were behind the American attitude. There was no theoretical reason why the 'merchant ships cast out of their employment by the war' should not be commissioned into the U.S.

navy and used as armed merchant cruisers, a practice which would not contravene the Declaration of Paris, except that the cost of equipping and manning them would fall on the Treasury rather than on private 'adventurers'. This, in fact, happened when the navy had to be expanded rapidly in 1861. A stronger reason was nostalgia. The American people were justifiably proud of the record of their privateers and were reluctant to believe that their exploits could never be repeated. The decision to abstain from the Declaration was one which the Union government was soon to regret.

Five years after the Declaration of Paris and six days after Brigadier General Beauregard's guns had opened on Fort Sumpter, Jefferson Davis, President of the Confederate States of America, issued a proclamation which recognised the intention of the United States to invade the Confederacy with an armed force and of 'subjecting the free people thereof to the domination of a foreign power'. He therefore invited,

> All those who may desire by service in private-armed vessels on the high seas, to aid this Government in resisting so wanton and wicked an aggression, to make application for commissions or Letters of Marque and Reprisal to be issued under the seal of these Confederate States.

Since the entire U.S. navy had fallen into the hands of the Union government, the south had no alternative to issuing Letters of Marque (which, it will be noticed, had become merged with Letters of Reprisal) if any war at sea was to be carried on, since the Confederacy had neither the funds nor the facilities to build a fleet. They were, in fact, in the same position that the U.S. minister had postulated to Lord Clarendon in the case of the United States being at war with Britain, that 'the only means we would possess to counterbalance in some degree their strength would be to convert our merchant vessels . . . into privateers'.

Such an argument found little acceptance in Washington and the government there waited only two days before issuing a counterblast to President Davis's proclamation.

> Whereas a combination engaged in insurrection have threatened to grant Letters of Marque to authorise the bearers thereof to commit assaults on the lives, vessels and property of good citizens of the country lawfully engaged in commerce on the high seas and in the waters of the United States . . . I, Abraham Lincoln, President of the United States . . . hereby proclaim

that if any person, under the pretended authority of the said [Confederate] States, or under any pretense, shall molest a vessel of the United States, or the persons or cargo on board of her, such person will be held amenable to the laws of the United States for the prevention and punishment of piracy.

This was definite enough but Lincoln could not have felt his moral position to be strong in view of the United States' firm refusal to accede to the Declaration of Paris only five years earlier. He therefore instructed his ministers at London and Paris to propose that the United States should now adhere to the Declaration. Britain and France both refused the suggestion, Lord John Russell replying that if Britain accepted this death-bed conversion she would 'be bound to treat the privateers of the so-called Confederate States as pirates' and that this would entail acting contrary to the strict neutrality she had already declared in the war. Both Britain and France, however, agreed to refuse privateers the right to bring their prizes into their ports, a right which the United States had accorded to French privateers in the wars between 1793 and 1814. This restriction crippled the operations of the southern privateers, since it meant that any prizes would have to be brought back to southern ports through the Union blockade.

Lincoln's threat to treat privateers as pirates had little effect on southern enthusiasm for serving at a substantial profit and applications for Letters of Marque flooded in, despite the requirement for sureties of $5,000 and $10,000 according to the size of the ship. The Letters were issued according to established American and British precedents, insisting that prizes be brought before a prize court and enjoining 'the strictest regard to the rights of neutrals'. In addition it was laid down that, 'Towards enemy vessels and their crews you are to proceed in exercising the rights of war with all the justice and humanity which characterize this Government and its citizens.'

Despite southern enthusiasm for privateering, the results were meagre. The most memorable venture was the cruise of the *Savannah*, a sixty-eight-foot schooner for which a Letter of Marque was obtained on May 18th, 1861 by T. Harrison Baker, a former ship's officer then serving in the Vigilant Rifles of Charleston. He enlisted a crew which comprised five officers and fifteen ratings who included, apart from a Chinese cook, three Irishmen, two Scots, a German and a Filipino. The ship was armed, in the absence of other guns, with a short 18-pounder, dated 1812, mounted amidships. *Savannah* slipped out of Charleston on June 2nd, and next morning took her first, and only, prize, the brig

77

Joseph sailing to Philadelphia with a cargo of muscovado sugar. An officer and six ratings were put aboard her and she was successfully sailed back to a southern port where a prize court condemned her as good prize and valued her at $30,000.

Late on the same afternoon, *Savannah* sighted another sail but this turned out to be U.S.S. *Perry*, a brig mounting six guns, which rapidly overhauled the privateer. Baker, realising that he could not escape, turned to fight, hoping to gain time for the onset of darkness. His crew, who were not naval men, immediately fled below and the antique gun was manned by the officers. Both sides fired at each other for twenty minutes without causing casualties or damage but Baker realised that he could not escape and surrendered his ship. He and his twelve remaining companions were immediately put in irons, where they remained until June 30th, when the *Perry* reached New York. Marched through a jeering crowd to the Tombs prison, they were put into cells normally reserved for felons. The Union government announced that they would be tried for piracy and the New York press howled for them to be hanged at the nearest yard-arm.

When news of the impending trial reached Richmond, President Davis wrote to President Lincoln pointing out that the Confederacy held a large number of Union prisoners, most of whom had so far been allowed to live on parole but who, since the imprisonment of the crew of the *Savannah*, had been put into confinement.

A just regard to humanity and the honor of this Government now require me to state explicitly that, painful as will be the necessity, this Government will deal out to the prisoners held by it the same treatment and the same fate as shall be experienced by those captured on the *Savannah*, that retaliation will be extended so far as shall be requisite to secure the abandonment of a practice unknown to the warfare of civilized man, and so barbarous as to disgrace the nation which shall be guilty of inaugurating it.

Undeterred by this threat Lincoln insisted on proceeding with the trial and on July 23rd the thirteen prisoners, still chained, appeared in court to answer a charge of piracy. Further proceedings were then adjourned for three months since one of the judges was injured in a carriage accident, but on October 23rd twelve of the prisoners, the thirteenth having turned State's evidence, pleaded not guilty. Despite a vociferous press campaign, the *New York World* announcing that 'the voice of the people demands that if these pirates are convicted they shall be hanged', the jury, after twenty hours of deliberation, was unable to agree and a re-trial was ordered for the new year. Meanwhile, in Philadelphia, the trial was proceeding of the crew of another privateer, the *Jefferson Davis*, and here one member of the crew, William Smith, prizemaster, was sentenced to death. The Confederacy repeated its threat of immediate reprisals against prisoners of war (see p. 204 below) and, on this occasion, Lincoln wavered. No action was taken against Smith and, four months later, all those captured on privateers, save one who had died in the Tombs, were sent to prisoner of war camps and eventually exchanged.

By this time Confederate privateering was a spent force. The Union blockade had become too effective to allow private-armed ships to operate at a profit on the open seas. Two years later the Union threatened to undertake privateering against the British. London was informed that Letters of Marque, valid against the British ships which continued to run the blockade, would be issued unless Britain took effective measures to prevent the building and equipping of Confederate warships in British ports. The threat succeeded. The notorious Laird 'rams' were not allowed to sail and compensation of $15½ million was paid for damage done to American shipping by the British-built (and largely British-manned) *Alabama*.

Despite the short flurry of transatlantic privateering between 1861 and 1862, the Declaration of Paris marked the end of more than five centuries of profitable private war-making at sea. It would, however, be wrong to hail this as a triumph of international law. By the middle of the nineteenth century it was the consensus among European seamen that the odds against the privateer were too long to attract speculative investment. The advent of steam power and the increasing range of maritime artillery greatly reduced the disadvantages under which regular navies had operated against privateers and, a few decades later, the coming of wireless clinched the argument. Privateering vanished not because it was banned at Paris but because it was no longer commercially viable.

In the wars of the twentieth century, or so the Germans claimed, any armed vessel was either a warship or a pirate and in either case it would be legitimate to sink her on sight. They further claimed that, under the long-recognised 'cruiser rules', an unarmed merchant ship should, when signalled to do so by a warship, heave to and submit to search so that it could be established whether or not her cargo was contraband of war. A century earlier the British had been staunchly defending this view against the whole world; they took a diametrically opposed stand when faced with the menace of submarines in 1914–18. They instructed the masters of unarmed

79

ships to ignore orders to stop and, where possible, to ram the summoning U-boat.

In March 1916 the German U 23, which was on the surface, ordered the British ship *Brussels* to heave to but her captain, Charles Fryatt, obeyed his orders and tried unsuccessfully to ram the submarine. He was taken prisoner and charged, 'not being embodied in the armed forces', with 'a *franc-tireur* crime against the sea-forces of Germany'. His accusers also claimed that he had with him a gold watch which had been presented to him for a previous attempt to ram a U-boat. Despite attempts by the American embassy in Berlin to arrange that he should be legally represented, he was brought before a hastily convened court-martial, found guilty of piracy and, on the same evening, shot.

It is hard to dispute the legality of the German case. Fryatt was not a member of the armed forces and his attempt to sink a U-boat which was conforming impeccably with internationally recognised rules for stopping and searching merchant ships could convincingly be held to be an act of piracy. The wisdom of pressing the charge and even more of the hasty execution of the sentence was quite another matter and it would seem that the Germans themselves had serious doubts on the subject since they never repeated the procedure although they had the opportunity of doing so.

The introduction of unrestricted submarine warfare in 1917 made the question academic since 'cruiser rules' were no longer used. The same considerations applied in the Second World War although the Germans did, on one occasion, raise the question of piracy. On August 10th, 1940 the Foreign Office in Berlin announced that anyone joining the Free French Navy would be treated as a pirate and 'shown no mercy'. The threat was never implemented.

6

For Love or Money

Once given the theory that war was a business for professionals, it followed that any professional could take part. The *Kriegsbrauch*, a work not noted for a liberal interpretation of military practices, ruled that among the bodies which could legitimately take part in a war was 'The regular army, and it is a matter of indifference whether . . . it consists of subjects or aliens'.

Once a man had enlisted and became a member of the profession, his nationality was irrelevant. A member of that most famous mercenary body, the French Foreign Legion, was asked by a visiting general what his nationality was. He replied simply, *'Je suis légionnaire'*. He might equally have answered, *'Je suis soldat'*.

If a man joins a foreign army the authority most likely to object is the government of his own country. Most countries have legislation approximating to the British Foreign Enlistment Act which aims to prevent British nationals enlisting for alien wars. In the Second World War there was the case of Prince Pierre Murat who, being a member of the Bonaparte family, was forbidden to join the French army and joined the British instead. As Captain Peter Murray he served in the 4th/7th Dragoon Guards but when the war was over the government of General de Gaulle threatened to proceed against him for accepting a foreign commission, an offence, he was informed, for which the penalty was death or life imprisonment with the forfeiture of all property in France.

It is unlikely that Captain Murray/Murat considered himself a mercenary any more than those who fought with the International Brigade in the Spanish Civil War would have done, but according to eighteenth-century definitions, such as that of Vattel, anyone is a mercenary who enlists in a foreign army, accepting military discipline in exchange for a stipulated sum of money. This would include anyone who receives the ordinary pay for his rank irrespective of whether he fought for the sake of a cause, simple love of fighting, a desire to make money or even because he had been press-ganged into enlisting.

Mercenaries first came into prominence in Europe in the mid-fourteenth century. The interregnum in the century-long conflict between France and England threw out of employment thousands of men who had no trade but war. Many of them became free-booters, bandits who fought and plundered for their own benefit and overran much of France and Germany. Others formed themselves into companies under proven leaders and rented their services to any state which required an army and could pay for it. Italy was their happy hunting ground, the more so since many of the multifarious city states refused to allow any of their own citizens to hold military command in case he was tempted to execute a military coup. Venice went so far as to forbid any of her subjects to join the army, preferring to rely entirely on mercenaries. Venice, being the richest of the Italian states, could afford regular pay for the best type of mercenaries. It was an unfortunate state which fell behind in the payments. Mercenary captains fought on a contract and would have no scruple in deserting an employer who failed in his side of the bargain. No question of natural loyalty arose, indeed some mercenaries were not above changing allegiance in mid-campaign if the enemy made a better offer. Others, notably the Englishman Sir John Hawkwood, were renowned for the conscientious way in which they fulfilled their contracts, not that that would prevent them changing sides when their contract expired and it was time to renegotiate terms. Hawkwood fought for Florence against Pisa, for Pisa against Florence, for Milan against the Pope and for the Pope against Milan. To each he gave good and loyal service. His position was similar to that of a professional footballer who can transfer his services from one club to another. Sir John, however, was given a tomb and an equestrian statue in the Duomo by the grateful city of Florence.

Mercenary warfare in Italy developed along lines which ideally suited the professional soldier if they suited no one else. Campaigns resembled games of animated chess. Gambits were foreseeable and foreseen and were met with appropriate counter-gambits; battles were rare and usually bloodless. At the Battle of Zagonara (1424), 'a great rout which was celebrated throughout Italy, no one died except Ludovico degli Obizzi and two of his men, who were thrown from their horses and drowned in a muddy ditch'. There was no point in killing an opponent. Prisoners were a better proposition since, if they were officers, they could be ransomed, and if they were common soldiers, they could be used for making up the numbers in one's own company. There was no profit in a corpse. Both sides shunned the idea of a decisive battle since it would entail both armies losing their employment. As Machiavelli wrote in *Il Principe*,

They have taken care to save themselves and their men from the terrors and fatigues of war. They do not kill each other in their combats, but take each other prisoner without a blow being struck. They make no night attacks on fortresses nor do the defenders ever make sorties against the camps of the besiegers so that there is no need to stockade or entrench these camps. Campaigns are never continued into the winter. All these customs have grown into the military system because they wish to spare themselves both fatigue and danger.

Since they had no national or religious allegiance, mercenaries lived in great amity with their opponents. Many of them were old comrades and might well soon be once more on the same side when the time came for contracts to be arranged for the next season's campaigning. The only people who hated them were the peasantry who resented having their crops trampled and their womenfolk raped whenever the mercenaries marched and counter-marched. Sometimes they took the law into their own hands. In 1173 the rebel lords Lovel and Leicester brought a body of Flemish mercenaries to England only to be defeated at Fornham Bridge, near Bury St Edmunds. The peasants thereupon pushed all the surviving Flemings into a bog.

Mercenary fighting underwent an abrupt change in 1480 when the first Swiss regiments entered the service of France. Most of the cantons had more men than their agriculture could support and, with typical Swiss business acumen, they decided to capitalise on the surplus. Having devised a highly effective tactical doctrine, they soon became the most formidable infantry in Europe. They also introduced into warfare a needless brutality which shocked Europe. After the Battle of Novara (1513) they butchered several hundred Germans, mercenaries like themselves, whose only crime was to have been on the losing side. It was a long step on the downward slope that led to the Thirty Years War.

Swiss regiments also served in the Austrian and Spanish services, but it was to the French that they gave their most distinguished and profitable services, continuing until the revolution when they disbanded themselves as a protest against the lack of discipline in the early republican armies. Many of them then took service with the British, in such regiments as Meuron's and de Watteville's, but they soon reappeared in the French army list and fought in all Napoleon's campaigns, two battalions of *2ᵐᵉ Suisse* taking part even in the Waterloo campaign. It was not until 1884 that the last Swiss regiments left the French service.

A relic of the Swiss mercenary tradition survives in the hundred and fifty men of the Swiss Guard at the Vatican. These, however, represent a different strain of mercenaries, the foreign bodyguards which some sovereigns preferred to have as an insurance against the treachery of their own subjects. As early as 886 Louis le Gros, King of France, had a personal guard of twenty-four Scottish gentlemen. The same number of Scotsmen accompanied Louis IX, St Louis, when he went on the Seventh Crusade. From 1497 onwards the Kings of France relied on Swiss bodyguards until the *Cent Suisses* died protecting Louis XVI in 1792.

The climax of mercenary warfare came with the Thirty Years War. Although in theory a struggle between Catholic and Protestant, both sides relied almost entirely on mercenary armies and did not enquire into the religious affiliations of their soldiers. Without the defection of a great mercenary leader the war might never have swollen into the great catastrophe that it became. At the very outset the Protestant King of Bohemia had to defend his capital, Prague, against the Catholic Emperor's troops. The Prince of Orange and the Duke of Savoy had arranged for Ernst von Mansfeldt with a strong mercenary army to support the king but he could not find the money to pay his own troops and von Mansfeldt's account went by default. At the crucial Battle of the White Mountain (November 8th, 1620) the mercenaries were absent, Prague and Bohemia were lost and twenty-eight years' more fighting failed to regain them.

Von Mansfeldt was frank about the situation of his men,

Neither they nor their horses can live on air. All that they have, whether it be arms or apparel, weareth, wastest and breakest. If they must buy more, they must have money, and if men have not it to give them, they will take it where they find it, not as part of what is due to them, but without weighing or counting it. This gate being once opened unto them, they enter into the large fields of liberty . . . They spare no person of whatever quality soever he be, respect no place, however holy, neither churches, altars, tombs, sepulchres nor the dead bodies that lie in them.

He died six years later, too soon to see how truly he had prophesied, and before Germany was reduced to a desert, when no one could pay his soldiers and the Swedish Marshal Tortensson was reduced to enlisting men to whom he could promise only rations and such plunder as they could find.

In the Thirty Years War mercenaries became big business. For many years the dominant figure was Albrecht von Wallenstein, the greatest of all the entrepreneurs of war up to his day. Since he had a

84

firm financial base in his wife's estates in Bohemia and his own vast booty, he was able to wait for payment, unlike von Mansfeldt. The Emperor, for whom he raised more than 100,000 men, owed von Wallenstein vast sums and sought to buy time to pay by creating him Prince of Sagan, Duke of Friedland and Duke of Mecklenburg. Eventually, at the Emperor's instigation he was murdered by his own officers. The troops he had raised were a motley collection from all nationalities and religions. Among his senior subordinates, apart from Germans and Austrians, were Scots, Italians and Flemings, a Pole, a Frenchman and a Romanian. There is a record of one of the regiments he raised to fight for the Catholic side breaking into mutiny when ordered to parade for the celebration of the Mass. Among his Bavarian allies were contingents of Greeks and Turks while his most formidable opponent, King Gustavus Adolphus, supplemented his Swedish troops with Scots, Hessians, Bohemians and Poles.

After the Thirty Years War the amount of finance involved in raising mercenaries became too large for any private citizen and the business was largely taken over by German princelings who started with the advantage that their overheads were lower. They did not have to offer bounties to potential recruits, they could conscript them. Even the most avaricious of princes, however, had some scruples about whom their men would serve. The rulers of South Germany provided troops for the Catholic powers while those of the North served the Protestant states. Wars against infidels were another matter and in 1660 Protestant Brunswick rented three battalions to Catholic Venice to fight the Turks while in 1687 Hessians in the Venetian service captured Negroponte (Euboea) from the same enemy.

The doyen of purveyors of mercenaries were the Landgraves of Hesse-Kassel. They, like the Swiss two centuries earlier, found themselves with a surplus of manpower and used it as a capital asset. They also had a good product to sell, since the Hessians had a fine reputation both for courage and discipline. Successive landgraves rented troops to Prussia, Holland, Denmark and, since they were loyal subjects of the Holy Roman Empire, to the Emperor. But their best customer was Britain, a customer acquired when William of Orange, on his expedition to seize the English crown, hired 3,400 Hessians to take the place of Dutch troops who were accompanying him to England. Once installed at St James's Palace he continued to hire Hessians, as did Marlborough after him, for the long war against Louis XIV. By 1727 Parliament had agreed that an annual payment of £125,000 should be made to secure for Britain first call on all Hessian troops.

It was an arrangement that suited everyone. It meant that no taxes had to be paid in Hesse-Kassel and the Landgrave was even able to provide for his subjects some public education and rudimentary social services. The British were able to avoid keeping in peacetime a standing army of any size, an institution they greatly mistrusted. Even the Hessian conscripts seem not greatly to have resented the arrangement. The only problems arose when Britain, contrary to her usual policy, found herself in 1744 opposed in war to the Emperor. In her army in the Low Countries Britain had 6,000 Hessians and, due to imperial obligations, a similar number were serving with the imperial army; hence there had to be some brisk redeployment so that the two contingents did not come face to face in battle. Fortunately in the next year the rebellion of the Young Pretender gave an excuse for sending 5,000 Hessians to Scotland.

The British use of Hessians most often remembered came during the War of American Independence. It is calculated that the Landgrave of the time made a profit on the war of 12,650,0000 thaler (£1 = 5.5 thaler). In return the British gained the services of a large number of excellent soldiers who deserted far less frequently than their British comrades. As might be expected, the colonists complained vociferously against the inhumanity of employing foreigners in what amounted to a civil war. They had never complained when British had sent Hessians to America to protect the same colonies from the French and the evidence suggests that the foreigners were far less likely to commit outrages than the British or loyalist soldiers. Of the protests made at Westminster against the use of Hessians it is sufficient to say that the loudest complaints came from William Pitt, Earl of Chatham, who, in his years of power, had hired more mercenaries than any man in Europe.

It should be noted that by 1776 the term Hessians had become used generically for all German mercenaries. In fact, apart from Hesse-Kassel, the British employed in America units rented from Hesse-Hanau, Brunswick, Waldeck, Ansbach-Bayreuth and Ansbach-Zerbst. Strictly, none of these troops were mercenaries but auxiliaries since the states they came from were bound by treaties with Britain whereby both contracting parties undertook to provide help for each other in time of need. In practice none of the small states ever found it necessary to call for British aid. Not that Britain was averse to acting as an auxiliary. The Battle of Dettingen, when the British beat the French in 1743, is generally remembered as being the last occasion when a King of England led his troops into action. It is also remarkable since Britain and

France were not at war at the time but were both acting as auxiliaries to factions in an Imperial quarrel.

Britain differed from the European powers because she maintained no foreign regiments in peacetime. Nevertheless, much of her infantry had mercenary origins. The First (Royal, later Royal Scots) Regiment of Foot started life as a Scottish regiment in the Swedish service but in 1635 moved to the French army as the *Régiment d'Hebron*, the title being taken from its colonel, Sir John Hepburn. It did not come to the British service until 1670. Similarly the Third (Buffs), the Fifth (Northumberland) and the Sixth (Warwickshire) Regiments all started as mercenaries in the Dutch army.

On the Continent foreign regiments were a usual feature of peacetime armies. In 1700 there were five French regiments in the Prussian order of battle and by the middle of the eighteenth century one-third of the strength of that army, including officers of all ranks, had been born outside Prussia. The Spaniards had regiments from the Netherlands, Switzerland, Ireland and Naples and there were so many Germans in the Danish army that all orders were given in German. On the eve of the revolution the French army had forty-six regiments of foreign infantry, including, apart from Swiss, Swedes, Flemings and Irish a large German contingent of such units as *Royal Allemand*, *Royal Nassau*, *Royal Bavière*, *Royal Anhalt*, *Royal Alsace* and *Royal Deux Ponts* (from Zweibrücken).

There seem to have been few cases of trouble when a mercenary in a foreign army found himself in action against troops from his native country. It was generally accepted that, unless a man was bound by some particular obligation before taking service abroad, he was no more than a professional on the other side. Even Irish historians of the 'Wild Geese', the Irish mercenaries of Jacobite sympathies who took service in the armies of France, Austria and Spain, seem unable to find cases where Irishmen captured by British troops suffered inconvenience above the lot of prisoners of war of all nationalities. The celebrated occasion at the Battle of Malplaquet, when the British Eighteenth (Royal Irish) met and defeated the *Royal Irlandais* of France, appears to have been marked by neither reluctance to engage nor special bitterness. It was a straightforward fight between two bodies of professionals who happened to be Irish.

The French revolution had the effect of transferring the French 'Wild Geese' to the British army. This was done at the suggestion of Count Daniel O'Connell who had been born in County Kerry in 1743 and commissioned into the French Irish Brigade at the age of fourteen. He fought, mostly against the British, throughout the Seven Years War, being wounded nine times at the siege of Gibraltar, and by the outbreak of the revolution he was Inspector General of French Infantry. Although he fought for the French at Valmy, he left the country when the king was imprisoned; he proposed to Pitt that six battalions of Irish could be formed for the British army out of men from the French service who now found it more difficult to practise Catholicism in France than in Britain. He became colonel of one of the new-formed battalions but, at the Peace of Amiens, he visited France to see to his wife's property and was unfortunate enough to be caught among the *détenus* (see p. 34–5) and spent the rest of the war at Verdun. At the restoration of 1814 Louis XVIII gave him back his rank in the French army, making him perhaps the only man who has simultaneously drawn full pay as a French general and a British colonel.

The heightened sense of nationality – one of the legacies which Napoleon left to Europe – spelled the end of the raising of foreign regiments. The only major exception was the Foreign Legion, raised in 1835 to relieve the French soldier of the task of policing the less hospitable parts of Africa, but subsequently to take a distinguished part in all French wars. Otherwise the question of serving in foreign armies only arose in acute form when, in 1940, a group of Americans living in London proposed to form a special company of the Home Guard. They were not strictly mercenaries since the Home Guard served without pay, but their ambassador, the defeatist Joseph Kennedy, protested strongly that, when the Germans invaded England, they would all be shot as *francs-tireurs*. The Foreign Office had their own doubts about the proposal. What, they asked, would happen if the Japanese in London made the same suggestion?

Nationality meant less at sea. Since the conditions of their trade determined that sailors ranged the world, there were always many seamen who served in ships belonging to nations other than their own, usually in search of better pay, conditions and, best of all, prize money. Service in a British warship was notably uncomfortable but no navy had more opportunity of sharing in prize money and in some cases the amounts paid were very large. When two Spanish frigates with cargoes of coin were captured in 1799 the captains of the British ships which took them each received £40,730, but each ordinary seaman on board was paid £182. 4s. 9½d, the equivalent of eleven years' pay. Such windfalls must have tempted men of many nationalities to enlist but equally many

88

British seamen who had been unlucky with prize deserted to join the U.S. navy where the regular pay and conditions were far superior to those in their own service.

Having to man both the largest navy and the strongest merchant fleet in the world, Britain could ill afford to lose experienced seamen and from 1575 the Crown issued frequent proclamations, none of them effective, forbidding enlistment in foreign ships. To enforce these decrees orders were sent to British ships to see that no British sailors were disobeying them. In 1640 an Admiralty instruction was sent to the captains which read,

> As you meete with any men of war, merchants or other ships belonging to any foreign prince or state, either at sea or in any road or other place where you or any of his Majesty's fleet shall happen to come, you are to send to see whether there be any of his Majesty's subjects on board them; and if any seamen, gunners, pilots, or mariners (either English, Scots or Irish), shall be found on board any of them, you are not only to cause such of his Majesty's subjects to be taken forth, committed, and disposed on board, or otherwise in such sort as they shall be forthcoming and answer their contempt of his Majesty's proclamation in that kind, but friendly to admonish the captains or commanders and officers in such foreign ships, that they do not receive or entertain on board any of their ships no more of his Majesty's subjects, that his Majesty may have no cause to resent it at their hands. But you are to have an especial care that no man be permitted to go on board the ships and vessels of any of his Majesty's friends and allies, to search for such of his Majesty's subjects as aforesaid, for whose fair and honest carriage you or the captain that sends them will not answer. And you are not in any wise to suffer any violence, wrong, or interruption to be given to any of his Majesty's friends and allies bearing themselves fairly or respectfully to you and his Majesty's fleet.

However apparent the 'fair and honest carriage' of the boarding party, the Admiralty was making the remarkably arrogant assumption that, in time of peace, any foreign captain would allow his ship to be searched for British deserters. This assumption had its basis in the centuries-old claim that the King of England was Sovereign of the Seas, a sovereignty that every foreign ship was compelled to acknowledge. So strictly was this claim enforced that when in 1553 Philip II of Spain approached England in his largest warship to marry Queen Mary Tudor, he was compelled to dip his flag in salute. When he at first demurred Lord Howard of Effingham,

89

Lord High Admiral, fired a shotted gun to compel compliance. In 1673 the Admiralty order on the subject read,

> If you chance to meet in his Majestie's seas any ships or fleet belonging to any foreign prince or state, you are to expect that they, (in acknowledgement of his Majestie's sovereigntie there), shall perform their duty in passing bye, strykinge their topsails, and taking in their flagges, and if they refuse to do it, you are to force them thereunto, not suffering in any wise any dishonour to be done to his Majestie, or derogation to his power and sovereigntie in these seas.

The extent of the monarch's dominion over the oceans was in some dispute. In Queen Anne's reign, legal opinion was not wholly certain, 'I take it,' wrote an eminent Admiralty judge,

> without any doubt, that the four seas, viz, East, South, West and North are within her Majesty's sea dominions as Queen of Great Britain.
>
> That the South and East parts of this dominion extend to the opposite shores; and that if a line be drawn from Berwick to the Naes [Lindesnes] in Norway, and another from Cape Finisterre [the north-western point of Spain] to Cape Clear, or the southernmost point in Ireland, I conceive the space within these lines have always been reputed a part of the British seas; but I cannot say this is the utmost extent of them outwards, there being some that carry them further . . . To the westward the British seas take in St George's Channel, and as far beyond Ireland as has been accounted and reputed to belong to the British seas, or according to the extent of possession thereof. Some will have it to reach Newfoundland or North America. [The Northern Seas] may extend northward to the coast of Norway, taking in the Hebrides, Orchades, and all the islands even to Islands [Iceland].

In 1694 a Danish warship off Deal refused to strike her colours despite two visits by naval officers who explained what was required. Thereupon the admiral sent orders to Captain Dean of H.M.S. *Stirling Castle* 'to come as neare as you can to the Danes' man of war rideing here in the Downs, and oblige him by fair means or force to strike his pendant and colours, as usuall'. To Dean's remonstrance the Danish captain replied that 'He would strike for no man in the world, for he had orders of his King not to doe so, and he would sink before he would strike.' When this defiance was received, *Stirling Castle* fired a broadside which was returned and several men were killed on both sides before the Danish flag was hauled down. The King of Denmark was quick to repudiate his captain, claiming that he had not given orders to deny the customary honours and undertaking to punish the offender. The fact was that Denmark exacted the same honours from all ships going into and out of the Baltic and the king may have feared that, if honours were denied in British waters, British ships would not only fail to salute as they passed on their way to the Baltic but would refuse to pay dues which formed a substantial proportion of the Danish revenue.

Britain relinquished her claim to salutes in the British sea in 1818 and before that time her insistence on searching foreign ships for deserters had played a large part in involving her in a war with the United States. The rights and wrongs of the dispute were very much more complicated than they are usually represented, but there can be no doubt that the arrogance with which many British captains went about their job was sufficient to ruffle many American feelings. There was, for example, the case of the U.S. frigate *Chesapeake* (36) which, in March 1807, was known to have embarked five deserters from the Royal Navy. As soon as the frigate had cleared the three-mile limit off Norfolk, Virginia, she was challenged by the elderly *Leopard* (50) with a demand to be allowed to search for deserters 'according to the customs and usages of civilized nations on terms of peace and amity with each other'. The American captain gave an assurance that there were no known deserters in the ship but refused to permit a search. It took three broadsides from *Leopard* to persuade him to change his mind and a boarding party found sixteen deserters and the body of another. They contented themselves nevertheless with removing the four survivors of the five for whom they had originally asked. All were undoubtedly deserters from the British but two were certainly and one probably American citizens and at the subsequent court-martial the only undisputed British subject was sentenced to death and hanged while the other three were awarded five hundred lashes each. In deference to American opinion the latter sentences were remitted and the men repatriated.

The faults were not all on one side. A month before the *Chesapeake* incident the Americans, with a show of force, had seized three men from the British armed-transport *Chichester* which was undergoing storm repairs at Gosport, Virginia. All three were British subjects, as the Americans admitted, but equally they were deserters from the U.S. navy. In most cases there was difficulty in deciding who was an American citizen. The

91

United States had been an independent state for little more than twenty years and while the British agreed that those living in the former colonies in 1783 and their children were indisputably U.S. subjects, they looked with suspicion on any British subject who claimed nationalisation since that date. Since the U.S. Naturalization Act of 1802 required five years of residence, it was clear that recent deserters from the Royal Navy could scarcely claim to be American citizens.

To complicate the problem even more a number of Americans saw the uncertainties as an opportunity to turn a dishonest penny. U.S. law required that all American sailors putting to sea must hold a certificate of protection, which declared that the holder was a U.S. citizen. They could be obtained from any notary, consul or customs official who was entitled to a fee of twenty-five cents for his trouble in issuing it. Any British deserter, who wished to improve his lot by exchanging the harsh discipline of his own service for the relative comfort of the American, had little trouble in finding an official prepared to supplement his income by the issue of certificates of protection. The most flagrant case came to light when H.M. Sloop *Éclair* stopped and searched the American merchant ship *Wareham* and discovered a bundle of blank certificates signed by William Lyman, U.S. Consul in London, who had obligingly supplied them to the captain in case any deserters came his way.

When war between Britain and the U.S.A. broke out in 1812, President Madison claimed that the Royal Navy had 'impressed and held in bondage' 6,057 American citizens. The list he produced of these men had many names repeated at least once and also included many who had purchased certificates of protection. The probability is that very few of the names represented men who had actually been pressed. A committee of the Massachusetts House of Representatives at that time took evidence from fifty-one shipowners who deposed that they had employed 1,560 sailors over twelve years (i.e. 18,720 sailor-years) but that they knew of only thirty-five cases of impressment by the British. Only twelve of these pressed men had been U.S. citizens and of these nine had been released at the request of a consul and one more had succeeded in deserting.

Nevertheless, a large number of Americans were serving in the Royal Navy at the time. At the outbreak of war in 1812 the Admiralty called for returns to show the number of Americans in the various fleets and enquiring whether any of them would be prepared to fight against their native country. The return from the Mediterranean Fleet showed that of 484 American volunteers 109 were prepared to serve against anyone, thirty-five were undecided and 340 would fight only against European enemies. When H.M.S. *Guerrière* (38) had her unfortunate encounter with U.S.S. *Constitution* (44) on August 19th, 1812, ten American volunteers on the British ship were allowed to remain below decks during the battle. Although reliable figures are hard to obtain, the evidence suggests that out of 460 men in the crew of the victorious *Constitution*, nearly two hundred were deserters from the British service.

It was not only Americans who were welcomed, and sometimes pressed, into the Royal Navy. The British were so desperate for sailors that they would enlist men from anywhere. In March 1808 the captain of H.M.S. *Implacable* (74) wrote that among his ship's company of 564 he had ratings from,

Canada 1; Jamaica 1; Trinidad 1; St Domingo 2; St Kitts 1; Martinique 1; Santa Cruz 1; Bermuda 1; Swedes 8; Danes 7; Prussians 8; Dutch 1; Germans 3; Corsica 1; Portuguese 5; Sicily 1; Minorca 1; Ragusa 1; Brazils 1; Spanish 2; Madeira 1; Americans 28; West Indians 2; Bengal 2.

Thus one man in every seven was born outside the United Kingdom and, the captain added, this 'may be considered applicable to every British ship with the exception that *very* few of them have *so many native* [i.e. British] *subjects*'.

The problem of manning British ships did not end with the Treaty of Ghent and Waterloo. Next time Britain went to war in Europe, in 1854, a fleet was sent to the Baltic and, as usual, it was seriously undermanned. On the advice of the Admiralty the admiral, Sir Charles Napier, sent the paddle-steamer, H.M.S. *Porcupine*, into Stockholm to try to enlist Scandinavian volunteers. The mission was successful and it is almost certain that William Johnstone, the first man on the lower deck to win the Victoria Cross, was a Swede.

The Hague *Convention on the Rights and Duties of Neutral Powers* (1907) prohibited the opening of recruiting offices on neutral territory. The permissibility of such recruiting had always been a matter of how benevolent the neutrality of the state concerned was towards the one that was doing the recruiting. No one had objected to Admiral Sir Charles Napier manning his ships in Stockholm in 1854, but in the following year the British consul was arrested for attempting to raise a British Legion in Hamburg.

The same Convention laid down that no belligerent warship should be permitted to stay in neutral waters for more than twenty-four hours 'except on account of damage or stress of weather'. This practice had been customary for centuries but when it was proposed at The Hague the German delegate protested that the time allowed was too short, only to be persuaded by the British and Japanese delegates. The Germans might have stuck to their objection more tenaciously if they could have foreseen the fate of the *Graf Spee* in Montevideo harbour in 1939.

Traditionally an exception was made when warships from opposing belligerents entered the same ports. On such occasions it was customary to insist that at least twenty-four hours should elapse between the departure of the two ships. As James I had ordered in 1605,

> If it so happen that any Shippe or Shippes of Warre do find Shippe or Shippes of Warre of thother [sic] syde in any of our Portes or Roades, our pleasure is that, during their abod there, all Violence be foreborne. Soe do we lykewise command our Officers and Subjectes, both on Sea and Land, that the Shippe which came in firste bee suffered to depart a Tyde or two before thother which came in laste, and that for soe long Tyme they shall staye and detain any Shippe of Warre that would offer to pursue another out of any of our Portes immediately.

All such regulations and Conventions were useless if the neutral power did not have the strength to enforce them. It was a great humiliation for England in 1639 when the Dutch admiral Van Tromp drove a huge Spanish fleet into English waters off the Downs and there captured or destroyed seventy out of seventy-seven ships. Britain's navy was weak at the time and she could do nothing but protest and, as Admiral Boscawen remarked in 1759, after he had defeated the French fleet in Portuguese waters, 'It is easier to satisfy the Court of Lisbon than for the French to build men of war.'

Once Britain had become the dominant naval power it was she who was most likely to invade neutral waters. On March 9th, 1796 boats from a squadron under Vice Admiral Waldegrave rowed into the harbour of neutral Tunis and cut out the frigate *Nemesis* and the corvette *Sardine*. There was perhaps some shadow of an excuse for this high-handed act since, in the previous year, *Nemesis*, then a British ship, had been seized in equally neutral Smyrna by two French ships without 'any opposition from the British frigate beyond a fierce remonstrance at the illegality of the measure'. Less justifiable was the action taken about the French ship of the line *Impétueux* (74) which was driven ashore by a British squadron at

Cape Henry, Virginia, in 1806. Not content with this success the British ships then anchored a bare mile from the American coast, sent boats across to collect the prisoners and set fire to the beached ship. 'However,' as a contemporary account ran, 'the affair happily passed off in the United States with very little notice.'

Not that the British were the only culprits. In 1904 the Russian warship *Reshitelni* took refuge in the Chinese harbour of Che-foo (Yentai) and the Japanese unhesitatingly sent in destroyers and brought her out. Eleven years later the German cruiser *Dresden*, last survivor of Von Spee's squadron at the Battle of the Falkland Islands, was located by three British ships in Cumberland Bay, Mas a Tierra, within Chilean waters. The German captain had asked the Chilean authorities to intern his ship but he had refused to immobilise his engine and still flew the German ensign. Nor was there a Chilean ship to guard him. The British orders from the Admiralty were, 'Object is destruction not internment' and they opened fire. Three minutes later *Dresden* hoisted the white flag and sent an officer across to protest. The officer was Lieutenant Canaris and he later became an admiral and head of German Intelligence. *Dresden* scuttled herself but the Chileans protested. Fortunately the senior British officer on the spot settled the more vociferous local claims for damage done to Chilean property by distributing £500 in gold and the government in Valparaiso was content with an apology.

Neutral airspace presents an even more difficult problem than territorial waters particularly in the case of small countries which the raiders would have crossed before counter-measures could be taken. In 1915 the Dutch were incensed by constant flights across their territory by Zeppelins on their way to attack England. Protests achieving nothing, the authorities at The Hague took to sending a warning telegram to their legation in London. So stately was the progress of the Zeppelins that the legation had time to telephone the Foreign Office who, in their turn, could alert the air defences before the airships arrived.

PART THREE

'MEANS OF INJURING THE ENEMY'

In a vital struggle all available weapons have always been used and always will be used.

Sir Hugh Trenchard,
The War Object of an Air Force, 1929

7

Ban the Crossbow?

Few human activities are less productive than attempts to outlaw particular weapons. However horrible any weapon may be considered, it is likely to be used if it might shorten the war. In 1137 the Lateran Council forbade the use of the crossbow against Christian enemies as being both hateful to God and destructive to mankind. Pope Innocent III confirmed this ban two years later and it had the general support of chivalric opinion which disapproved of all weapons other than the sword and lance. It was Richard Coeur de Lion who reintroduced the crossbow into European war and there were many who said that it was a clear expression of divine displeasure when Richard himself was killed by the bolt of a crossbow while besieging the castle of Chaluz in 1199. A later pope, Pius II, declared that night attacks were 'against all the laws of war' but they continued to be used.

There was no papal interdiction against the use of muskets when they were first introduced but there was much strong feeling against them. It was mercenaries employed by Bologna who first used muskets in battle when fighting the Venetians in 1439. Great consternation was caused when it was found that their missiles could penetrate both plate armour and chain mail but the implication is that they were not very effective since the Venetians won the day and proceeded to massacre all the musketeers, fellow mercenaries though they were, on the grounds that their weapons were 'a cruel and cowardly invention'. Ninety years later when Pierre du Tuerrail de Bayard, *chevalier sans peur et sans reproche*, was on his death-bed, he thanked God that he had never given quarter to musketeers. Were not, he asked, the sword, the lance and the crossbow the proper weapons for knights? It seems that technological innovation had outstripped the Lateran Council's prohibition.

The most that has ever been generally agreed is that weapons which cause unnecessary suffering should not be used. In the eighteenth century Vattel ruled that,

All damage done to the enemy unnecessarily, every act of hostility which does not tend to procure victory and bring the

99

war to an end, is a licentiousness condemned by the law of nations.

A few years later, Martens was more specific.

> It is contrary to the laws of war to load cannon with nails, pieces of iron, &c, to load muskets with two balls, or with disfigured balls, the first augmenting too much the number of sufferers, and the latter wantonly increasing the pain.

The Hague Rules could be no more definite than to say that,

> The right of belligerents to adopt means of injuring the enemy is not unlimited. It is especially forbidden . . . to employ arms, projectiles, or materials calculated to cause unnecessary suffering.

The Rules are, however, more specific in renouncing the use of 'poison or poisoned weapons'. This formalised a very longstanding prohibition. Grotius had declared against 'the administration of poison by hired assassins' in the seventeenth century and later Martens had maintained that,

> Since the beginning of the seventeenth century the use of empoisoned weapons has been looked on as unlawful . . . It is also against the laws of war to send among the enemy persons attacked with plague or any other contagious disease.

Until the coming of poison gas (see p. 106 below), the easiest way of using poison against the enemy was by contaminating the wells. Vattel wrote that, 'A general unanimity prevails in condemning the practice of poisoning waters, wells and springs, because (say some authors) we may thereby destroy innocent people.'

Clearly the danger to the non-combatant population, particularly the crop-raising peasantry, was undesirable but Vattel omits another strong reason for desisting. Once a well is poisoned it would be very difficult to purify it if its location was reoccupied by the army which did the poisoning. To poison a water source is an admission of defeat. One German jurist, Wolff, disagreed with the generally accepted view. In his *Jus Gentium* of 1749 he wrote,

> Naturally it is lawful to kill an enemy by poison . . . there is no difference whether you dispose of him by the sword or by poison

100

(which is self-evident, because in any case you dispose of him, and he can no longer resist or injure you).

Coincidentally one of the few occasions in which well-poisoning has been used in recent centuries was the work of a German. When the Germans evacuated Swakopmund in South-West Africa in 1915 the South African troops who occupied the town found that six wells had been contaminated with arsenical sheep dip. General Botha therefore wrote to his German opponent claiming that The Hague Rules had been broken and that he would hold responsible whoever ordered the poisoning if he was captured. Lieutenant Colonel Franke replied that it was his duty to prevent water falling into the hands of his enemy since, in that climate, water must be considered a war material.

> Accordingly the officer in charge when Swakopmund was evacuated had several sacks of salt thrown into the wells. But we found that the salting of the water could be rendered ineffective in a short time. Thereafter we tried cattle dip, and we found that an enemy occupying the town would for some time have to rely on water brought from a distance.

He added that all the contaminated wells had been marked with warning notices since, in his reading of The Hague Rules, only secret poisoning was prohibited. There followed a long and inconclusive exchange of letters which revolved around the question of whether or not the concentration of arsenic in the wells was lethal. If, as Colonel Franke contended, it was merely disabling, it was legitimate.

Vattel would not necessarily have disagreed with this verdict. In his opinion,

> It is very allowable to divert water – to cut off the springs – or by other means [than poison] to render them useless, that the enemy may be reduced to surrender. This is a milder way than that of arms.

The Confederate General Joseph Johnston adopted this view when he was retreating from Vicksburg and his pursuer, Sherman, wrote, 'In retreating [Johnston] caused cattle, hogs and sheep to be driven into the ponds of water and there shot down so that we had to haul their dead and stinking carcasses out of the water.'

This, wrote an English jurist soon afterwards, was only equivalent to 'turning the water' and the same would apply to the Boer, de Witt, who caused a typhus epidemic in Bloemfontein in March 1900 by cutting off the water supply and compelling the town and its garrison to rely on infected (but not deliberately infected) wells.

Another point on which historical opinion agrees was that the assassination of foreign heads of state and other consequential persons was illegitimate. Grotius condemned it and Vattel described it as, 'infamous and execrable, both in him who executes it and in him who commands it . . . because such an act is pernicious to human society and the practice of it would be destructive to mankind'.

It was in this spirit that Charles James Fox, as Foreign Secretary, wrote to his French opposite number, Talleyrand, to tell him of a plot to assassinate Napoleon. The originator, an *émigré* called Guillet, was arrested in Paris and confined in an asylum for criminal lunatics where he soon died.

There are few examples of deliberate attempts to kill an enemy head of state or even an enemy commander in chief. In the Sino–Japanese War of 1894 Imperial Commissioner Sung posted notices in Northern Manchuria offering rewards of 10,000 taels for the decapitation of three named Japanese generals but, like every other Chinese initiative in that war, nothing came of it. On November 8th, 1940 the Royal Air Force made a deliberate attack on the Bürgerbräukeller in Munich where Hitler was, mistakenly, believed to be celebrating the anniversary of his Munich *putsch*. At the time the attempt was widely remarked in the British press but, perhaps significantly, it is mentioned neither in the British *Official History* nor in the memoirs of Winston Churchill.

On one other form of warfare opinions in the 'polite nations' have always been agreed. No one disputed that spying was a necessary evil but equally it was agreed that, if detected, spies could suffer death. The reasons for executing spies differed. Vattel's view was that only the lowest of men would undertake such treacherous work since, 'A man of honour, who is unwilling to expose himself to an ignominious death at the hands of a common executioner, ever declines serving as a spy'.

A century later an echo of Vattel's opinion survives in the writings of A. W. Kinglake, the historian of the Crimean War. 'The duty of gathering knowledge by clandestine means is one so repugnant to the feelings of an English gentleman, that there is always a danger of him neglecting it, or performing it ill.'

The Germans disagreed and the *Kriegsbrauch* suggested that 'ruthless measures by way of precaution and exemplary punishment – usually death by shooting or hanging' were justified not 'on account of dishonourable disposition on the part of the spy . . . but principally on account of the particular danger which lies in such secret methods. It is, as it were, a matter of self-defence.' The *Kriegsbrauch* added that, since the penalty was so heavy, it should not be inflicted without a trial 'however summary (if the swift course of war permits)'. The British were not so insistent on the death penalty and the *Manual of Military Law* lays down that 'Custom permits their punishment by death, although a more lenient penalty may be inflicted', while the French ruling was that 'in the case of individuals not soldiers, the court may, if there are extenuating circumstances, reduce the penalty'.

Deception is an essential part of the spy's trade but in naval warfare one piece of deception has always been universally recognised as proper. A warship may fly any flag she pleases until the moment she opens fire. To fire under false colours has always been 'an act of perfidy by which they lose all claim to the protection of the laws of war'. One man who nearly suffered severely under this rule was the French privateer Duguay-Trouin. In 1694 his depredations in the Channel were temporarily checked when his forty-gun ship *Diligente* was overwhelmed by six British warships. The Frenchman, who was unconscious when his ship surrendered, was treated with every courtesy and accommodated in the captain's cabin of H.M.S. *Monk* (60). When he was landed at Plymouth he was given parole and entertained by every captain in the squadron which had taken him. This civilised captivity continued until H.M.S. *Prince of Orange* (50) put into the Hamoaze and reported that *Diligente* had earlier fired into her while wearing British colours. Duguay-Trouin was immediately transferred to the town jail and would have been prosecuted had he not contrived, with the help of a young woman, to escape. It was to avoid this kind of embarrassment that, as late as March 1942, the blockship H.M.S. *Cambeltown,* a former U.S. lease-lend destroyer, sailed into St Nazaire under the German flag but hauled it down and hoisted the White Ensign before using her guns.

It is rare for a new weapon to be introduced without the enemy complaining that it is unlawful. There is, however, no record of complaints when Hannibal's army started hurling earthenware jars containing serpents at their enemies. It was probably administrative rather than humanitarian considerations that allowed this form of warfare to fall into disuse. When the British used rockets against Flushing in 1809 the governor protested that they were 'contrary to the usages of civilised nations' but in this case they were abandoned because it was decided that they were too inaccurate to be useful. In 1881 the Egyptians complained that the use of searchlights by the British fleet bombarding Alexandria was 'discourteous and improper' and in 1918 the Germans lodged a formal protest that some American troops were using shotguns in the trenches and that these were 'calculated to cause unnecessary suffering'.

The first prohibition of a specified weapon by international agreement took place in St Petersburg in 1868. The Russians had called an international conference which would lay down 'the technical limits at which war ought to yield to the requirements of humanity'. As the preamble to the Declaration of St Petersburg stated,

> The progress of civilization should have the effect of alleviating as much as possible the calamities of war; that the only legitimate object which States should endeavour to accomplish during war is to weaken the military forces of the enemy; that for this purpose it is sufficient to disable the greatest possible number of men; that this object would be exceeded by the employment of arms which needlessly aggravate the sufferings of disabled men or render their death inevitable.

The assembled powers had no difficulty in subscribing to this admirable sentiment but they could agree on very little else. The only practical step taken by the conference was the prohibition of explosive bullets weighing less than 400 grams (13½oz). The only bullets of this kind existed in the Russian army which had introduced them five years earlier with the object of blowing up ammunition waggons. Since the other signatories – Austria-Hungary, France, Great Britain, Italy, Prussia and Turkey – had no such projectiles and had no plans for making them, they happily agreed to the Russian proposal to ban them. The ban remained in force until, during the war of 1914–18, it was found that small explosive bullets were effective against balloons and aircraft whereupon they were immediately brought into service.

The next agreement to prohibit a weapon came thirty-one years later at the first Hague Conference. This time it was proposed to outlaw 'bullets which expand or flatten easily in the human body'. The British fought against this suggestion, claiming that modern bullets, such as those of the Lee Metford, were,

> not sufficient to stop a charge of cavalry or a rush of fanatics . . . Even the savage enemies of England looked on them with contempt . . . In one of our small wars in India a man perforated

104

five times by these bullets was still capable of walking to the English hospital at a considerable distance to have his wounds dressed.

The European powers were not impressed by this plea and voted to ban the dum-dum bullet, which was generally believed not to be worth using. Britain agreed to adhere to the Convention eight years later.

On the same day that most of the powers agreed that prohibition, Austria-Hungary, Belgium, Bulgaria, China, Denmark, France, Germany, Greece, Italy, Japan, Luxembourg, Mexico, Montenegro, the Netherlands, Persia, Portugal, Romania, Russia, Serbia, Siam, Spain, Sweden-Norway, Switzerland and Turkey put their signatures to a further agreement which provided that,

> The Contracting Powers agree to abstain from the use of projectiles the sole object of which is the diffusion of asphyxiating or deleterious gases.
> The present declaration is only binding on the Contracting Powers in the case of a war between two or more of them.

Britain at first refused to sign unless all the other powers did so but she and Nicaragua eventually joined in 1907. The United States would not adhere on the grounds that no one could know if asphyxiating shells were inhumane without trying them. Her case was put by Captain A. T. Mahan, U.S.N., the distinguished naval historian and theorist.

> Until we know the effects of asphyxiating shells, there is no saying whether they will be more or less merciful than missiles now permitted . . . It is illogical and not demonstrably humane to be tender about asphyxiating men with gas, when all are prepared to admit that it is allowable to blow the bottom out of an ironclad at night, throwing four or five hundred men into the sea to be choked with water, with scarcely the remotest chance of escape. If, and when, a shell emitting asphyxiating gases has been successfully produced then, and not before, will men be able to vote intelligently on the subject.

A more valid objection would have been to the unsatisfactory drafting of the Convention. In the first place it limited the prohibition to 'projectiles the sole purpose of which is the diffusion of . . . gases', leaving open both the possibility of diffusing them by other means and of using gas in projectiles which also exploded or, even distributed pamphlets, since gas would not be the 'sole object'. Moreover the word deleterious (*délétères*) was open to a wide variety of definitions.

The French certainly believed that, to be banned, gas had to inflict serious, perhaps lethal, damage. From the start of the 1914 war some of their troops were supplied with *cartouches suffocantes*, projectiles weighing half a pound which were fired from special large-calibre rifles. The gas used was ethyl bromo-acetate which affected the eyes, nose and throat. According to a confidential circular from the Ministry of War the gas was '*irritant*' but not '*délétère*' and it is probably true that it would be unlikely to be lethal in any circumstances likely to be met on the battlefield.

In practice the *cartouches suffocantes* appear to have been so ineffective that the Germans did not know about them and did not use them as an excuse when they launched their own, more famous, gas attack near Ypres on April 25th, 1915. In this they released a hundred and fifty tons of chlorine from 6,000 cylinders, letting the wind carry it across to the allied lines. They could thus claim that they were not in breach of The Hague Convention since they were not using projectiles. With less conviction they could claim that chlorine was not lethal, although it could hardly be held not to be deleterious. According to the British *Official History*,

> Chlorine has a powerful irritant action on the respiratory organs, and all mucous membranes exposed to it, causing spasms of the glottis, a burning sensation in the eyes, nose and throat, followed by bronchitis and œdema of the lungs. Frequently there is evidence of corrosion of the mucous membrane of the air channels and of the cornea. Prolonged inhalation or exposure to a high concentration of the gas will cause asphyxia, or, if not fatal, produce cardiac dilution and cyanosis (blueness of the skin) as a result of injury to the lungs.

The Germans could also claim that, on humanitarian grounds, they had abstained from making the gas far more lethal by combining the chlorine with phosgene, a technique they had already mastered.

The tactical results of this first gas attack were spectacular. A gap eight thousand yards wide was torn in the French line and, had the Germans been prepared to exploit their opportunity, Ypres could have been taken without difficulty. The gas, however, caused comparatively few casualties. Despite the horrific reports widespread at the time, telling of 5,000 dead and 10,000 seriously affected, the number of gas casualties from that attack was only 625 of whom three died. In addition the Germans treated about 200 French prisoners for chlorine symptoms. The great gap in the line had been torn not by gas but by panic among the low-grade troops who held the sector. A similar attack a few days later against well-trained Canadian troops, equally unprepared, achieved only small gains.

While the discharge of gas from cylinders may not have been contrary to the letter of The Hague agreement, it was a wildly inefficient way of diffusing it, being dependent on the wind. Although the most frequent wind in that part of Flanders comes from the west, into the faces of the Germans, the most damaging attack occurred during the Battle of Loos in September 1915. A British discharge of chlorine was caught by a veering wind and caused 2,639 casualties, including seven fatalities, among our own troops, whereas German gas casualties amounted to only 106 men. Inevitably, therefore, more efficient methods of discharging gas were sought and by the middle of 1916 both the French and the Germans were using gas-shells. That the British did not use them until late in 1917 was due not to a careful regard for The Hague agreement, but to the great difficulty they experienced in providing even high-explosive shells in sufficient quantity. Manufacturing capacity for gas-shells was non-existent.

Although war gases improved in both type and methods of delivery, protective measures largely kept pace, so that, as a means of injuring the enemy, gas was never a major factor. On the western front British gas casualties represented only one per cent of deaths and 3.3 per cent of non-fatal injuries – 17,000 dead and 180,000 non-fatal – yet notably larger in proportion to Germany. These modest proportions did not affect the growth of a thriving myth, based on illusory casualty figures which were inflated by the press, the pacifists and the chemists, which declared that gas would be used, especially against non-combatants, in any future war. It was with this in mind that in June 1925 many of the powers signed the Geneva Gas Protocol which prohibited the use in war of, 'asphyxiating, poisonous or other gases, and all analogous liquids, materials and devices . . . unless as a measure of retaliation in kind'.

Having thus closed the loopholes left at The Hague in 1899, the Protocol went on to outlaw bacteriological warfare.

By 1939 thirty-two countries, including Britain, France and Germany, had ratified the Protocol. There were, nevertheless, significant absentees from the signatories: Japan, the U.S.S.R. and the United States although it might have been supposed that the widespread practical experiments made between 1915 and 1918 would have met the objections raised by Captain Mahan in 1899.

It is possible that the memory of the Geneva Protocol played some part in the abstinence from gas warfare that marked the war of 1939–45. It is more probable that it arose from more practical considerations. In the first place the military commanders on both sides opposed the use of gas. In the First World War it had been shown to be of limited use and both sides felt that it would not be cost-effective in a later conflict in which the armed forces of all the belligerents and the civilian populations of some (notably Britain and Germany) were equipped to deal with it. To use gas entails great inconvenience to the troops. No one wants to fight a campaign encumbered by a mask and anti-gas clothing, indeed it would not be worthwhile unless the results expected appeared much greater than experience showed likely. In particular Hitler, who had been gassed in 1918, showed, until the last weeks of his rule, a marked revulsion against its use.

Even more effective was the deterrent factor. Both sides believed that their opponents had a more dangerous gas-capability than they possessed themselves and were reluctant to embark on a course of action which might rebound against them. There were times when civilian governments came near to ordering the use of gas against the advice of their military chiefs. In February 1945, in the aftermath of the devastating air attack on Dresden, Göbbels proposed the authorisation of two new German gases, Tabun and Sarin, and Hitler, already moving into his Gotterdämmerung phase, momentarily agreed with him. On the other side of the Channel, Winston Churchill, in July 1944, called for a report including 'a cold-blooded calculation . . . as to how it would pay to use poison gas, by which I mean principally mustard [gas]'. When his service advisers told him that high explosive was, ton for ton, a more effective way of killing Germans, he turned his attention to the possibility of spreading anthrax in Germany by dropping infected cattle-cake, only to be advised, once more, that it was an inefficient way of making war. Churchill was also dissuaded from using chemical warfare by the steady opposition from President Roosevelt, an opposition which makes it the more surprising that the U.S.A. did not ratify the Geneva Gas Protocol of 1925 until 1974.

There seems little doubt that the fear of retaliation induced the belligerents to eschew the use of gas in the Second World War, a theory supported by the only two occasions on which gas was used after the Geneva Protocol – by Italy in Ethiopia and by the Japanese in China – both in circumstances where there was no possible fear of retaliation.

The Geneva Protocol's concession that gas could be used as 'a measure of retaliation in kind' is the first mention of retaliation in any international agreement and yet retaliation is the only defence that a belligerent has against an enemy who breaks the rules. Dr Lieber's views on retaliation have been quoted earlier (p. 13) but although he recommends that 'it should only be used . . . cautiously and unavoidably', he can give no clear guidelines as to what form the retaliation should take. In some cases the type of riposte is fairly straightforward. If your enemy uses gas, it would be reasonable to use the same type of gas against him. What is perhaps the most well-remembered reprisal in history was of this type. On April 27th, 1813 United States troops seized the provincial capital of Upper Canada which was then called York but is now better known as Toronto.

> Contrary to the articles of capitulation, the public buildings and all the records were burned, the church was robbed, the public library pillaged to the last book, and much private property plundered and destroyed.

This vandalism, contrary to the pledged word of the American commander, was the work of uncontrolled and ill-disciplined soldiers but Washington made no offer of compensation. London therefore sent orders for reprisals. The opportunity came on August 24th, 1814 when, under General Robert Ross, British troops occupied Washington D.C. Great care was taken to safeguard private property but all the public buildings were systematically fired. The officers of the army were horrified and, when it was reported to him, the Prince Regent 'thought it was a barbarian act'. When the Americans came to repair the damage they painted the presidential mansion white to conceal the marks of the fire and it has remained the White House to this day.

A far more questionable reprisal occurred on April 14th, 1917 when the Western allies were anxious to retaliate for the sinking of two clearly marked hospital ships, *Asturias* and *Gloucester Castle* by U-boats. There were no German hospital ships on the high seas and in any case attacks on them would have been unacceptable. Instead, a force of French and British aircraft attacked Freiburg-im-Breisgau, a beautiful little town devoid of military objectives. As was to be expected, the bombing had no effect on the war at sea but, in case it should be repeated, the Germans moved 400 French and British officer prisoners to Freiburg. The British retaliated once more by moving a similar number of German officers into

Ramsgate, Margate and Southend, all port towns exposed to air attack.

The abortive Brussels Conference of 1874 debated at interminable length the question of what constituted legitimate reprisals. Finally the Belgian delegate said,

Why should not the Committee . . . leave the matter in the domain of unwritten law, under the sanction of public opinion, until the progress of science and civilization brings about a completely satisfactory solution?

The matter has remained in that optimistic limbo ever since.

On June 24th, 1859 a Swiss banker of evangelical tendencies wandered on to the battlefield of Solferino in the hope of interesting Napoleon III in a commercial scheme outlined in a paper which he had written entitled *Memorandum on the Financial and Industrial Company of the Mills of Mons-Gemila, Algeria (Capital 1,000,000 francs)* by J. Henri Dunant, President of the Company. Dunant was horrified by what he saw at Solferino but,

The appearance of the battlefield is nothing compared with the despair of the poor wretches who lay in heaps, one, two, even three days without care, without help, believing themselves abandoned. I have seen old soldiers, brave *zouaves*, who cried like children. It would break your heart. In the corners of churches I found many who had simply been forgotten, others who for days had been brought nothing to eat or drink. Many, despite their terrible wounds, had never been bandaged, men whom a little quicker assistance might have saved. Still others remained for days without having their bandages changed because no one gave them a thought. Almost all were naked, still covered with blood and swarming with flies and maggots. There they lay on the stones or on straw, pieces of which stuck in their wounds, surrounded by a hideous filth and horrible stench. And day after day.

The doctors have done all they could. But there were not enough of them.

From Dunant's experience in organising volunteer help for the wounded at Solferino sprang the International Red Cross, the national Red Cross societies and the Geneva Convention of 1864 'for the amelioration of the condition of wounded soldiers in armies in the field', an agreement which, four years later, was widened to include the wounded at sea. The Geneva Conventions sought the neutralisation of all hospitals and ambulances with their personnel, both regular and, if properly constituted, volunteer. It established the Red Cross (or the Red Crescent) as a symbol of this neutralisation and the groundwork laid by the early Conventions was extended by supplementary agreements in 1906 and in 1929, when the work of the Red Cross for prisoners of war was first officially recognised. The Red Cross organisation in all its facets is the greatest achievement of international agreements by establishing a neutral body which can deal openhandedly with all belligerents and act as a clearing house for information, medical materials and comforts for the sick and for prisoners and can also deal with vast sums of charitable and governmental money.

Nevertheless it would be wrong to think that the care of the wounded was needlessly neglected before 1864. Certainly by the eighteenth century it was customary to treat the enemy's wounded as if they were those of one's own army. In 1742, at the suggestion of John Pringle, the father of British military medicine, the French and British agreed that their hospitals should be considered as non-belligerent and not subject to bombardment or invasion. This did not mean that the wounded had an easy time. The basic problem was that there was so little that could be done for them. Fifty-one years before Solferino a physician wrote home from another battlefield,

To some a simple inspection of their wounds, with a few words of consolation, or perhaps a little opium, was all that could be recommended. Of these brave men the balls had pierced organs connected with life; and in such cases prudence equally forbids the rash interposition of unavailing art and the useless indulgence of delusive hope.

Just how unavailing the medical art could be is revealed by the statistics of a British military hospital for ten weeks in 1814. Of those who underwent surgery to the head 1 in 5 died; for operations to the thorax the proportion was 1 in 2.3; to the abdomen 1 in 4.3; in amputations to arms or legs 1 in 5.3; in compound fractures 1 in 3. The death rate for operations for gangrene wounds of the spine was a simple 1 in 1.

It was an open question whether it was better for a severely wounded man to be left on the battlefield or to be taken to a hospital such as that at Celorico which is described in the two following accounts.

> Two small rooms, crowded with sick; no ventilation; no chamber utensil; the patients nearly all delirious.

> Two patients occupied each bed, and when one died, another was brought in to fill his place and share, in mind as well as body, the infection of his disease.

This overcrowding into unsuitable buildings was due neither to neglect nor callousness. It resulted simply from the impossibility of transporting large numbers of sick and wounded men. Sprung carriages were seen in few European countries outside the cities and all that remained were an inadequate number of primitive farm carts. Sometimes cavalry horses were pressed into service and a man who had just received a musket ball extracted after it had broken two ribs and passed through his liver, described how, after he had been hoisted on to a charger, 'I had to ride twelve miles. The motion of the horse made the blood pump out, and the bones cut the flesh to a jelly.'

By the time Henri Dunant and the Red Cross came on the scene, conditions were changing for the better with the introduction of anaesthetics and antiseptics; Florence Nightingale had revolutionised the running of hospitals and, most important of all, the coming of railways was making it possible to evacuate the wounded with speed and comparative comfort so that the overcrowding of hospitals was no longer inevitable. Nothing can detract from the nobility of Dunant's vision or from the value of the work of the Red Cross ever since 1864, but it was the advances in science and technology that made their triumphs possible.

The neutralising of hospitals and medical personnel is less easy at sea. The sick bay in a warship is just as likely to be hit by bombardment as any other part of the ship. The Hague Convention of 1907 could only decree: 'In case of a fight on board a warship, the sick wards shall be respected as far as possible.'

It was, however, possible to agree on the distinctive markings to be used on hospital ships and to agree that they would be subject to search by the opposing side. The actual idea of a hospital ship is far from new. The British had one with the fleet at the Glorious First of June in 1794. They had given it the astonishingly inappropriate name of *Charon*, the ferryman of hell.

8

Starvation

As has been seen, The Hague rules laid down that, 'It is especially
forbidden . . . to employ arms, projectiles, or materials calculated
to cause unnecessary suffering.'

They are silent about the evils of withholding the most vital
material of all – food – and yet starvation is among the most
lingering causes of death and, at times, a painful one. To deny a
hostile army subsistence has always been considered a legitimate
operation of war. In doing so some non-combatants are bound to
suffer but, until the late nineteenth century, with the spread of
industrialisation and the growth of large cities, the starvation of a
whole population would not have been feasible. It is true that
during the Thirty Years War Germany experienced widespread
starvation, but it had not been deliberately devised and had taken
decades of unrelenting war to achieve. Laying waste the country in
the path of an invading army was a trick that the Scots had often
employed to keep out English armies and in 1689 the French
deliberately devastated the Palatinate to secure their flank against
incursions from Germany. In those days, when every general
depended on the resources of the country for his food, when roads
were few and waggons scarce, a wide belt of ravaged country was as
effective as a chain of fortresses.

Such tactics were at a discount in the eighteenth century since
they could not be reconciled with the concept of war as something
in which only soldiers and sailors took part; only in Portugal did
they survive. A small country, surrounded on three sides by a
powerful neighbour, Portugal was constantly in danger of invasion
across her long and indefensible frontier from Spain. 'Driving the
country', clearing it of supplies, transport and people, was traditionally her best defence. She had used it in the war of the Spanish
Succession and again in 1762, when the Spanish general who hoped
to march on Lisbon penetrated no further than Castello Branco
before being starved into turning back, leaving his sick and
wounded to the care of his enemies.

It was this system that Wellington employed when Massena
invaded the country in 1810. The old laws were used to leave an
area of swept country in front of the *Armée de Portugal*. The

clearance did not work as well as Wellington had hoped but his opponent had only been in the country a few weeks before he reported to Paris, 'All our marches are across a desert; not a soul is to be seen anywhere; everything is abandoned . . . The women, the children and the aged have all decamped. We cannot find a guide anywhere.'

The marshal protested to Wellington against 'a system that instantly spreads the evils and violence of war to a whole kingdom, bringing more evils than twenty years of continual war'. He received a dusty answer and it was not many months before his army was in full retreat to Spain since, according to the official French account,

> All the magazines formed by the army were exhausted. Foraging parties brought back nothing although they had ranged as far as twenty leagues from headquarters. The army was down to its final reserve of fifteen days' biscuit; there was no possibility of waiting until the harvest.

In that campaign the French army lost, apart from its battle casualties, 15,000 men, almost a quarter of its original strength, from disease, starvation and skirmishes as the soldiers fought the remaining peasantry for the little food that was available.

When Napoleon set out to conquer Russia in 1812 the defenders did not have to apply a 'scorched earth' policy with the care that had been used in Portugal. Since it was ten times the size of Massena's army, the *Grande Armée* created its own devastation. Before the invasion Napoleon had remarked that 'on the plains of Russia nature produces fodder beneath the hooves of the horses' but his central striking force alone included 375,000 men and 100,000 horses and even if the advance guard could feed itself, there was no hope that those who followed would be able to glean a living from the desert that was left. To this self-inflicted dearth, the Russians added their own quota.

> They destroyed their magazines, and burnt their establishments, even large houses . . . Long before we arrived, everything had been made ready for lighting and spreading the fires by the Cossack rearguard, and they ignited the fires as soon as we appeared. In various houses, especially those containing provisions, we found inflammable material methodically prepared and arranged for this purpose.

114

When, despite these obstacles, the *Grande Armée* reached Moscow the Russians would not allow them to forage. Hence they were forced to retreat along the road by which they had advanced, through country already picked clean. Napoleon's army was destroyed but the Russians were in little better case. Kutusov's men, who followed the French as they fell back, suffered 90,000 casualties, most of them the result of under-feeding as they marched through the same exhausted and snow-covered countryside.

Both in Portugal and in Russia the process of driving the country was a limited operation in pursuit of a set military objective – the obstruction of an army advancing on a given route. So too was the next notable use of the technique, Philip H. Sheridan's desolation of the Shenandoah Valley in 1864. As Confederate armies had several times made use of the Shenandoah for their threats to Washington and Maryland, General Grant ordered Sheridan to make it impassable. He succeeded.

I have destroyed over 2,000 barns filled with wheat, hay and farming implements, over 700 mills filled with wheat and flour; I have driven in front of the army over 4,000 head of stock, have killed and issued to the troops not less than 3,000 sheep. A large number of horses has also been obtained.

As he reported jubilantly, 'a crow flying across the valley would have to carry its own rations'.

The famous march through Georgia was a different type of operation. Instead of trying, as Sheridan had done, to obstruct the march of an enemy army, Sherman set out to destroy the war-potential of the Confederacy and to break its will to continue the war.

The destruction of the roads, houses and people will cripple their military resources . . . I can make Georgia howl. If the people raise a howl against my barbarity and cruelty, I will answer that war is war . . . If they want peace, they and their relations must stop the war.

His soldiers were instructed to 'forage liberally' and by their commander's own estimate they did damage worth $100 million, of which not more than a fifth was 'legitimate foraging' and the rest, again in Sherman's words, 'simple waste and destruction'.

While it must be conceded that instances of murder and rape were astonishingly few, Sherman's march through Georgia marks a long step away from the concept of moderation in war since it was a premeditated attempt to exert military pressure on non-combatants in the hope that they could influence their government to make peace. It was a significant move towards total war. Sherman was, of course, acting within his instructions. *General Order N° 100* ruled that,

Military necessity . . . admits of all destruction of property, and obstruction of the ways and channels of traffic, travel and communication, and of all withholding of sustenance or means of life from the enemy. (Article 14)

It is lawful to starve the hostile belligerent, armed or unarmed, so that it leads to the speedier subjection of the enemy. (Article 17)

This was the nineteenth century speaking in terms that would not have occurred to commanders of earlier generations. Napoleon did not think along those lines. When he sent Massena to take Lisbon he specifically ordered him not to reach his objective before the harvest was in 'because I could not feed the city, whose immense population is accustomed to live on sea-borne food'. Perhaps it had not occurred to him that starvation might help to break the Portuguese will to resist.

The task of starving an enemy nation belongs principally to navies and is, naturally, impracticable when that nation is self-supporting for food. It is ironic that Britain, the major power most susceptible to starvation by blockade, has always been the most extreme exponent of the right of her fleet to enforce a blockade.

Before the twentieth century the aim of British blockades was not to cut off food supplies to her enemies, principally France. To have adopted such a strategy would have seemed absurd to Hawke, St Vincent, Nelson and the other blockading admirals. The intention, apart from keeping enemy warships in their ports, was to cripple the enemy economy. Far from preventing food from reaching France the British, in the Napoleonic Wars, were doing their best to sell it to them. To counter the effect of the Continental System, they built up a huge smuggling system by which thousands of tons of food, for the most part coffee, tea and sugar, were covertly introduced into French-occupied Europe. Dozens of small boats traded between Heligoland and the North German ports, the Royal Navy escorted fleets of merchantmen into the Baltic and hundreds of mules trudged over the Balkans from

116

Salonica with British colonial produce. Any neutral ship was welcome to trade with the enemy, provided they did their trade in British goods and with a British licence.

Napoleon thought along the same lines. His aim was to denude Britain of gold, thereby making it impossible to continue the war. To his brother Louis, King of Holland, he wrote, 'If you need to sell your gin, the English need to buy it. Settle the point where the English smugglers are to come and fetch it, and make them pay in money, never in goods.'

He was ready to give special sittings to the artist Louis David so that he could paint a portrait commissioned by the Marquess of Douglas for a fee of a thousand guineas to be paid in coin. He lost his best chance of stirring up civil disturbance in Britain when, after the harvests of 1809–10 failed, he sold his inveterate enemy 1½ million quarters of wheat, insisting that he receive gold in payment.

The international laws which are supposed to govern the imposition of a blockade are particularly involved, a quagmire in which there is no firm standing. The rules changed at the whim of the dominant naval power and would be the severest that could be imposed without inconveniencing beyond endurance the most influential neutrals. These neutrals, it may be noted, always changed their reading of the rules when they became belligerents. In the case of an enemy ship carrying enemy goods the rules were simple: ship and cargo became lawful prize to the captor. If an enemy ship was, however, partially laden with neutral goods, the neutral might be able to recover them, if they were not ruled to be contraband of war. Similarly enemy cargoes in neutral ships might be released if, once again, they were not contraband of war. No satisfactory definition of contraband of war has ever been achieved.

According to Grotius a neutral who supplied a belligerent with goods primarily for use in war could be assumed to be on the side of that belligerent and such goods could be seized. There were, however, goods that were equally useful in peace and war (*res ancipitis usus*) and with these, known as conditional contraband, the blockader should be guided 'by his necessity, the neutral's knowledge of it and the justice of his cause'. Grotius's ruling might suffice a judge in chambers but was singularly useless to the captain of a frigate enforcing a blockade, since Grotius omitted to define which goods were useful in war and left conditional contraband in a peculiarly fuzzy kind of limbo.

As Britain's seapower grew so did the scope of her definition of contraband. In 1590, soon after the defeat of the Armada, Queen

117

Elizabeth's government announced that neutrals would not be permitted to carry to Spain, Portugal or the Azores,

> Any kind of provisions, munitions of war, powder, artillery, arms, sails, cables, anchors, cordage, masts, peas or other provisions for land war, or apparel or furniture for ships (except what shall be necessary for their own ships' use).

Forty years later the list had been expanded and included,

> Ordnance, arms of all sorts, powder, shott, match, brimstone, copper, iron, cordage of all kinds, hempe, saile, canvas, Dantsic pouldavis, cables, anchors, masts, rafters, boate oars, balks, capraves, deale board, pipe staves, and vessells and vessell stuffe, pitche, tarre, rozen, okam, corne, graine, and victuals of all sorts, all provisions for shipping, and all munitions of warre, or of provisions for the same.

As Britain widened the list of contraband articles, the rest of Europe was trying to narrow it. In 1659 France and Spain agreed on only 'armoury, warlike materials and saltpetre' whereas in England the Admiralty judges included,

> Canvas, masts, pitch, tarr and other naval accommodations, as also wine, oil, brandy, fish, corn, salt, flesh and all other things that tend as provisions unto the support of life, as well as powder, guns, or other instruments of war.

The basis of the disagreement was usually the question of naval stores. Britain (and her northern allies) had easy access to the Baltic, the prime European source of such stores, and she was determined that France and Spain should not do likewise by means of neutral shipping. It is significant that the United States, which had its own sources of naval stores, agreed with this view of contraband as early as the Jay Treaty of 1794, a time when she agreed with little else about British blockading policy.

Britain continued to tighten her definition of contraband so long as she had the naval power to do so. When, however, in 1780 the Royal Navy was greatly overstretched by war with France, Spain and the American colonies, the neutrals revolted. On the occasion that two Russian ships loaded with hemp and flax were seized on their voyage to Bordeaux, Catherine the Great declared that neutral vessels had the right to trade freely with belligerents except in contraband of war from which she specifically excluded naval stores. To enforce this declaration she organised the first Armed Neutrality of the North, a combination which included Russia, Sweden, Denmark, Prussia, Austria, Holland, Portugal and Naples. Faced with this threat, Britain did not modify her list of contraband, but merely ceased to enforce it with all its vigour.

Nevertheless Catherine's declaration that 'Free ships make free goods' was not one that Britain could countenance for long, blockade being such an essential weapon in her armoury. As Nelson told the House of Lords it was,

> A proposition so monstrous in itself, so contrary to the law of nations, and so injurious to the maritime interests of England as to justify war with the advocates of such a doctrine so long as a single man, a single shilling, or a single drop of blood remain in the country.

During the whole of the quarter century of wars which followed the French revolution Britain enforced blockade as she saw fit despite the short-lived reformation of the Armed Neutrality and despite the sullen if impotent resentment of American traders. She had the naval power and she used it ruthlessly. It was not until the Crimean War that she was prepared to conciliate neutral opinion in regard to contraband, and then only because trade with Russia was too small to be worth ruffling the neutral dovecotes. In a *Declaration to the Neutrals*, issued on the outbreak of war, she reserved all her rights but announced that she did not intend to enforce them.

> Her Majesty will waive the right of seizing enemy property on board a neutral vessel, unless it be contraband of war. It is not Her Majesty's intention to claim the confiscation of neutral property, not being contraband of war, found in enemy ships.

As far as the Russian war was concerned, this was unexceptionable but, as soon as the war was over, Britain subscribed to the Declaration of Paris which, in addition to abolishing privateering (see p. 75) attempted to regulate blockades.

> 2. A neutral flag covers belligerent merchandise, except for contraband of war.
> 3. Neutral goods, except contraband of war, cannot be seized under a belligerent flag.
> 4. Blockades, to be recognized, must be effective. That is to say that they must be maintained by a sufficient force to deny access to the enemy coast.

Britain's adherence to the declaration caused a storm of protest. Lord Derby accused the Foreign Secretary of having 'gratuitously surrendered the foundation of England's greatness'; even as late as 1927 a passionate attack on the agreement was made in the House of Lords, but Parliament ratified the government's signature and Britain carefully observed the provisions of the Declaration until she was next involved in a major war.

The most notable absentee from the signatories of the Declaration of Paris was the United States of America, which had always been a staunch upholder of neutral rights. Her failure to sign was partly due to her refusal to abandon privateering but, as her Secretary of State, William M. Marcy, pointed out, the articles on blockade evaded the central problem.

> The weakness . . . is the impossibility of securing the proper observance of the second article in the absence of an authoritative definition of contraband. Under the present practice what is or is not contraband depends upon the wishes of the belligerents as announced from time to time during the war.

Five years later the United States was faced with the problem herself and changed her attitude. On April 16th, 1861 President Lincoln declared the secessionist states to be blockaded even though those states had 3,000 miles of coast and the U.S. navy consisted of only seventy-six ships of which thirty-two were small sailing vessels. Nevertheless this small fleet, as far as it was able, imposed contraband control with all Britain's rigour. They even introduced a novelty which almost involved them in a war with Britain and perhaps France.

The accepted customs of war had always permitted diplomatic personnel to travel freely on the high seas, but, in the view of Washington, representatives of the Confederacy were not diplomats but rebels. On November 8th, 1861, off Cuba, U.S.S. *San Jacintha* fired a shot across the bows of the British mail packet *Trent*, which hove to. The *San Jacintha* despatched a boarding party which, despite protests, removed James M. Mason and John Sliddell, who had been appointed as Confederate representatives to Britain and France respectively. When Captain Wilkes of the *San Jacintha* landed his prisoners he received a hero's welcome. Congress passed a joint vote of thanks to him and asked the President to give him a gold medal.

News of the arrest of the two envoys reached London on November 28th, whereupon the press and the opposition demanded war against the U.S.A. to avenge Britain's honour. The government was reluctant to stir up trouble with America but, in view of the vociferous demands, the fleet was mobilised and large reinforcements, including a brigade of Foot Guards, were embarked for Canada. Meanwhile the Crown's law officers were havering. First they recommended that the Union government were within their rights to detain the two men; then they decided that the correct course would have been for *Trent* to be taken before a prize court which could have decided whether anything (or anyone) on board was lawful prize. Fortified by this opinion the British minister in Washington was instructed to protest against a breach of international law, to express the hope that Captain Wilkes had acted against his orders and to demand an apology and, within seven days, the release of the two men. The French supported the British stand.

Washington was now faced with a dilemma. They were unwilling to risk serious trouble with Britain and France, yet it would be difficult to disavow Wilkes after the lionisation with which he had been greeted. They compromised by releasing Mason and Sliddell and paid compensation for the arrest of the *Trent*. On the other hand they refused to apologise, saying merely that Wilkes had acted incorrectly in the manner in which he had effected the arrests. Thus the affair blew over with everyone dissatisfied. The Foreign Secretary agreed to receive Mason when he reached England but said only that he hoped he would enjoy his stay in London. As *The Times* remarked, the two men were 'about the most worthless booty it would be possible to extract from the jaws of the American lion'.

The British blockade of Germany and Austria and the German attempt to blockade Britain in the First World War made nonsense of all previous attempts to regulate this form of naval warfare. Both blockades were distant affairs, far from the close 'effective' blockades envisaged in the Declaration of Paris. Nor were the arrangements for dealing with suspected ships the same. The submarine had changed the rules.

Winston Churchill remarked that the use of submarines to sink trading ships was comparable with 'the spreading of pestilence and the assassination of individuals'. In this he reflected the peculiar horror that seafaring men have always had of a menace that strikes unseen from beneath the surface. As early as 1778 an American, David Bushnell, had devised a submersible, the *Turtle*, which carried a primitive kind of torpedo. Piloted by the intrepid Sergeant Ezra, *Turtle* made an attack on H.M.S. *Eagle* (64) in New

York harbour. No damage was done to the battleship and Ezra narrowly escaped with his life but Bushnell was ostracised by his compatriots and had to move to Georgia where he lived under an assumed name. Similarly, when another American, Robert Fulton, offered his submersible *Nautilus* to the French navy in 1800, Admiral Villaret-Joyeuse refused it since 'to make war on the enemy in this way would bring such disapproval that those undertaking it would, if captured, be hanged. That is no death for a military man.'

In 1914, the Germans, seeing in submarines a way of lessening the disparity in strength between the High Seas Fleet and the Royal Navy, demonstrated their potency by sinking three British armoured cruisers, *Aboukir*, *Cressy* and *Hogue*, off the Dutch coast on September 22nd. It was their intention to use U-boats to blockade Britain but they had planned to do so by orthodox means. The orders to their navy, which applied equally to submarines and surface vessels, laid down that, 'An enemy ship may be destroyed if it seems inexpedient or unsafe to bring her in, but before destruction all persons on board are to be placed in safety with their goods and chattels if possible.'

It was on these lines that their small submarine fleet started to operate in 1914. Having found an isolated merchantman, the U-boat would surface and order the ship to heave to. A boarding party would be despatched, according to the 'cruiser rules' by which blockade had been enforced for centuries. The only difference was that, since few prize crews could be carried on a submarine, it was more often necessary to sink the captured ship rather than bring her into port. Care was, nevertheless, taken to put the passengers and crew into their boats. As U-boats then had short ranges, this was seldom far from a coast and it was not unknown for the Germans to signal their position so that they could be quickly rescued.

Unfortunately submarines have built-in limitations. While they are potent offensive weapons, they are weak in defence. In 1914 a U-boat in the attack was more than a match for an armoured cruiser, but it was as vulnerable to counter-measures as a coastal steamer. A small artillery piece could damage it irreparably with a single well-aimed round. Thus a U-boat on the surface was a sitting target, even for a trading ship which had been supplied with only an elderly cannon. The British had made no secret of the fact that they would be arming their merchant fleet. In March 1913 Winston Churchill, First Lord of the Admiralty, said in the House of Commons,

If British ships had no armament, they would be at the mercy of any foreign liner carrying one effective gun and a few rounds of ammunition. It would be obviously absurd to meet the contingency of considerable numbers of foreign armed merchant cruisers on the high seas by building an equal number of cruisers ... The proper reply to an armed merchantman is another merchantman armed in her own defence.

This argument, plausible as far as it went, ignored the possibility of the Germans using submarines to enforce a blockade. No one was liable to suffer unduly if two merchantmen armed with six-inch guns fired at each other but one round from such a gun could destroy a submarine. Churchill's statement also ignored the difference between a cargo boat lightly armed for its own defence, a concept which had obtained for centuries, and an armed merchant cruiser, a large vessel commissioned into the navy, manned by naval personnel and performing any naval function for which she could be used. Such A.M.C.s were fighting ships and, according to all precedent, were liable to be sunk on sight by any means available.

With the arming of merchantmen, it became extremely dangerous for U-boats to apply the stop-and-search routine that custom demanded. Their task became more difficult still when the British set out to make German observance of the 'cruiser rules' impossible. They made it an offence for the captain of a ship to stop when ordered to do so and gave orders that the U-boats were to be attacked either by gunfire or ramming. Despite the fate of Captain Fryatt (see p. 80), several British skippers were prosecuted for failing to obey these orders. As early as February 1915 Q-ships, ostensibly merchantmen with a heavy but concealed armament, were sent out to lure submarines into a sense of security. Everything was done to confuse British ships with those of neutrals; their names and ports of registry were painted out and orders given to hoist neutral colours in cases of need. This was a legitimate *ruse de guerre* (see p. 103). The penultimate voyage of the *Lusitania*, however, caused some embarrassment. Carrying President Wilson's personal representative, she hoisted the Stars and Stripes when the presence of a U-boat was reported off the Irish coast. Wisely Colonel House did not come on deck and was able to say truthfully that he had seen nothing of the incident.

All these British moves made it impossible for the Germans to comply with the recognised procedures and on February 5th, 1915 they declared the waters round the British Isles to be a war zone in which any allied merchant ship was liable to be sunk,

Without it always being possible to avert the dangers threatening the passengers and crew on that account. Even neutral ships are exposed to dangers in the war zone as, in view of the misuse of neutral flags ordered by the British Government and the accidents of naval warfare, mistakes will not always be avoided.

The war zone came into force on February 18th, and the early days passed quietly. In thirty-seven days twenty-five merchantmen were sunk, but only fifty-two lives were lost, thirty-eight of them in one ship which blew up and was probably loaded with explosives. There was, however, an ugly incident on March 28th, when a U-boat stopped the liner *Falaba*. Ten minutes, later extended to twenty-five, were allowed for the passengers and crew to take to the boats, but before that time a British armed trawler appeared on the scene and the U-boat torpedoed *Falaba* which, thanks to thirteen tons of explosive in her holds, blew up. More than a hundred lives were lost.

The sinking of *Falaba* caused a worldwide sensation, the more so since one of the dead was a U.S. citizen, but the furore was soon drowned in the most famous sea 'atrocity' case of all time, the sinking of *Lusitania* with the loss of 1,201 lives on May 7th, 1915.

The indignation aroused by that sinking was largely misplaced. *Lusitania* had been built with an Admiralty subsidy. She therefore carried mountings for twelve six-inch guns and was listed as an Armed Merchant Cruiser in *Jane's Fighting Ships* and *Brassey's Naval Annual*. To all appearances she was a combatant unit of the Royal Navy. In fact her owners had been told in 1914 that she would not be used as an A.M.C. but this had not been announced and, as far as Walter Schweiger, the commander of U-20, which carried copies of both *Jane's* and *Brassey's*, could tell she was an active warship. Following a positive identification, he fired a single torpedo at her.

The fact that *Lusitania* sank in eighteen minutes surprised no one more than Schweiger who, like most U-boat captains at that time, had little faith in the effectiveness of his torpedoes. The cause of her rapid sinking was almost certainly the explosion of sixty-eight tons of gun-cotton in her holds, though she also carried large quantities of ammunition to say nothing of other military stores and a small detachment of Canadian soldiers. The fact that she also carried a large number of American citizens was unfortunate but was not the fault of the Germans who had made it plain in New York that it was unsafe to embark in her. If the U.S. government did not know that she carried a large cargo of contraband of war this could only be because it had been decided to turn a blind eye to her cargo.

The British turned the sinking of *Lusitania* into a great propaganda exercise aiming to prove that Germany had abandoned all restraints in naval warfare. Not only were there violent anti-German riots both in Britain and in some of the Dominions, but also ugly scenes at sea particularly when, later in 1915, the Q-ship H.M.S. *Barralong,* having sunk U-27 and U-41, machine-gunned the survivors in the water. In the circumstances it is hardly surprising that the Germans abandoned all restraints and, in 1917, declared unlimited submarine warfare.

On their side the Germans claimed that British tactics made it impossible to maintain a blockade in the traditional way. They claimed that there was no moral difference between sinking professional sailors who, even if they were not members of the armed forces, knew the dangers they were running, and the British blockade which was deliberately setting out to starve women and children whose only offence was to live in Germany. The infliction of starvation on a whole nation was a new development made possible only by the growth of very large towns. Germany, particularly after she had acquired access to Poland and the Ukraine under the terms of the Treaty of Brest–Litovsk, could not be absolutely short of food but, thanks to the demands made by the war on the railways and their consequent deterioration, the food available could no longer be efficiently distributed. Starvation was a purely urban phenomenon but it was no less an effective weapon. The average meat consumption of town-dwellers fell from its peacetime level of 1,050 grammes a week to 135 grammes and the fat consumption from 210 to 49 grammes. Since it became all but impossible to obtain cheese, milk and eggs in the towns the effect on the health of the inhabitants was very serious. Deaths from tuberculosis doubled. More died from the disease in the first half of 1918 (41,847) than in the whole of 1914 (41,730). By the end of 1917 the overall death rate from all causes for children between one and five rose by 49.3 per cent, and for children between five and fifteen by 55 per cent. German figures calculated after the war showed that between 1915 and 1918 the blockade was responsible for 726,766 deaths and that the death rate among civilians was, by 1918, running at 37 per cent above the level for 1913. These figures are sufficiently impressive, but they tell only part of the story. The blockade demoralised the entire population. Every urban worker was short of essential foodstuffs and his production level inevitably fell; so did his will to work for a victory that seemed always to recede. It disheartened the nation.

Although the United States, when she entered the war, enforced the blockade with all the severity of Britain and France, the second of President Wilson's Fourteen Points for ending the holocaust was, 'Absolute freedom of navigation upon the seas . . . alike in peace and war.'

Between the two world wars lengthy, though largely unavailing, efforts were made to devise a practicable system for making submarines conform to the 'cruiser rules'. Eventually, in November 1936, representatives of Hitler's Germany put their names to the London Submarine Protocol, to which, before 1939, forty-seven other states, including Britain, France, Italy, Japan and the United States, adhered. This reaffirmed the 'established rules of international law' and laid down that,

1. In their action with regard to merchant ships, submarines must conform to the rules of international law to which surface vessels are subject.

2. In particular, except in the case of persistent refusal to stop on being duly summoned, or of active resistance to search and visit, a warship, whether surface vessel or submarine, may not sink or render incapable of navigation a merchant vessel without first having placed passengers, crew and ship's papers in a place of safety. For this purpose, the ship's boats are not regarded as a place of safety unless the safety of the passengers and crew is assured, in the existing sea and weather conditions, by the proximity of land, or the presence of another vessel which is in a position to take them on board.

It is scarcely credible that those taking part in the drafting of this protocol sincerely believed that it would have much effect. It was an attempt to put the clock back, to consider the submarine in the same light as one of Nelson's frigates. All the evidence from the previous war showed that submarines were incapable of working within these rules. The British Admiralty seems to have had no illusions in the matter. Less than two years after the Protocol was signed they announced that, in case of war, they would again arm merchant ships for defensive purposes and, as soon as war was declared, they instituted a convoy system, a clear indication that they did not believe the Germans would observe the reiterated rules.

The sinking of the liner *Athenia*, ten hours after Britain and Germany went to war in 1939, seemed to show that their scepticism was justified. In fact the sinking was a tragic error. Captain Lemp of U-30 was under orders to conform to the Protocol and fired at her under the impression that she was an Armed Merchant Cruiser. It may have been a mistake that he should not have made, but it was nevertheless a mistake. For the first nine months of the war the Germans with few exceptions obeyed the rules, notably in the case of the surface raider *Graf Spee*, whose captain succeeded in capturing nine British merchantmen without causing the death of a single British sailor. It was not until May 24th, 1940 that Hitler decreed that 'All restrictions on naval action in English and French waters are hereby cancelled and commanders are free to employ their forces to the fullest extent.' No announcement was made of this decision until August 17th, when neutrals were warned that any ship approaching the British Isles was liable to attack by U-boats, mines and aircraft.

Meanwhile the British were trying, rather pathetically, to repeat their triumph of the previous war. Although they had an almost mystic faith in the blockade weapon which had served them so well, in May 1940, it leaked like a sieve and Germany had her eastern and southern frontiers open to almost any kind of import. The evacuation from Dunkirk was already under way and their only large continental ally was disintegrating when the chiefs of staff blithely reported to the cabinet that,

It is probably only a matter of months before hoarding by the peasant population creates a really acute shortage of food in the industrial areas, including Germany herself . . . Denial of food-stuffs is likely to produce widespread starvation in many of the industrial areas, including parts of Germany, before the winter of 1940.

It is a matter of history that not until the later months of 1944 did the people of Germany start to have less food than the strictly rationed British.

9

Bombardment – Old Style

Until the middle of the nineteenth century the use of artillery for purposes other than disabling troops on the battlefield was, except in one set of circumstances, a pointless exercise. As late as 1815 the most powerful cannon practicable to move on land weighed, with its limber, rather more than four tons. Even on good roads five pairs of bullocks were needed to move it at a rate, in fine weather, of eight miles a day, about half the speed of marching infantry. Its maximum rate of aimed fire was one round in two minutes and for sustained firing twenty rounds in an hour was seldom exceeded. Its missile was a solid iron ball weighing twenty-four pounds and it could throw this to a range of less than a mile and a half.

From this specification it is clear that no one would employ such a clumsy and inefficient weapon unless to do so was unavoidable. This would only arise if an army was faced with solid fortifications which only constant and heavy battering could reduce. Such obstacles were only to be met in permanent fortresses and, in consequence, the art of using such guns – siegecraft – became a highly specialised branch of military science, one so set about with ritual that it resembled a huge, lethal ballet.

Sieges were also the only occasions when civilians were deliberately involved in fighting. In a besieged town the non-combatants shared the hardships and most of the dangers with the troops of the garrison. They were, however, a different type of non-combatant. It could be assumed that they lived in a fortress town by their own choice, recognising that any fortress was likely to be besieged. Moreover, they were not agricultural workers and consequently they were not useful to the invading army except insofar as they could be used as a bargaining counter with the garrison commander, who might be blackmailed into making concessions to spare them suffering. Anyone who lived in a fortress town was expendable and of their own choice.

The first act of a siege was the investment of the fortress, the encircling of the walls by the attacking army so that supplies could not be sent in. Next came the temporary earthworks, known as batteries, which were thrown up to protect the cumbersome siege guns when, in the fullness of time, they arrived. Simultaneously a

128

trench was dug parallel to the walls and once this, the first parallel, was complete a ceremony marked the opening of the siege. In the seventeenth and eighteenth centuries the investing troops would march into the trench with their colours flying, bayonets fixed and bands playing. They then planted their colours on the parapet as a challenge to the garrison. Although the defenders were not obliged to cease firing during this rite, the formalities had to be meticulously observed. In 1647 when Louis, Prince de Condé laid siege to Lerida, Paris complained that, contrary to tradition, the bands of the French army had included violins. Condé replied that it was the Spanish custom to include strings and that he had done so as a compliment to the garrison. Although the British abandoned the ceremony in Marlborough's days on the reasonable grounds that it incurred unneccessary casualties, the French continued until the last recorded occasion when Lafayette's division invested Yorktown in 1781 and astonished Cornwallis's garrison.

At this stage the commandant of the fortress might wish to disencumber himself of the non-combatants within the walls. There was no general ruling on whether he should be allowed to do but there were precedents on both sides. All depended on the investing general's opinion of whether he could quickly bombard the place into submission, in which case he could afford to let the civilians go, or whether he must starve the place into surrender. When Edward III laid siege to Calais in 1346, the governor sent out all the poor people, those without stocks of food, and the King not only let them pass but gave each a free dinner and twopence as alms. Half a century later when the English were besieging Rouen, the defenders drove out 12,000 *bouches inutiles*, but the investors refused to let them through and the wretched crowd did its best to live through the winter on a diet of grass and roots. When the Prussians besieged Strasbourg in 1870 their commander offered to permit the evacuation of all women, children and sick, an offer which was inexplicably refused. Later, at the instigation of delegates from the Swiss Federal Council, 4,000 non-combatants were allowed to leave. Similarly in 1904 the Japanese proposed to the Russian commandant of Port Arthur that women, old men and boys under sixteen should quit the fortress provided that they brought with them not more than one package, which would be liable to search, and that the number leaving was notified in advance. The Russian command agreed to this offer.

At the beginning of the twentieth century it was the German view, as expressed in the *Kriegsbrauch*, that,

If the commandant of a fortress wishes to strengthen its defensive capacity by expelling a proportion of the population, such as women, children, old people, wounded, &c, then he must take these steps in good time, before the investment begins. If the investment is completed, no claim to the free passage of these classes can be made good . . . The very presence of such persons may accelerate the surrender of the place, and it would be foolish of the besieger voluntarily to renounce this advantage.

The contemporary British guidance was similar, but added,

It is therefore left to the consideration of the besieging commander whether or not he will permit such individuals to leave.

All persons dwelling within the zone that will usually exist between the opposing forces in the first stage of a siege are treated as inhabitants of the invested locality. Humanity, however, makes it desirable that the commander of the besieging army should, if the conditions of the case permit, allow them to withdraw into the fortress.

As late as September 29th, 1944 the practice of both sides on this point was put to the test when the German commandant of Calais asked for a truce so that the inhabitants of the town could be evacuated. His opposite number, Major-General D. C. Spry, commanding 3rd Canadian Division, granted twenty-four hours and, according to the *Official History of the Canadian Army,* 'The unfortunate people of Calais streamed out of the city by the eastern roads, to be received and looked after by our Civil Affairs staff.'

One of Napoleon's marshals, Gabriel Suchet, had a different solution. When he invested Lerida in 1810 there was no question of violins as in Condé's time. The strength of the place lay in its citadel built in the centre of the city and Suchet's scheme for subduing it was brutally simple. In his own words,

My soldiers were ordered to make a concentric movement to push the inhabitants, along with the garrison, towards the upper streets and the citadel. They were dislodged by musketry from street after street, house after house, in order to force them into the castle. That work was still firing, and its guns augmented the danger and panic of the civil population, as they were thrust, along with the wreck of the garrison, into the ditch and over the drawbridge. Pressed by our soldiers, they poured into the castle yard before the governor had time to give orders that they should not be admitted.

15,000 people, men, women and children, soldiers and civilians were crammed into the citadel when every gun and mortar within range was opened on them and, wrote the marshal, 'every shell fell in the narrow space containing the multitude . . . The scheme had a prompt and decisive effect.' Five hundred civilians were killed during the night and the governor surrendered in the morning.

The second act of siege would begin when the heavy artillery had been put into position for firing on whichever part of the walls had been selected as most susceptible to battering. At this stage it was customary to summon the garrison to surrender. If they agreed, which was unusual, they would save their church bells since a long tradition dictated that if a single siege gun opened fire the bells, or an equivalent ransom, would become the property of the artillery commander of the investing army, since they were suitable for melting down and casting into cannon.

The most famous summons in history was that sent by General Verdier to José de Palafox, Governor of Saragossa in 1808. The Frenchman sent a note containing a single word – *Capitulation?* Palafox replied with equal terseness *'Guerra y cuchilla'* – war and the knife. Rather more formally, a Confederate general summoned a northern garrison on October 12th, 1864.

To: O.C. Troops at Resaca, Ga.
Sir, I demand the immediate and unconditional surrender of the post and garrison under your command, and, should this be acceded to, all white officers and soldiers under your command will be parolled in a few days. If the place is taken by assault, no prisoners will be taken.
Most respectfully,
J. B. Hood, Major General.

It should be noted that the offer of clemency applied only to white troops, a reflection of the Confederate view that coloured soldiers were not legitimate combatants. Earlier that year, when they had taken Fort Pillow on the Mississippi, they had massacred the whole garrison, the blacks because they were black, the whites because 'they were fighting with niggers'. At Resaca the matter was never put to the test. The colonel in command replied,

To General Hood,
Your communication of this date received. In reply, I have to state that I am somewhat surprised at the concluding paragraph, to the effect that, if the place is taken by assault, no prisoners will

be taken. In my opinion, I can hold this post. If you want it, come and take it.

I am, General, etc.

Clark R. Weaver.

In the event General Hood did not attack.

One of the last examples of summoning a garrison to surrender occurred as late as May 1940. When the Rifles were defending Calais, a summons was carried in by a German officer accompanied by two allied prisoners of war. Brigadier C. N. Nicholson's reply was thought worthy of being recorded in English in the German War Diary.

The answer is no as it is the British army's duty to fight as well as it is the German's.

The French captain and the Belgian soldier having not been blindfolded cannot be sent back. The allied commander gives his word that they will be put under guard and will not be allowed to fight against the Germans.

A somewhat impertinent summons was recorded by a British naval captain from Riga in 1812.

General Grawart, who commands the troops of the enemy in this neighbourhood during the absence of Marshal Macdonald, sent on the 27th [August] to summons General Essen [commanding the Russians in Riga] to surrender, assigning as a reason for doing so that his battering train would arrive in the course of a fortnight.

General Essen did not consider that this was a sufficient reason to throw in his hand and it would not even have sufficed for Milan, a city so rich and difficult to defend that it had an Imperial dispensation that it might surrender to any hostile army that crossed either the Adda or the Ticino rivers, provided that no friendly force was within reach.

Occasionally it was possible to frighten a fortress into surrender without firing a shot. In 1798 Sir Charles Stuart managed to secure the surrender of the fortress of Ciudella, which gave the British the possession of Minorca, by erecting impressive batteries for guns he did not have and by drawing up all his men, who scarcely outnumbered the garrison, in single file where they could not be seen clearly. Having thus given the governor a false impression of overwhelming strength, he sent in a summons and was rewarded with capitulation. This was exceptional and tradition was that no fortress should be surrendered unless there was a breach in the wall large enough for an attack to be able to break in or if the place had no more than two days' rations left – that margin being necessary for the attackers to provide food for garrison and inhabitants.

When one of these two conditions was nearly reached, the governor had a nice decision to make. If a court-martial held that he had surrendered the place needlessly he could be sentenced to death. On the other hand, he might be executed by the victorious side if he hung on too long and caused unnecessary casualties to both sides. In France Louis XIII forbade surrender before several assaults had been beaten off from a practicable breach. Louis XIV was less demanding and required only one assault to be withstood. His orders remained in force until the revolution, when the beleaguered republic was likely to guillotine any commander who did not defend his post to the last extremity. Napoleon restored the orders of Louis XIV.

Once the governor, who usually took care to call a council of war so as to ensure the agreement of his chief subordinates, decided to capitulate, tradition required that he sent a drummer to the walls, presumably in a quiet sector, and that a white flag would be raised while the *chamade*, the drum call to a parley, was beaten. Negotiations would follow and there would be keen bargaining about whether the garrison deserved the honours of war and, if so, to what extent. If the garrison's defence had been half-hearted, they would be required to march out without arms except for the officers' swords which would be carried under the arms, with their points to the rear. Colours would be cased and there would be no music. If, however, they were held to have distinguished themselves they would receive the full honours. When Breda fell to the Spaniards in 1624,

The governor with the officers and soldiers, both horse and foot, to march out of the town armed soldierlike, viz: the foot with flying colours, drums beating, completely armed, bullets in mouth, matches lighted on both ends, their pouches full of powder and shot. The horse with their trumpets sounding, standards displayed, armed in such sort as when they march towards the enemy. No soldier shall be questioned or detained for any pretext whatever, not though he had formerly been in the enemy's service. All without exception to march the best and most commodious way to their next garrison, without injury, hindrance or wrong done to their own persons, their arms, horses or baggage. And it shall be lawful for them to take with them their wives, children, household stuffes, horses and carts.

Best of all was the right to march out over the breach, thus demonstrating that it was fully practicable. This could cause embarrassment. When José Imaz treacherously surrendered Badajoz to the French in March 1811, he stipulated that he should be given the fullest honours of war. Being desperate for time, the French agreed but the ceremony was a fiasco. Far from being able to march out over the breach the garrison could not even scramble over it. They had to be turned about and left by the gate.

If a governor decided to stand an assault he risked the lives of everyone in the fortress, soldiers and civilians alike, together with all their property. As Martens wrote in 1788,

> If the place, after being duly summoned, refuses to surrender and is taken by assault, those found in it are obliged to submit to the discretion of the victor: all the garrison can expect is to have their lives spared if they immediately lay down their arms.

Nothing is mentioned about those who have no arms to lay down.

Over the centuries a tradition had grown up that those who survived a successful assault had the right to do as they wished with a town that they had captured. This, however, was not one of the laws of war but a law of nature. The storm of a strongly-held breach was the most horrifying experience that a soldier could undergo and many of those who came through it became utterly uncontrollable in the immediate aftermath. Their commanders would have been delighted if the sack that usually followed a storm could be prevented. The characteristic orgy played havoc with the discipline of an army and temporarily destroyed its fighting power. It frequently also destroyed stocks of provisions which were badly needed by the attackers. Experienced generals realised that some disorder could not be avoided but some did not appreciate the extent to which it might go. After the storm of Magdeburg in 1631 Jan Tilly, the Imperialist commander, said grudgingly, 'Three hours' plunder is the shortest rule of war. The soldier must have something for his toil and trouble.'

It was three days, rather than three hours before he could induce his troops to abandon their rampage and by that time Magdeburg was a smoking ruin and the population had been reduced from thirty thousand to five thousand, the greater part of whom were women who had been abducted to the Imperial camp before the wrecking of the city got fairly under way. Even Wellington, whose army was under extremely strict discipline, realised that it was useless not to wait forty-eight hours before issuing his order that, 'It is now full time that the plunder of Badajoz should cease.'

As was inevitable in assaults, the officer casualties had been so high that the maddened men were deprived of their natural leaders and, until their insensate fury died down with exhaustion, there was nothing that could be done to stop them.

The behaviour of the defenders could also drive the attackers to frenzy. In 1894 the Japanese took Ryojun (later renamed Port Arthur) from the Chinese. The garrison had not put up a desperate defence and casualties in the assault were small but the storming parties found exposed on a gateway the mutilated and tortured bodies of some Japanese soldiers. According to *The Times* correspondent on the spot,

> Thursday, Friday, Saturday and Sunday were spent in murder and pillage from dawn to dusk, in mutilation and every kind of nameless atrocity, until the town became a ghastly inferno, to be remembered with a fearsome shudder until one's dying day.

Compared to the climacteric horrors of the last act of a siege, the storm and sack, the bombardment which preceded it was a comparatively mild ordeal for the civilians living within the walls. Towards the end of the eighteenth century Martens wrote,

> Except in cases of necessity, it is now admitted that the besiegers ought to direct their artillery against the fortifications only, and not, intentionally, against the public edifices, or any other buildings, either within or without the ramparts.

From the soldiers' point of view, this precept was more of a logistic necessity than a humanitarian concession. The problems of transporting the ammunition for the voracious battering guns were sufficiently great without adding to it the need to bring up supplies for howitzers and mortars. The battering guns at Badajoz in 1812 consumed 31,861 rounds of shot and 2,523 barrels of powder, a quantity which required the use of 1,050 waggon loads to be brought from the nearest port 129 miles, or sixteen days' waggon journey, away. This imposed a vast strain on the army's limited transport resources and one that could not be supplemented by adding to it the need to bring as much again for the high-angle weapons. It is noticeable, however, that when the same army attacked San Sebastian 13,987 mortar and howitzer shells were thrown into the interior of the town but there the army was in close touch with the sea and the transport difficulty was minimal. It is hard to resist the conclusion that sparing the townspeople was more a question of cost-effectiveness than any concern for the safety of civilians.

In the nineteenth century technological advance removed some of the logistic restraints on bombardment. By 1870 the Krupp siege guns with a range of three and a half miles could make a serious effect on the interior of a town and both the piece itself and its ammunition could be moved by railway. The question remained whether the indiscriminate shelling of civilians was a useful operation. The first to make the experiment was General Carl Wilhelm von Werder when he invested Strasbourg in 1870. He was unwilling to tie down the number of troops necessary for a formal siege and hoped to terrify the inhabitants into demanding that the garrison should surrender. After giving formal notice, he opened his bombardment on August 23rd, continuing it for four days and nights during which most of the public buildings and many private homes were destroyed or damaged. On the first day the plan seemed likely to succeed. Following some panic the municipality was induced to offer a ransom of 100,000 francs a day for the cessation of the shelling. Then the mood changed and it became apparent, even to the besiegers, that far from terrorising the non-combatants the bombardment was rallying them to the defence of their city. Von Werder called off the shelling and instituted a siege.

The lesson of Strasbourg was lost on Bismarck at the siege of Paris. Backed by an outcry, which he orchestrated himself in the Prussian press, he forced the High Command to undertake long-range shelling of the city. Few of the soldiers supported him. Some, led by von Moltke, opposed him because the supply of ammunition would put a further strain on his tenuous communications. Others, notably the Crown Prince Frederick, objected both on humanitarian grounds and because, as Strasbourg had suggested, the bombardment would not be effective. Bismarck overrode them, declaring that 'two or three shells' would frighten the Parisians into surrender. The bombardment, starting with the outlying forts but soon switched to the city itself, was a total failure. Twelve thousand shells were fired and damaged 1,400 buildings, killing ninety-seven people and wounding 278 more. As for stimulating a demand for surrender, in the opinion of Elihu B. Washburne, the U.S. minister at Paris, 'it apparently made the people more firm and determined'.

The Hague Rules did their best to regulate the use of bombardment but the thought behind them was more attuned to the artillery of 1870 than that of the twentieth century.

The attack or bombardment, by whatever means, of towns, villages, dwellings, or buildings which are undefended is prohibited.

The officer in command of an attacking force must, before commencing a bombardment, except in cases of assault [*sauf le cas d'attaque de vive force*], do all in his power to warn the authorities.

In sieges and bombardments all necessary steps must be taken to spare, as far as possible, buildings dedicated to religion, art, science or charitable purposes, historical monuments, hospitals and places where the sick and wounded are collected, provided they are not used for military purposes.

It is the duty of the besieged to indicate the presence of such buildings or places by distinctive and visible signs, which shall be notified to the enemy beforehand. The pillage of a town or village, even when taken by assault, is prohibited.

Although the Rules make no suggestion about how buildings, other than hospitals, should be marked to avoid being shelled by land-based guns, the Ninth Hague Convention (1907) which dealt with Bombardment by Naval Forces, recommended that each such building should be marked with, 'Large stiff rectangular panels, divided diagonally into two coloured triangular portions, the upper portion black, the lower portion white'.

This naval Convention also contained the curiously outdated provision that,

After due notice has been given, the bombardment of undefended ports, towns, villages, dwellings or buildings may be commenced if the local authorities, after a formal summons has been made to them, decline to comply with requisitions for provisions or supplies necessary for the immediate use of the naval force before the place in question.

10

Bombardment – New Style

The last revision of The Hague Rules was agreed in 1907, only four years after the Wright brothers had achieved powered flight and two years before Blériot succeeded in flying across the Straits of Dover. It could not be expected therefore that the idea of bombardment from the air would have received much attention, although an agreement reached in 1899 declared that, 'The Contracting Powers agree to prohibit . . . the discharge of projectiles and explosives from balloons or by any other new methods of a similar nature.'

Germany, France, Russia and Italy were among the nations which declined to renew this declaration in 1907 so that Italy was not in breach of her agreement when, in 1911, she inaugurated aerial bombing during her war with Turkey. In the same year a participant in one of the rash of conferences of international lawyers which were striving to frame rules for air warfare, remarked, 'I regret very much that the progress of science has made aviation possible.' It was a comment which must have been echoed by the many people who in the years to follow took any part in the abortive business of trying to regulate war in the air.

Up to the outbreak of war in 1914 (and subsequently) discussion revolved endlessly around the problem of what constituted a legitimate target for bombing. A lawyer who in the summer of 1914 published a book, *Aircraft in War*, came to the dispiriting conclusion,

> I can see nothing in international law to prevent an hostile aircraft from dropping bombs on Chelsea, Wellington, Albany or Knightsbridge barracks, or on the clothing factory or depots at Pimlico, or on Euston, King's Cross, Waterloo and the other great railway termini. Many commercial undertakings which hold orders from the War Department or Admiralty would be liable to bombardment also. So probably would be the War Office and the Admiralty and the headquarters of the Eastern Command and the London District. The various Territorial Force headquarters all over London also appear to be possible legitimate objects of attack.

Since aiming a bomb in those days consisted of little more than pushing it over the side of the flying machine, it was clear that little accuracy could be expected and that a good deal of incidental damage would occur in the neighbourhood of these multifarious but legitimate targets.

The first air raid on a major city occurred in April 1915 when a Zeppelin succeeded in dropping some bombs on London. Zeppelins, however, were too vulnerable to fighter aircraft and raids were soon discontinued. Meanwhile the generals were too busy trying to find sufficient aircraft for the close support of the land battle to be interested in sparing planes for the dubious business of attacking targets far from the fighting which, at best, could only promise long-term results. A few French and Royal Naval Air Service machines were used to attack vulnerable targets provided by the German iron industry in Lorraine but the results were far from spectacular. On the other side, the Germans started a series of raids against England which, although aimed at military targets, seldom managed to hit them. It was the start of a terrible escalation.

On May 25th, 1917 twenty-one Gotha bombers set out to attack targets in London but, running into heavy cloud, changed course and attacked Folkestone, a military port, and Shorncliffe, a military centre. No warning was given to the two towns and casualties were, by the standard of the day, heavy – ninety-five killed and 195 injured, almost all of them non-combatant. One raider was shot down. Twenty-one more Gothas struck at London on June 13th, and, without loss to themselves, killed 162 and injured 432. A formation of the same size lost a single plane when, on July 7th, they again attacked London and killed fifty-four people, injuring 190.

There ensued in London some panic and a violent outcry against the government for the obvious inadequacy of the defence which consisted principally of fighters slower than the bombers they were trying to intercept. Lloyd George, the prime minister, had a talent for the public gesture and appointed Jan Smuts, the veteran South African, to report on what steps could be taken to combat the raids. His recommendation was the formation of a separate service whose primary task would be retaliation against Germany.

An air service . . . can be used as an independent means of war operations. Nobody who witnessed the attack on London on [7th] July could have any doubt on that point . . . The day may not be far off when aerial operations with their devastation of enemy lands and destruction of industrious and populous centres on a vast scale may become the principal operations of war, to which the older forms of naval and military operations may become secondary and subordinate.

As a result the Royal Air Force was formed with two aims, to give the impression that Lloyd George's government was doing something to stop the air raids and to carry out retaliation for what the public regarded as terror raids on Britain. To ensure that both points were not overlooked by the voters Lloyd George first offered the new secretaryship of state to one newspaper magnate and, when he refused it, to another. Hugh Trenchard, who later became known as the Father of the R.A.F., wrote soon after the formation of the new service, 'An impossible organisation was set up by politicians simply in order that they could say, "I am bombing Germany".'

The only innovation in the early R.A.F. was a small Independent Bombing Force which, before the war ended, dropped 543 tons of bombs on Germany, but without causing much damage.

After the Armistice the politicians, led once more by Lloyd George, wished to abolish the R.A.F. on grounds of economy but they had fathered a monster which they could not throttle. Sir Hugh Trenchard had become a convert to the idea of air power and advocated the retention of the force with all the zeal of a proselyte. To justify its continuation meant finding a role that could not be carried out equally well by the army and the navy. Since Trenchard had ended the war in command of the Independent Bombing Force it was natural that he should choose the idea of winning the next war by the destruction of the enemy's war potential. According to his doctrine, as enunciated in 1923, 'To win [the next] war it will be necessary to pursue a relentless offensive by bombing the enemy's country, destroying his source of supply of aircraft and engines, and breaking the morale of his people.'

It would, he wrote, be 'better to have less fighters and more bombers to bomb the enemy and trust to their cracking before us'. It was not an original policy. In 1916 Colonel Barrés of the French service had asserted that 'the end of the war would be brought about by the effective bombing of open towns' and, while Trenchard was developing his theory of strategic bombing, General Giulio Douhet was putting forward parallel views in Italy. Nevertheless only in Britain did the idea that long-range bombing could win a war take root. Germany, Italy and France built large fleets of bombing planes but these were primarily intended for support of the armies. Trenchard was prepared to neglect this role in favour of using the R.A.F. to 'attack direct the centres of production, transportation and communication from which the enemy's war effort is maintained'.

> It is well known that the moral effect of Air Attack is out of all proportion greater than the material effects achieved. While, therefore, serious material damage may be expected from bomb attack, the most probable cause of chaos in the community will be the *moral* collapse of the personnel in the working of the vital public services, such as transport, lighting, water and food distribution.

The idea of setting out to cause chaos and the moral collapse of non-combatants was a sharp departure from all the traditional concepts of limiting war as far as possible and particularly where civilians were concerned. When objections were made on this score, Trenchard replied,

> As regards the question of legality, no authority would contend that it is unlawful to bomb military objectives wherever situated . . . Among military objectives must be included the factories in which war material (including aircraft) is made, the depots in which it is stored, the railway termini and docks at which it is loaded or troops entrain or embark, and in general the means of communication and transportation of military *personnel* and *material*. Such objectives may be situated in centres of population in which their destruction will result in casualties also to the neighbouring civilian population . . . The fact that air attack may have that result is no reason for regarding the bombing as illegitimate provided all reasonable care is taken to confine the bombing to the military objectives . . . What is illegitimate, as being contrary to the dictates of humanity, is the indiscriminate bombing of a city for the sole purpose of terrorizing the civilian population.

Given the many targets which Sir Hugh considered as legitimate and allowing, as he did, that a proportion of the bombs would go astray, there were few parts of any town that could not be considered as either a military objective or close enough to it to be within the area of legality. The dividing line between this idea and 'the indiscriminate bombing of a city for the sole purpose of terrorising the civilian population' was so narrow that, when Trenchard's ideas came to be put into practice, his successors found it invisible.

Trenchard insisted that 'reasonable care' should be taken that the bombs went to the right place but, between the wars, little attention was paid in ensuring this. On the one hand, lessons drawn from the many imperial policing actions undertaken by the R.A.F. were used to give an over-optimistic view of the accuracy of bombing techniques. From Iraq the future Air Chief Marshal Embry reported that, flying at 3,000 feet, the average bombing error of his Vickers Vernon aircraft was ten and a half yards. In May 1932 the Cabinet Committee on Coastal Defence noted that, 'We were informed by the Chief of the Air Staff that accuracy of aim has improved so much that on the North West Frontier of India aircraft are able to bomb the house of a particular sheikh.'

These feats, carried out without opposition under conditions which could never be expected in Europe, appear to have convinced Trenchard and his successors that bombers would have no difficulty in reaching their targets and bombing them with pinpoint accuracy. They opposed the development of long-range fighters to protect bomber formations and the fitting of armour to protect a bomber's crew. Navigation was neglected and it was not until 1938 that a trained navigator was added to bomber crews, since previously it had been assumed that the pilot would be able to manage. Bomb sights remained rudimentary. The efficiency of the fighter aircraft as a means of defence was greatly underrated. Each expansion scheme for the R.A.F. postulated a bomber force at least twice as strong as the fighter squadrons and had it not been for the intervention of a civilian, Sir Thomas Inskip, the R.A.F. would not have had enough fighters to win the Battle of Britain.

Parallel to the assumption that bombers would find and hit their targets was an overestimation of the casualties that bombing would cause. The Air Staff in Britain estimated that every ton of bombs dropped over a built-up area would cause fifty casualties of which one-third would be fatal, that is that every ton would kill 16.6 people. This compared with a figure of 11.7 deaths per ton from the German aeroplane raids in 1917–18 (Zeppelins had only achieved 2.8 per ton) and 1.4 deaths per ton caused by the British Independent Bomber Force in the First World War. If the air staff sincerely believed in their figure of 16.6 deaths for every ton of bombs dropped on a built-up area, it is even harder to understand how a line was to be drawn between Trenchard's legitimate bombing and bombing to terrorise the civilian population.

While the strategy of a bombing campaign designed to win a war was being evolved in Britain, a series of international conferences was held in the attempt to establish acceptable rules for air war. All proved abortive. One failed because there was no agreement on what constituted a military target and the acceptable risk to those living near armament factories. Another proposed that all bombing aircraft should be prohibited. For some time this suggestion was resisted by Britain who wished to retain bombers for imperial policing. When she agreed to renounce the practice, the conference foundered on the problem of civil aircraft that could be converted into bombers. A suggestion that all civil airlines should be controlled by the League of Nations failed to gain widespread favour. In an attempt to solve the problem of causing civilian casualties in military targets one ingenious theorist wrote in 1924,

> Offices, factories, business premises, etc, have this in common that they are not, for the most part, tenanted by their habitual population for the whole twenty-four hours. Centres of human activity and industry by day, they are practically deserted by night. Is it unreasonable to demand that they should be subject to air attack only at night? Is it not a just and reasonable condition to attach to the recognition of their liability to air bombardment that such bombardment must be rigidly and absolutely restricted to the hours when it is unlikely to entail disastrous loss of life.

The fact that the author of those words was employed by the Air Ministry emphasises the extent to which the accuracy of bombing, particularly in darkness, had been exaggerated.

Not only in Britain was it believed, as Stanley Baldwin put it, that 'the bomber will always get through'. Although in Germany Hermann Göring boasted of the inviolability of the airspace of the Third Reich, the Japanese had no such illusion. They appreciated not only that they could not stop bombers but that their cities with huge populations living in houses largely constructed of wood, fabric and paper were the most vulnerable in the world. Japan therefore planned her own form of deterrent in the hope of frightening enemy pilots. One of her grounds for refusing to ratify the 1929 Geneva *Convention relative to the Treatment of Prisoners of War* was her decision not to treat bomber crews as prisoners. By Japan's reasoning, and assuming she maintained peace with the Soviet Union, no major air power had bases from which bombers could fly to Japan, drop their bombs and return. There was a danger, however, that they might reach the great cities and, having made their attack, land and expect to be treated as prisoners. If, it was argued, the crews knew that they would be treated as murderers and criminals they would refuse to undertake such missions.

This theory, which greatly undervalued the gallantry of American airmen, was not put to the test until April 18th, 1942 when U.S.

aircraft from carriers made their first raid on Tokyo and other Japanese cities. The crews of two Flying Fortresses were captured and treated as common criminals until July when a regulation was issued making any air attack on non-military targets an offence punishable by death or imprisonment. Eight airmen were thereupon sent before a court which conducted its proceedings entirely in Japanese. Three airmen were sentenced to death and executed, five were given life imprisonment. Thereafter captured flying crew were frequently executed, usually without the formality of a trial. There is, however, no record of the Japanese having taken proceedings against any of their own airmen who had regularly indulged in terror bombing of the Chinese.

As soon as war broke out in 1939 Hitler showed that he had no scruples about using bombers as a terror weapon in the Polish campaign and his Soviet allies did the same in Finland. In the West the anticipated holocaust was delayed. The Germans were pursuing a policy of letting sleeping dogs lie, but Hitler said to General von Brauchitsch on October 9th, 'The ruthless employment of the *Luftwaffe* against the heart of the British will to resist will follow at the appropriate moment.'

Britain and France had opened hostilities with a declaration that they would not 'initiate air action against any but purely "military" objectives in the narrowest sense of the word [and that they] would refrain from attacks on civil populations for the purpose of demoralization'. They were forced to abide by this assurance by the French fear of reprisals and the British realisation that they did not have available aircraft which could make a significant impact on the German war potential. Before the Western war burst into life in the spring of 1940 the R.A.F. had established from some abortive attacks on the German fleet that the use of unescorted bombers in daylight was impracticable.

The start of strategic bombing, attacks on objectives other than those directly involved or trying to take part in the fighting, can be dated from May 15th, 1940. The R.A.F. missions were flown in what was believed to be retaliation for German terror bombing but, as is so often the case with retaliation, the original attack had been misunderstood and the misunderstanding had been made more acute by mistakes on the German side. On May 14th the Germans had bombed Rotterdam heavily, but in no sense could it be called an 'open city'. There were fortifications on the outskirts which were being stubbornly defended by Dutch soldiers. On the previous afternoon the Eighteenth German Army had sent to

General Schmidt, whose XXXIX Corps was trying to capture the city, an order which read, 'Resistance in Rotterdam will be broken by every means; if necessary destruction of town will be threatened and carried out.'

Schmidt on the following morning sent a demand for the surrender of Rotterdam, threatening the destruction of the city if his demand had not been agreed by twelve-thirty p.m. that day. He arranged an air attack for one-thirty p.m. Immediately after the deadline had passed Schmidt heard that the Dutch were prepared to negotiate and at once sent a signal cancelling the air attack. Discussions were in progress when at one-thirty-five p.m. bomber squadrons were seen approaching the city. Schmidt immediately fired red flares, the prearranged signal to stop the bombing. Half the attackers, Heinkel 111s, turned away but about fifty planes dropped ninety-four tons of bombs on Rotterdam. It is possible that Göring, as head of the *Luftwaffe* overrode Schmidt's cancellation in order to give a practical demonstration of the power of his aircraft, but it is equally probable that the cancellation miscarried – it had to be transmitted by a roundabout route – and the aircraft that bombed had failed to see the flares. In any case General Schmidt apologised for the attack when, at half past three, the city surrendered.

The attack on Rotterdam was represented in the West as a barbarous onslaught on an undefended city. In truth the city was being defended and the attack was made in error. Nor was the reported figure of 30,000 deaths a true one, although the accurate figure of 930 civilians killed was serious enough. It was nevertheless in response to the early inaccurate reports that on May 15th, ninety-nine British bombers struck at oil installations and railways in the Ruhr. The damage they did was very slight but the fact of the attack was enough to induce Hitler to include in his directive of May 24th,

The *Luftwaffe* is authorised to attack the English homeland in the fullest manner, as soon as sufficient forces are available. This attack will be opened by an annihilating reprisal for English attacks on the Ruhr.

As it happened neither the *Luftwaffe* nor the R.A.F. had available sufficient suitable planes to conduct strategic bombing in the immediate aftermath of the Rotterdam raid and few attacks on British or German cities occurred until August 25th, when a small number of German planes set out to attack oil storage tanks at Thameshaven and aircraft factories at Rochester and Kingston-on-

Thames. Some lost their way and, probably by mistake, unloaded their bombs on the City and East End of London where, notably in Bethnal Green, they caused a heavy loss of civilian life. Again reprisals were started and on the following night the R.A.F. made an attack on Berlin. The damage was slight but, in 'protective retaliation', Hitler, in a speech on September 4th, proclaimed,

> Mr Churchill is demonstrating his invention, night attacks . . . They say they will make large-scale attacks on our cities, we will erase theirs. We will stop these night-time pirates, so help me God. The day will come when one of us will break.

Despite this oratory, it appears that he still intended to confine his attacks to military targets. On September 14th, when the heads of the navy and the *Luftwaffe* advised him that 'our attacks on targets of military importance will not suffice to produce mass psychosis and large-scale evacuation, since the residential areas are some distance from the docks', he replied that he 'wished to reserve deliberate attacks on residential areas as a final means of pressure and as a reprisal for British attacks of this kind'. This, as it happened, was unimportant since, in the opinion of the British, the indiscriminate night bombing of London had started seven days earlier.

The fact was that no one could define a military objective with any degree of precision. Everyone agreed that warships, barracks, ordnance and aircraft factories were legitimate targets but there were large areas where there could only be doubt. Railways were generally conceded to be fair game, but could the same be said of roads? It could scarcely be denied that it was legitimate to create an obstacle to bar the march of an armoured division but how this was to be done was a matter of debate. In the Battle of France the Germans had deliberately encouraged refugees to take to the roads and had used aircraft to spread panic among them and this undoubtedly blocked military movement. When the Seventh French Army was retreating to the Loire the staff reported, 'Movement has been rendered almost impossible by the afflux of refugees encumbering the roads with their cars and carts. The villages and crossroads are indescribable bottlenecks.'

Could it be held that the stampeding of civilians was not in this case an operation undertaken in pursuit of an immediate military objective which could not be attained by any other method?

Even if a legitimate target could have been defined neither the *Luftwaffe* nor the R.A.F. were capable of hitting it except by the type of low-level attack which was impossible against serious opposition. The heavy bombers of 1940, the Heinkels and the Wellingtons, would be fortunate if their bombs fell within a mile of their targets, even assuming that they could find their way to their targets. Despite the best endeavours of the aircrew, attacks on military objectives were indistinguishable from terror bombing.

In any case, some of the senior air force officers drew fairly wide definitions of legitimate objectives. In September 1940 Sir Charles Portal, then A.O.C. Bomber Command, referred to 'such a town as Essen, the whole of which can for practical purposes be regarded as a military target' and no doubt there were those in Germany who would have said the same about Coventry which, with its many factories, was vital to the British aircraft industry. The only consolation was that neither side had the capability of breaking their enemy's morale. The Germans had designed the *Luftwaffe* primarily as a tactical force to act in support of the army and, when they came to use it to break the British will to resist, found it quite unable to mount a sustained offensive on the scale required. The R.A.F., on the other hand, had been principally organised as a strategic bombing force and could not carry out the role. Pre-war economy could justly be held responsible for its lack of aircraft with the range and bomb load needed for crippling attacks but, for a fraction of the cost of a single squadron of bombers, they could have carried out the research necessary to make bombing a success. They had no accurate bomb sight and, in the words of Sir Henry Tizard, Britain began the war in 1939.

with the most inadequate bombs, with rudimentary ideas of accurate bombing under conditions of war, with little if any experience of flying in a 'black-out' . . . and a fixed idea that Bomber Command would have to rely on sextant navigation over Germany, because any form of radio navigation would be dangerous.

In consequence hundreds of British lives and millions of pounds-worth of aircraft were lost in scattering bombs almost at random around the German countryside. Nor was the R.A.F. prepared to recognise the uselessness of most of their efforts. The belief in the effectiveness of their bombing was buoyed up by such assertions as that made by a senior adviser to Bomber Command on September 4th, 1940, 'However little damage appears in a photograph, an objective must have suffered damage in proportion to the weight of bombs dropped over it.'

It was not until the summer of 1941 that an analysis of air

photographs produced by a member of the War Cabinet Secretariat went some way to puncturing their complacency.

> An examination of photographs taken during the night bombing in June and July points to the following conclusions.
> 1. Of those aircraft recorded as attacking their target, only one in three got within three miles.
> 2. Over the French ports, the proportion was two in three; over Germany as a whole, the proportion was one in four; over the Ruhr it was only one in ten.
> 3. In the full moon, the proportion was two in five; in the new moon it was only one in fifteen.
> 4. In the absence of haze, the proportion is over one half, whereas in thick haze it was only one in fifteen.
> 5. An increase in the intensity of A.A. fire reduces the number of aircraft getting within five miles of their target in the ratio of three to two.
> 6. All these relate only to aircraft recorded as *attacking* the target; the proportion of the *total sorties* which reached within five miles is less by one-third. Thus, for example, of the total sorties only one in five get within five miles of the target, i.e. within the 75 square miles surrounding the target.

The conclusion to be drawn from this, the Butt report, was that in the twelve months before it had been submitted (i.e. August 1940 to July 1941) only 5,000 tons of the 25,000 tons of bombs that had been delivered arrived within five miles of their target. To achieve this 4,200 aircrew had been killed and 900 more had become prisoners of war. 846 bomber aircraft had been lost. The cost-effectiveness of this could not be calculated at the time but after the war it was discovered that the damage done to the German armed forces and war industry had been negligible and that the number of German civilians killed was smaller than that of aircrew lost.

Despite the Butt report, the bombing offensive went on with ever-increasing severity largely because, in 1941 and for some time afterwards, the British had no other effective way of striking at their enemies. As Churchill wrote in 1940,

> There is one thing that will bring [Hitler] down, and that is an absolutely devastating, exterminating attack by very heavy bombers from this country upon the Nazi homeland. We must be able to overwhelm them by this means, without which I do not see a way through.

Churchill was not so certain of the overwhelming effects of strategic bombing as he seems in that comment. In 1917 he had written,

> It is improbable that any terrorization of the civil population which could be achieved from air attack would compel the government of a great nation to surrender. Familiarity with bombardment, a good system of dug-outs or shelters, a strong control by the police and military authorities, should be sufficient to preserve the national fighting spirit unimpaired.

In September 1941 he was still of the same opinion.

> It is very disputable whether bombing by itself will be a decisive factor in the present war. On the contrary, all we have learnt since the war began shows that its effects, both physical and moral, are greatly exaggerated . . . The most we can say is that it will be a heavy and, I trust, seriously increasing annoyance.

Hitler had already come to the same conclusion. Assessing in February 1941 the effects of the *blitzkrieg* against Britain, he wrote, 'The least effect of all (as far as we can see) has been made upon the morale and will to resist of the English people.'

The continuation of the bombing offensive was largely dictated by the mood of the British people. They had been subjected to a sustained campaign of terror bombing, deliberate or unintentional, which had killed more than 30,000 civilians and damaged 3½ million homes before the main strength of the *Luftwaffe* had been diverted to the Russian front. Moreover their morale had been greatly lifted by the true stories of the heroism of the bomber crews. Since the Butt report was a closely-guarded secret the public had no means of knowing that four-fifths of that heroism was wasted.

As the strength of Bomber Command grew the campaign turned almost imperceptibly into one of undisguised terror. On October 30th, 1940 the British cabinet decided that, 'Whilst we should adhere to our rule that our objectives should be military targets, at the same time the civilian population must be made to feel the weight of war.'

On the same day the directive to Bomber Command said,

> It is desired that regular concentrated attacks should be made on objectives in large towns and centres of industry, with the primary aim of causing very heavy material destruction which

will demonstrate to the enemy the power and severity of air bombardment and the hardship and dislocation which will result from it.

Nine months later, in July 1941, the chiefs of staff were recommending that

The most vulnerable point in the German nation at war is the morale of her civilian population under air attack, and until this morale is broken it will not be possible to launch an army across the Channel with any prospect of success.

By September 1942 the chief of the air staff claimed that

The advantage of bombing for devastation is of course that the vast majority of bombs have a direct effect on something – at best an important factory, at worst the morale of the German people – whereas the very high proportion of bombs which I expect will miss a small target will often do no good at all.

'We were,' he added a year later, 'thrown back upon the general blasting of industry by means of big attacks in which few bombs are wasted.' At about the same time, A.O.C. Bomber Command was opposing the creation of the Pathfinder Force to increase the accuracy of bombing on the grounds that 'the majority of our bombs are landing in the built-up area of the Ruhr reasonably close to the intended target'.

The use of phrases such as 'bombing for devastation', 'general blasting' and 'bombs are landing in built-up areas . . . reasonably close to the intended target' all show that the R.A.F. had been forced to abandon Trenchard's definition of legitimate targets as those in which deaths to non-combatants were merely incidental. The entry of the United States into the war gave some hope that more accuracy might be expected. The Americans had more sophisticated bomb sights than the British and their Flying Fortress bombers had been designed to be able to defend themselves on daylight raids. They hoped to be able to pinpoint their targets and hit them. Unfortunately the U.S.A.A.F. had greatly overestimated the invulnerability of their aircraft and, after a series of very expensive sorties, they had to fall back on 'general blasting'. It was not until, in March 1944, the Mustang long-range fighter began to become available that accurate bombing became a practical possibility.

Despite the opinion of the Deputy Director of Bomber Operations, himself an experienced bomber pilot, that in eight attacks on Essen in the early spring of 1942 nine out of ten pilots had dropped their bombs between five and one hundred miles from the target, the R.A.F. went on pounding away at Germany. Their incomparable bravery and stamina were not matched by results. Sir Arthur Harris, who had led Bomber Command since February 1942, was convinced that the efforts of his airmen could make a greater contribution towards winning the war than any other branch of any other service in any nation. He pursued this aim with the single-minded persistence of Sir Douglas Haig but with a greater facility for expressing his views. In the summer of 1943 he wrote to the chief of the air staff,

> It is my firm belief that we are on the verge of a final showdown in the bombing war . . . I am certain that given average weather and concentration on the main job, we can push Germany over by bombing this year.

With this objective he organised a series of massive operations each aimed at a major centre of German production which was to be bombed to destruction. The most efficacious of these was that undertaken against Hamburg in July and August 1943. In a series of heavy raids 8,600 tons of bombs were dropped causing 42,000 casualties, the great majority of them civilians. 40,385 houses, 275,000 flats, 2,632 shops, 277 schools, twenty-four hospitals, fifty-eight churches and a zoo were destroyed or damaged. The equivalent of seven weeks' production from the city's factories was lost to Germany.

Before the war ended the supply of devastation targets had almost been exhausted and it seemed as if those who controlled the strategic bombing command were hard put to it to find employ-ment for the great organisation they had created. In September 1944 a great attack was launched against Darmstadt, a town with very little military potential but one which, being almost totally undamaged, was extremely suitable for testing a new system of target-marking. Sixty-nine per cent of the built-up area was des-troyed. The purpose of the shattering Anglo–American attacks on Dresden in February 1945 was, according to the Air Ministry, to 'show the Russians when they arrive, what we can do' and because the city was 'far the largest unbombed built-up area the enemy has got'.

The campaign of strategic bombing, of devastation bombing aimed, in the words of Sir Arthur Harris, 'at undermining the morale of the German people', was as ruthless an attack on non-combatants as had ever been waged by one belligerent against another. Its advocates defended it on one or both of two grounds – retaliation and its effect on hastening the end of the war. The inspiration for the campaign was British and the British carried the heaviest weight of bombs to Germany and dropped them more indiscriminately than their partners. Certainly the British had grounds for retaliation. They had been savagely bombed and few doubted that Nazi Germany would have bombed Britain to destruction if she had possessed the potential to do so. As late as 1944 the German V-weapons, V for *Vergeltungswaffe* (reprisal weapons), showed that Britain's enemies had little concern for accuracy with high explosives and did not dispute the right to reprisals. It would be hard, however, to describe the British retaliation as being conducted, in Dr Lieber's words, 'cautiously and unavoidably'. During the blitz of September 1940 to May 1941 the *Luftwaffe* aimed 13,651 tons of bombs at London. The R.A.F. only dropped monthly totals smaller than this on two occasions (December 1943 and February 1944) between July 1943 and the end of the war. In three months (July and October 1944 and March 1945) the R.A.F. dropped more than 60,000 tons, more than four times the German total for the nine months of the blitz, in each month. In addition the U.S.A.A.F. dropped more than the blitz total in each month between February 1944 and April 1945. Civilian air raid deaths in Britain throughout the war amounted to 60,000; in Germany 800,000. There can be little doubt that, considered as retaliation, the imbalance was overwhelming.

The argument that bombing for devastation greatly hastened the end of the war can only be described as not proven. It was not until late in 1944 that German war production started to decline and by that time other factors, notably the advances of the Soviet and Anglo–American armies, were playing a major part in destroying German morale. In so far as the decline in production was the product of air attacks, it largely reflects the accurate bombing in daylight of the U.S.A.A.F. when flying under escort from long-range fighters. The evidence of Albert Speer, Reich Minister for Armaments and War Production and the man most likely to be able to judge, was that the R.A.F. campaign was not a significant factor in Germany's defeat. When interrogated in 1945 he claimed that,

> The purpose of the night attacks directed exclusively against city centres had been 'incomprehensible' to him; their effects on industry were very slight . . . He considers that area bombing alone would never have become a serious threat. He particularly

152

emphasises the factor of civilian morale, and especially labour morale, which was excellent throughout and resulted in rapid resumption of work after attacks . . . The powers of resistance of the German people were underestimated and no account was taken of the fatalistic frame of mind which a civilian population finally acquires after numerous air raids.

The American attacks, which followed a definite system of assault on industrial targets, were by far the most dangerous. It was in fact these attacks which caused the breakdown of the German armaments industry.

If Speer's evidence is accepted it would seem doubtful whether Bomber Command's aim of shortening the war by destroying the German will to resist had been achieved or that their casualties of 47,268 aircrew lost on operations, to say nothing of 8,090 killed in accidents, were cost-effective. It seems possible that those lives and the 7,449 British bombers lost on night operations might have made some other more effectual contribution towards ending the war.

It was not only the British who resorted to bombing for devastation. In the Far East the Americans found themselves driven to it. According to General Henry H. Arnold, Commanding General U.S.A.A.F.

Japan, unlike Germany, had not concentrated her industries and . . . they were scattered out and were small and closely connected in site with the houses of their employees; that thus it was practically impossible to destroy the war output of Japan without doing more damage to the civilians than in Europe.

Consequently they initiated a campaign of incendiary bombing against the major Japanese cities. On the night of March 9th, 1945 three hundred and thirty-four bombers attacked Tokyo, burning out 15.8 square miles of the city and killing 83,793 of its inhabitants. Osaka, Kobe and Kagoya were similarly treated in the same month. From this it was only a short step to drop the atomic bomb on Hiroshima on August 6th. The atomic bomb was the most indiscriminate weapon ever devised but it has for many centuries been clear that 'excess and indiscriminate violence' feed upon themselves.

PART FOUR

PRISONERS OF WAR

'For you the war is over.'
Unknown German soldier to the author, Poggio Berni,
Italy, September 21st, 1944

11

'Gaignes de Guerre'

Prisoners of war are a nuisance and at no time more so than at the moment of their capture. They must be disarmed, guarded, escorted to the rear and, eventually, fed and all these services must be supplied at a time when the captors are likely to be more than usually short of manpower and supplies. When an enemy army disintegrates it presents its conquerors with an administrative problem that it is unlikely to have foreseen and certain not to have prepared for. A classic example can be found in May 1943 when the German and Italian armies in Tunisia surrendered and threw a vast number of prisoners in the hands of the Anglo–American forces. Some indication of the chaos caused can be deduced from the fact that none of the authorities concerned can, to this day, agree on the number of prisoners taken. The Army Group responsible reported that they had taken 244,500; the British *Official History* makes the number only 238,243; the American equivalent goes as high as 275,000. It would not be true to say that no preparations had been made for this huge influx. British IX Corps, the formation responsible for the final thrust on Tunis, had established an Advanced Prisoner of War Cage which was manned by forty men commanded by a twenty-year-old lieutenant. Their only weapons were pistols and, although they were supplied with no transport, they had enough coils of barbed wire to make their cage fifty yards square. At times the cage 'contained' more than 10,000 prisoners who disarmed each other, guarded each other and, inaccurately, counted each other so that a ration state could be prepared. The guards allotted were far too busy trying to find food for them to have time for guard duty. The only concession to security was a small piquet at the gate which told prisoners where to go and, more important, gave warning of the approach of senior allied officers.

The trouble that prisoners cause makes it the more surprising that over the course of history the plight of the prisoner has, in general, improved. In ancient times few prisoners were taken. The strongest captives might be retained to become slaves, the rest were quickly despatched. This was less a measure of inhumanity than of administrative convenience. H. A. L. Fisher, writing of the Crusades, commented that 'The generous nature of Richard Coeur de Lion shines with ineffectual glory' but neither generosity nor ineffectualness shone when he massacred 2,700 survivors of the garrison of Acre on the plea of military necessity although he was negotiating for their ransom at the time. Eight centuries later and seventy miles to the south, Napoleon Bonaparte followed his example and disposed of 2,500 Turkish soldiers, survivors of the storm of Jaffa.

> Buonaparte, who had expressed much resentment at the compassion manifested by his troops, and determined to relieve himself of the maintenance and care of the prisoners, ordered them to be marched to a rising ground near Jaffa, where a division of infantry formed against them. A signal gun was fired. Vollies of musquetry and grape instantly played upon them.

Like Coeur de Lion, Bonaparte pleaded military necessity, the impossibility of feeding the prisoners. They might also have claimed that their enemies were infidels and therefore outside the rules of civilised warfare. Not that the infidels against whom the crusaders fought were always ruthless with their prisoners. They were, however, likely to take reprisals for barbarities practised against them and, after the Battle of the Horns of Hattim (1187) Saladin personally killed Reginald of Chatillon on the grounds that he had treacherously broken a truce and that he was in the habit of robbing Muslim pilgrims.

In the last Crusade of all a Franco–Hungarian army was endeavouring to drive the Turks eastwards along the Danube and had no compunction in killing all the Turco–Bulgar prisoners they took in the fortresses of Vidin and Rachowa [Orykhavo]. When they went on to attempt the siege of Nicopolis [Nikopol] they were surprised and defeated (1396) by the army of Sultan Bajazet (or Bayezit). The sultan reserved twenty of the richest of his captives for ransom and sent into slavery in Turkey all those under twenty years of age. With their hands tied the remainder were paraded before him in groups of four. After he had inspected each group he nodded to his executioners who beheaded them, occasionally pausing to dismember them first. Even allowing for fourteenth-century exaggeration, it seems that three thousand men were killed before the sultan tired of the sight. Some years later Bajazet himself was defeated by Timur the Tartar, a potentate whose practice was to bury his prisoners alive. For so notable a captive as the Sultan of Turkey a special fate was reserved. He was put into a wheeled cage and dragged behind the baggage of Timur's army until, unregretted, he died.

158

The most famous case of killing prisoners was immortalised by Shakespeare. Henry V could plead military necessity at Agincourt and it is noticeable that no contemporary French account reproached him for his action. It is also worth remarking that 1,500 live prisoners were in English hands at the end of the day. There was a recent precedent for King Henry's decision to kill his prisoners. Thirty years earlier King João I of Portugal had, with English support, been defending his kingdom against a Castilian army. At the Battle of Aljubarotta (August 14th, 1385) João beat off one great assault but when another threatened he found that he could not guard his prisoners and fill his line of battle. He despatched the prisoners and won a victory.

At about the time that King João was defeating the Castilians, Abbot Bonet was writing in his *Tree of Battles*,

> If a knight, captain or champion takes another in battle, he may freely kill him, but if he were to lead him to his house and then, without further reason, decide to kill him, I consider that he would have to answer for it before justice.

Bonet was writing at about the time that, according to economic historians, feudalism was giving place to capitalism and the fact that this change was clearly observable in military affairs added a stronger reason than chivalry or Christian feeling to the tendency to keep prisoners alive. As the feudal levy, raised through knight-service, was replaced by armies of mercenaries, the soldiers were requiring a share in the profits of war. When the prisoners were murdered at Aljubarotta there were murmurings in the Anglo–Portuguese armies of 'So perish four hundred thousand francs'. There were few more promising sources of income for a soldier than the ransoming of prisoners.

Any mercenary would insist on a clear statement of the division of booty (including ransoms) being written into his contract. Before the Agincourt campaign Henry V agreed with one Thomas Tindall for the raising of six men at arms and eighteen horse-archers. The contract was somewhat complicated by the fact that since King Henry claimed to be King of France he had to find some other phrase to describe the occupant of the French throne in Paris. The paragraph dealing with ransoms reads,

> And if it should happen that the Adversary of France, or any of his sons, nephews, uncles or cousins-german, or any King of any Kingdom, or his lieutenant, or other chieftain having command from the said Adversary of France, shall be taken in the said

159

voyage [i.e. campaign], our said Lord the King shall have the said Adversary, or other person of rank above said who may be so taken, and shall make reasonable agreement with the said Thomas, or those by whom he may be taken. And respecting other profits of *Gaignes de Guerre* our said Lord the King shall have as well as the third part of the *Gaignes* of the said Thomas, as the third of the third part of the *Gaignes* of the people of his retinue in the said voyage taken, as the *Gaignes* of the prisoners, booty, money, and all gold, silver and jewels, exceeding the value of ten marks.

Put more simply this meant that for ordinary prisoners the immediate captor fixed a ransom and paid over one-third of it to his immediate superior, in this case Thomas Tindall. Tindall, for his part, paid to the King one-third of his gross profits – the ransoms of prisoners he took himself and the thirds of ransoms he received from his retinue. The rules were different if anyone won the jackpot. Captured kings, their close relations and their senior commanders could not only command huge ransoms but were important pieces on the strategic and political chessboard. Such prisoners belonged to the king but he would 'make reasonable agreement' with the captor. At Nevill's Cross (1346) King David of Scotland was captured by John Coupland. The ransom obtained by Edward III was 100,000 marks (£66,666) and Coupland was rewarded by promotion to knight banneret and an annuity of £500.

The amount demanded by kings for the ransom of important prisoners depended on their calculation of what the market would stand and there was a danger of being too greedy. When John II of France was taken at Poitiers he agreed a ransom of four million gold crowns. Further negotiations with Paris reduced this sum to three million but even this was too much, since John died in London with 1,400,000 *écus* still outstanding. The attempt to pay John's ransom almost reduced France to bankruptcy and before the country had had time to recover, 200,000 gold ducats had to be found to redeem Bajazet's prisoners from Nicopolis. The Agincourt campaign, therefore, was something of a financial disappointment for the English Crown. Two important prisoners, Marshal Boucicault and the Duke of Bourbon, died before the amounts demanded by Henry V were forthcoming. Another Agincourt captive, the Duke of Orleans, was still enjoying English hospitality twenty-one years after the battle and Henry VI decided to cut his losses, sending him home after exacting from him an oath that he would never again serve against England.

At lower ranks there were more realistic prices. The ransom for an archer was usually two pounds and Geoffrey Chaucer, who was captured while acting as secretary to the Duke of Clarence, cost his employer fifteen pounds. The custom was that knights and other men at arms should be ransomed for the equivalent of a year's income. Honoré Bonet advised captors that,

> If he does not wish to let his prisoner go, he should ask reasonable and knightly ransom, such as it is possible for the prisoner to pay and according to the usage of arms and of his country, and not such as to disinherit his wife, children, relations and friends; for justice demands that they should have the wherewithal to live after the ransom has been paid. If he do otherwise he is not a gentleman but a tyrant and no knight.

Saladin, whose army was not recruited on a profit-sharing basis, often preferred tactical advantage to cash. When he captured any of the Frankish knights of the Kingdom of Jerusalem, he was likely to demand, in place of ransom, the surrender of some castle or castles which were in the charge of his captive's retinue. Edward IV of England was another who was not interested in ransoms, a fact that goes far to explain the ambivalent behaviour of his army at Bosworth Field. His orders were to let the common soldiers go and kill off those of gentle blood. He set an example after the Battle of Tewkesbury when he had the Duke of Somerset hauled from sanctuary in the abbey and beheaded. Little sympathy need be wasted on Somerset. During the battle he had brained one of his divisional commanders, Lord Wenlock, on the unfounded suspicion that he had failed to support him.

Evidence is scarce about the fate of those prisoners who could not afford a ransom. Some no doubt were murdered to save having to feed them; some were turned loose but, as mercenary armies became more common, many merely changed sides. In the days when deaths from disease habitually exceeded battle casualties by at least four to one, there was always room for a trained soldier. In the sixteenth and early seventeenth centuries most armies consisted largely of men who were fighting for money and *gaignes de guerre* rather than for patriotic reasons or because they had been forced to join. Such men were always ready to join the opposing side if the alternative was death. Desertion to the enemy was not the disgraceful crime it became with the rise of national armies. The Thirty Years War was, ostensibly, a religious struggle but it took more courage than most men possessed to stand on religious scruples when confronted with the usual fate of intransigent prisoners. It was a recognised pastime to stand prisoners tied together in long files, and lay wagers on how many of them a single musket ball would penetrate. Such stories go far to explain why, after the Battle of Nordlingen (September 1634), 4,000 good Protestants – Swedes, Scots and Germans – took service under the Catholic banners. One man who took care not to put too much stress on religious niceties was Sydenham Poynyz, a Londoner who had served in one of the Scots regiments in the Dutch service. From there he transferred himself to the army of the Elector of Saxony, then fighting on the Protestant side.

> I was taken Prisoner by Count Butler, one of the Emperour's Coronells, an Irishman and the same man that killed afterwards Walleston [Wallenstein, see p. 84]. Though I wrote to [the Elector] to tell hym what State I was in and that he would be pleased to pay my ransom or els I must starve in prison, or serve to Emperour (which was the custome on both sides in those German Warres) and I could never get any answer from hym of my Letter, neither in Word or Writing.

Poynyz therefore joined the Catholic side and did well. It seems probable that he became a Catholic and certainly he married a rich Catholic lady but this did not prevent him from accepting a senior command from the Puritan faction when the Civil War broke out in England.

After the Thirty Years War armies became more national in character but they still contained many foreign regiments which had great difficulty in keeping up their strength especially when their employer was at war with their country of origin. The Irish Brigade in the French service was constantly trying to suborn British prisoners into changing sides. Corporal Todd of the Twelfth Foot, who was captured with a detachment of pioneers in 1761, was immediately approached by Irish officers who 'brought brandy, wine, bacco stuff and several things to sell much cheaper than we could buy them in our own cantonments' and who tried to get them to enlist, offering a bounty of ten ducats and rapid promotion. When the whole detachment refused,

> One of the men of the Irish was very impertinent and said that the English were all scoundrels, that he had lived and been brought up in it many years, but would not return to Brittain any more upon no conditions. I replied, 'So much the better for Brittain' whereupon he drew his sword and made a lunge at me and cut me over the right eye in so shocking a fashion that the pioneers thought he had taken my eye out.

At this the French intervened, arrested the Irishman and sent a doctor to tend Todd's wound.

The American War of Independence saw much changing of sides. The British soon exhausted their supply of recruits and, especially after Saratoga, relied increasingly on loyalist Americans for their numbers. On the colonial side ever-increasing offers of bounties and grants of land were made to tempt British and Hessian regulars to fight in their ranks. At the end of the war the American General Nathaniel Greene commented, 'We fought with British soldiers and they fought them with those of America.' Twenty years later Napoleon was relying increasingly on foreign troops to supplement his forces but he was in the position of being able to conscript whole armies to his own. One regiment had a notably varied career. It started as a Tyrolean regiment in the Austrian service but was captured complete in Bonaparte's great Italian campaign of 1796. At that stage the French sold it to their Spanish allies for two dollars a head and it became known as a Swiss regiment and was employed as part of the garrison of Minorca until the British captured the island in 1798. They then volunteered for the British army and, under the title of Stuart's Minorcans, fought so well in the Egyptian campaign of 1801 that they were one of the few foreign regiments to escape disbandment at the Peace of Amiens. In 1805 it achieved the distinction of being the only foreign regiment to be taken into the British infantry of the line and, as the Ninety-Seventh (Queen's Germans), they earned Wellington's approval in Portugal.

Most wars were short between Waterloo and the outbreak of war in 1914 and there were few attempts to turn prisoners to fight against their original allegiance. It was not until 1914 that the Germans attempted to form an Irish Brigade and the idea came not from the High Command but from the Foreign Office. Their instrument was Sir Roger Casement and he signed an agreement with the Wilhelmstrasse by which,

With a view to securing the national freedom of Ireland, with the moral and material assistance of the Imperial German Government an Irish brigade shall be formed from among the Irish soldiers, or other natives of Ireland, now prisoners of war in Germany.

Recognising that it would be impossible to enrol Irish officers in the prison camps, it was agreed that the brigade would have German officers until suitable Irishmen could be procured 'either from Ireland or the United States'. Nor was it intended to use the new formation directly against their old comrades in arms on the Western Front but,

> The Imperial German Government undertakes, in certain circumstances, to send the Irish Brigade to Ireland with efficient military support, and with an ample supply of arms and ammunition to equip the Irish National Volunteers in Ireland who may be willing to join them in the attempt to recover Irish national freedom by force of arms.

The 'certain circumstances' referred to were detailed as being a German naval victory on such a scale that the invasion of Ireland became a practicable possibility, and since no one was optimistic about such a victory, Casement was induced to agree to an alternative objective, to assist the Turks in driving the British out of Egypt 'since a blow struck at the British invaders of Egypt to aid Egyptian national freedom is a blow struck for a kindred cause to that of Ireland'. Wisely Casement kept this alternative objective to himself.

Even without this aberration he had a stormy reception when he attempted to enlist the 2,500 Irish prisoners who had been concentrated at a special camp at Limburg. It was a hopeless task since, at that stage of the war, his audience consisted of long-service regulars whose loyalty lay not to Ireland or England but to their regiments. One member of his audience told how his listeners 'behaved all right for a quarter of an hour, and then they found out who he was, and they hissed and booed him out of the camp'. Another prisoner wrote that,

> On one occasion he was struck, and on another I saw him get pushed. When he was struck, he swung his umbrella round him to keep the prisoners off him, and when he was pushed, he walked out of camp . . . A couple of German sentries came on the scene the second time, and he went out of camp with them.

The Irish Brigade came to nothing except to ensure that Casement was hanged. Nothing that he or the Germans could do would persuade more than fifty-two men to enlist and twenty of these insisted on leaving as soon as they realised what was expected of them. Only one recruit was used on an actual operation. Corporal Joseph Dowling of the Connaught Rangers, after having been severely beaten by his infuriated fellow prisoners, was promoted to sergeant major by the Germans and on April 12th, 1918 was sent ashore in a small boat launched from a submarine. He was found during the morning slightly drunk and clinging to a rock off the coast of County Clare. He was sent to prison for life.

Despite Casement's fiasco the Germans made the same mistake in 1940. Their great victories of that summer gave them a vast supply of prisoners who were living in primitive conditions and ninety Irishmen were sent to a special camp with comfortable quarters where they were subjected to a barrage of lectures, many given by members of the I.R.A., on the need to liberate Ireland. Ten volunteers were obtained but six of them were immediately discarded on the justifiable suspicion that they only intended to escape. Two more were rejected as unsuitable for training but the remaining pair, after a course of instruction, were sent to Norway for transport by submarine to Scotland. Before they could sail one of them had talked so freely and constantly of his mission that his controllers thought it better to cancel the operation. As one German security officer remarked of the 1940 Irish Legion, 'We found the Irish even worse than the Poles when it came to making decisions.'

In May 1943 the German Foreign Office made an attempt to recruit a unit from among all the British prisoners which would play its part in the crusade against Bolshevism. This was originally called the Legion of St George but the name was soon changed to the British Free Corps in the belief that the new name would have greater appeal to Irishmen. The part of Casement was played on this occasion by John Amery, the bankrupt son of a distinguished political family whom the Germans mistakenly believed to be a person of some social consequence in England. Dissolute, spend-thrift and wholly egocentric, Amery was probably sincere in his detestation of Communism, having run guns to the Spanish Nationalists and subsequently offered his services to the Finns and Italians. Both countries found no use for him and, when his politics were becoming unpopular even with the Vichy government, he was taken from France by the Germans who used him for broad-casting to England and for lecture tours to the occupied countries. The *Wehrmacht* disapproved of the plan to raise a British Free Corps but they were induced to let Amery tour some prison camps where he put about the story that the B.F.C. was already at brigade strength with a full complement of senior officers. On occasions he announced that the unit was being raised with the approval of the British government for use on Germany's Eastern Front.

Oratory raised few recruits but more enrolled after having been sent to a *Straflager* (*Dulag* IIIA at Lückenwalde) where conditions were peculiarly abominable. There they were told that they could only escape from the squalor and harsh discipline by volunteering for the B.F.C. Some more were blackmailed into enlisting by the threat of heavy penalties for minor infringements of German law while on working parties. The Wilhelmstrasse ordered eight hundred uniforms, each differentiated from the normal German field uniforms by embroidered Union Jacks, and it must have been a disappointment when only thirty recruits could be obtained. Some of these had been enthusiastic supporters of Sir Oswald Mosley; the remainder showed other signs of feeble-mindedness. One youth – he had been captured at the age of thirteen as a ship's boy – was credulous enough to suppose that John Amery was the British Foreign Secretary.

Such training as this motley band received came from one Thomas Cooper, child of a British father and German mother, who had served in Russia with the *Waffen S.S.* His efforts made little impression since, with the apparent connivance of the German authorities, the B.F.C. spent most of their time in drinking and wenching. When they were quartered in Hildesheim their conduct was so disorderly that the *Burgomeister* asked for them to be removed from the town.

By the early months of 1945 the German manpower situation was so desperate that they attempted to commit the B.F.C., now renamed *Sonderkommando E* of the *Waffen S.S.*, to action. When orders arrived to move to the Eastern Front all but six of the gallant band reported sick and one of the fit men was so unreliable that he was allowed no ammunition for his rifle. They suffered no action casualties and eventually succeeded in surrendering to the British. The wretched ship's boy was rewarded with a six-month sentence and Cooper was sent to prison for life.

While the attempt to recruit prisoners to fight against their own side is almost certainly a waste of effort, it does not seem to be contrary to the Geneva Convention. When two representatives of the B.F.C. visited Colditz – an expedition which demonstrates clearly how out of touch with reality the B.F.C. was – the *Kommandant* refused them admittance on the wise grounds that violence might result. He did, however, allow recruiting leaflets to be sent to each officer and thereby provoked a protest from the senior British officer. He chose to base his protest on Articles 2 and 3 of the Convention which forbid insults to a prisoner's honour.

It should be noted that the British had made an even less successful attempt on the same lines. When 130,000 Italian prisoners were taken in the Wavell–O'Connor offensive of 1940–41, Yak Mission was sent from London to raise a Garibaldi Legion from among the captives. The mission consisted of six officers, one of whom could speak Italian, and six other ranks and it was issued with £40,000 in cash for pay and expenses. Although it was led by Peter Fleming, not a single Italian was persuaded to join

12

The Honour System

The emergence of national standing armies which followed the Thirty Years War was a great benefit to prisoners of war. Once the state took over the business of raising and paying its army there was an end to the financial interest which officers and soldiers had previously held. The raising of troops as a financial venture and of serving in the hope of large profits vanished since, as the state was paying all the overheads, the state could reasonably expect to pocket all the proceeds. In earlier times a prisoner was, subject to deductions, the property of his captor who was bound to invest in him at least enough money to keep him alive so that he would be ransomable. In the late seventeenth century the prisoner became the responsibility of the state. Not that this was a new idea. In the fourteenth century Bonet had written,

> If it is the case that the soldier is in the King's pay or that of another lord, the prisoners or other possessions acquired should be the lord's in whose pay the soldier is . . . What the soldier conquers should be his lord's; for what he does he does not by his own industry or his own initiative.

In Bonet's time that had been, at best, the theoretical position. The rise of the mercenary made it impractical since mercenaries served for profit and prisoners were a prime source of profit. If there were no ransoms there would be fewer mercenaries. With the nationalisation of armies, the lot of prisoners was bound to improve. The capturing state would be bound to establish some kind of ration scale for them and, since it was likely to have lost some men of its own to the enemy, it would be glad to be relieved of having to subsist them by exchanging them. In particular the generals and the admirals were glad to be able to rid themselves of the trouble of prisoners who had to be guarded and fed and to regain in their place trained soldiers whom the enemy held.

By the middle of the eighteenth century commanders made it their business to conclude, as early as possible in the war, an agreement (known as a cartel) with their opponents. The Cartel of Sluys (Écluse) made between the French and British during the

Seven Years War is a typical example. It covered all British and French land forces, including foreign auxiliaries in their pay, in any part of the world and laid down that all prisoners already held, 'Of whatever quality, type and condition they may be, without reserve [and] wherever they may be, shall be exchanged or ransomed within one month from the date of signature of this Cartel.'

Prisoners taken after signature were to be returned within fifteen days of capture and, since it was unlikely that the numbers for exchange on a rank for rank basis would be equal, a table of ransoms was included. A field marshal was worth £2,500 and a private of the line cost 40p, guardsmen being rather more expensive at 70p. Regimental officers were to be ransomed for the equivalent of one month's pay. Both sides undertook to keep careful accounts, to give receipts for prisoners received, and to settle outstanding balances monthly.

Sick and wounded prisoners were to be attended by medical men from their own army, who were to be given safe-conducts and escorts to bring them from the outpost line. When their services were no longer required they could return and their patients would be sent back by the shortest practicable route as soon as they were fit to travel.

There was also a list of people who were not subject to capture and who would be returned to their own army immediately without ransom or exchange. Such men were auditors general and their staffs, the staffs of chancellories of war, secretaries to generals, intendants, treasurers, almoners, chaplains, surgeons, physicians, hospital personnel, postmasters 'together with their couriers and postillions' and, to ensure the comforts of the senior officers, *maîtres d'hotel, valets de chambre et tous autres domestiques'.* Provosts General and their staffs were also included since both sides recognised that the better discipline was enforced on both sides the better it would be for the civil population in the area.

While in captivity each private soldier was to receive the same ration of bread as was issued in the army of his captors and a cash allowance of sixpence a day. Fresh bedding straw would be issued every eighth day. A commissary, under safe-conduct, would be attached to the prisoners of his own nation to ensure that each man received his due. Neither side would press for the return of deserters, although application could be made for those accused of serious crimes and plunder found on deserters would be returned. It was also agreed that no attempt would be made to induce prisoners to serve in the opposing army.

So successfully did the Cartel of Sluys operate that at the end of the war there were only a hundred and thirty-seven French prisoners left in British hands and Corporal Todd, whose encounter with the Irish has already been mentioned, was exchanged nine days after capture.

In the interval between capture and exchange, officers could expect to receive parole. This enabled them to avoid confinement and to live in such comfort as was available provided they reported to the authorities at stated intervals. When no agreement for rapid exchange was in force, they might be permitted to go home provided that they gave written undertaking not to serve before they were exchanged. Parole was no new arrangement. After Poitiers King John had been allowed to go to Paris to oversee the collection of his vast ransom. Since so much money was involved he had to leave in England forty hostages, including three of his sons, as surety for his return. Unfortunately his second son, the Duke of Anjou, fled to France whereupon the King felt that his honour demanded that he return to England. Parole was also given after Agincourt. According to Froissart,

> When the English had all reassembled, they discovered that the number of their prisoners was twice that of themselves. In view of the risk they might otherwise run, they decided to ransom them on the spot. The French found their captors most obliging, and many were released on their own undertaking to come to Bordeaux with their ransom money before Christmas.

Another incident of the Agincourt campaign illustrates the extent to which the two sides trusted each other. A small number of knights had been taken at Harfleur and, while their ransoms were being collected, they were marching with the English army. When, on St Crispin's Eve, it became clear that a battle was impending and that the odds were going to be strongly against the English, the Harfleur captives were released on the understanding that, if the English won, they would return to captivity, which they duly did.

Only officers could expect parole. The argument was that an officer was, by definition, a gentleman and could therefore be trusted to keep his word. Equally his captor was bound to take his word and let him have a measure of freedom and it became understood that if a paroled officer was closely confined the parole lapsed. Bonet, usually enlightened where prisoners were concerned, did not approve of this custom. He maintained that if the prisoner had given his word he must abide by it 'notwithstanding . . . his captor keeps him shut up in a strong tower, and also arranges strong guards to watch him'. He based this argument partially on the inviolability of an oath and partly because, 'He is at fault for having put himself in a position to be taken prisoner. And if a man, by his own fault, find himself in such a case, the peril and risk are on his own head.'

Later opinion did not accept this harsh judgment and in 1809 Wellington was writing to General Kellermann,

> British officers who have given their parole, and who enjoy some liberty and the freedom which the laws and customs of war have, in former times, given to prisoners of war, will never violate the parole that they have given; and I can assure you that if an officer who, having given his word, dared approach me, I would send him back immediately to the enemy. But those whom you keep guarded as prisoners, who have nothing to look forward to but a long captivity, will escape as they can, despite what you can do by way of guards. Be certain, *Monsieur le Général*, that it would be better to give them their parole, and that the word of a British officer is more secure than all the guards and sentinels on earth.

This was the attitude that Eméric Vattel had, in 1758, praised so highly in *Les Droits des Gens*:

> We extol the French and the English when we hear accounts of the treatment which prisoners of war on both sides have experienced from these generous nations. And what is more, by a custom which equally displays the honour and humanity of the Europeans, an officer, taken prisoner of war, is released on his parole and enjoys the comfort of passing the time of his captivity in his own country, in the midst of his family; and the Power who have released him rest as perfectly sure of him as if they had him confined in irons.

It was not to be expected that rebels would qualify as prisoners of war since they were liable to execution for treason. Little clemency was shown to the Highlanders who fought for the Young Pretender. Not only had they given a great shock to the English (and the Lowland Scots) but terrible stories, mostly apocryphal, of the barbarities practised by the clansmen had been circulating in the Anglo–Scots army. James Wolfe, later the hero of Quebec but in 1746 a young regimental officer, was far from being an inhumane man but after Culloden he wrote in a letter,

> The rebels, beside their natural inclinations, had orders not to give quarter. We had an opportunity of avenging ourselves for

171

that . . . and we did not neglect it, as few Highlanders were made prisoners as possible.

In his despatch on the battle the Duke of Cumberland wrote that 'we gave quarter to none', but he added that an exception was made of fifty French soldiers with the Rebel army. They had committed no treason but were legitimate enemies and entitled to be treated with civilised consideration.

The next rebellion Britain had to face was more momentous but, since it happened three thousand miles away, a less alarming affair. The American colonists were in arms against the Crown but those taken prisoner were treated as if they were foreign enemies. Those holding commissions (except the commanders of small privateering ships) were allowed parole to an extent that shocked some of the British and all of the Loyalists. On November 20th, 1776 the Town Adjutant of New York wrote in his diary,

> The rebel officers who have been taken prisoners lately are suffered to walk in every part of this town on their parole and in their uniforms . . . Our treating them so well and keeping so many of them in a town of such great consequence as this is, may be attended with fatal consequences. It is perfectly easy for them to set fire to the remainder of the town; and we know they would not scruple to commit an act of that nature, especially as they know the greater part of our stores and provisions are now deposited in it, we should not put it in their power to do what might distress the army in a very high degree.

It was not only the Town Adjutant who had such fears and, when a serious fire did break out, a harmless American naval officer who was walking past in uniform on his way to keep a breakfast appointment was set upon by a mob of New Yorkers. Only the intervention of British soldiers prevented them from hurling him into the flames.

As always the way prisoners are treated depends largely on the character of the man in charge of them and it is pleasant to record that Admiral John Byron, who made so little of a name for himself as a commander at sea, won the hearts of his naval prisoners by his frequent visits to them and by his meticulous attention to their complaints. His successor, Rodney, a much less sympathetic character, sent to England seventy-one privateer officers under the threat of being tried as rebels. Either by Rodney's orders or by the malignancy of the captain of the ship in which they travelled, H.M.S. *Yarmouth* (64), they were confined throughout the fifty-one days of the voyage in a space so restricted that they could not sit upright nor could they all lie down at the same time. Eleven of them died on the voyage.

Not all the faults were on one side. The newly formed Congress showed a tendency to interfere in matters which they would have done well to leave to their soldiers. They voted that Hessian prisoners should be sold as slaves and were only diverted from this course when it was pointed out to them that the King's troops held far more prisoners than they did and were in too good a position to use reprisals. The Congress also behaved dishonourably when they revoked the terms that General Horatio Gates had granted to Burgoyne at Saratoga. It is true that Gates's terms were extremely favourable but the grounds for refusing to ratify them were a technicality, which did not even have the virtue of being true. As a result, Burgoyne's army was kept in deplorable conditions. One sergeant wrote,

It was not infrequent for thirty or forty persons, men, women and children, to be indiscriminately crowded together in one small open hut, their provisions and firewood on short allowance; a scanty provision of straw their bed; their blanket their only covering. In the night time those who could not lie down, and the many who sat up from the cold, were obliged frequently to rise and shake from them the snow which the wind drifted in at the openings.

Much of this ill-treatment was due to the unpreparedness of the Americans to receive so large a number of prisoners – an explanation which recurs with depressing frequency in all wars. This, however, was not the whole explanation. One American colonel was brought before a court-martial by his own people for his cruelty to the 'Convention Army' and another threatened the officers, who had been promised parole, that if any of them moved more than ten rods (fifty-five yards) from their quarters, they would receive 'two hundred lashes, without the benefit of court-martial'.

It was a sad episode, untypical of the way prisoners were usually treated in that war but unfortunately typical of what occurs when politicians interfere with matters best left to the responsible combatants. Burgoyne himself, a sick man, was allowed to go to England on parole and eventually exchanged for 1,047 private soldiers.

The cartels of the eighteenth century had been effective but unenforceable. They were gentlemen's agreements and the outbreak of the French revolution threatened the whole concept on which they were based. During the Reign of Terror the National Convention tried to reject the whole set of customs referring to prisoners of war. On May 26th, 1794 they issued a decree which included the words,

> When the results of battles put into your power either English or Hanoverians, bring to your remembrance the vast tracts of country the English slaves have laid waste . . . Republican soldiers, therefore, when victory shall put into your power either English or Hanoverians, strike; not one of them must return to the traitorous land of England, or be brought into France. Let the British slaves perish, and Europe be free.

This seemed to indicate that the French were returning to barbarism but the Duke of York, although he had recently narrowly escaped capture while in command of the Anglo–Hanoverian army in the Netherlands, made a dignified reply in a general order which, he laid down, was to be read to the troops at three successive roll-calls and, in translation, circulated to the French outposts.

> His Royal Highness desires to remind that mercy to the vanquished is the brightest gem in a soldier's character, and exhorts the brave troops whom he addresses not to suffer their resentment to lead them to any precipitate act of cruelty on their part, which may sully the reputation they have made in the world.
>
> His Royal Highness believes it would be difficult for brave men to conceive that any set of men, who are themselves exempt from sharing in the dangers of war, should be so base and cowardly as to seek to aggravate the calamities of it upon the unfortunate people who are subject to their orders. It was indeed reserved for the present times to produce to the world the proof of the possibility of the existence of such atrocity and infamy. . . . In all wars, which from the earliest times have existed between the English and French nations, they have been accustomed to consider each other in the light of generous as well as brave enemies, while the Hanoverians, for a century the allies of the former, have shared this reciprocal esteem . . . The British and Hanoverian armies will not believe that the French nation, even under its present infatuation, can so far forget their character as soldiers, as to pay any attention to a decree, as

174

injurious to themselves as it is to the persons who passed it. On this confidence, His Royal Highness trusts that the soldiers of both nations will confine their sentiments of resentment and abhorrence to the National Convention alone; persuaded that they will be joined in them by every Frenchman who possesses one spark of honour, or one principle of a soldier.

Despite the convolutions of the Duke's literary style, this message seems to have been appreciated by both armies and, as far as the taking of prisoners was concerned, things went on as before.

The Convention's decree was what might have been expected from Robespierre and the Reign of Terror but it is surprising to find the Directory making the same mistake, on a smaller scale, four years later. Soon after Nelson had shattered the French Mediterranean fleet at the Nile, Paris saw fit to decree that any men 'natives of, or originally belonging to, neutral countries or countries in alliance with France' who were taken on board British ships of war would be treated as pirates; that they would, in practice, be executed. London reacted sharply and immediately and on November 20th, 1798 it was announced that,

If that decree should, in any instance, be carried into effect against such persons taken in any vessel or vessels the property of his Majesty, or of his Majesty's subjects, and navigated under the British flag, it was his Majesty's determination to exercise the most rigorous retaliation against those subjects of the French republic whom the chance of war had then placed, or might thereafter place, at his Majesty's disposal.

The French took no steps to implement their decree and they would have been most unwise to do so. There were only 2,800 British prisoners in France while in England there were more than 30,000 French and Dutch, most of them sailors. If it came to reprisals the French were in a weak position and by their own fault. The large number of prisoners they held were a serious embarrassment to the British who had no proper arrangements to keep them. They had started the war on the assumption that, as was the custom, the enemy would be ready to make cartels of exchange and ransom. This the republic failed to do and accommodation had to be improvised to house growing numbers of prisoners. The earlier practice had been to keep prisoners in old battleships of the kind, known as 'accommodation ships', used as floating barracks for British sailors waiting to be posted to active ships in the fleet. This was an adequate if uncomfortable solution for prisoners who were only likely to stay for a few weeks while a cartel was arranged. As the Revolutionary War dragged on without cartels, the number of prisoners mounted and older and mouldier ships had to be pressed into service. Conditions deteriorated until prisoners of war were worse accommodated than convicts. The hulks were damp and airless, so unhealthy that in some of them the death rate was as high as thirty per cent, and things were made no better when some of the contractors engaged to victual the ships were less than honest. Nor were all the officers put in charge of the prisoners the upright and humane characters they should have been. The most undesirable was Lieutenant Peter Ennis (or Innes) of the Caithness Legion of Fencible Infantry who commanded the escort to a detachment of prisoners sailing from Falmouth to King's Lynn on board the transport *Marquis of Carmarthen* in 1797. So tyrannical was Ennis's behaviour and so abominable the food that the Frenchmen mutinied and a member of the crew was killed. Ennis therefore ordered his soldiers to open fire and did not stop them until six prisoners had been killed and thirty wounded. Then, having identified the ringleader, he shot him in cold blood and threw his body overboard.

Despite Ennis the situation had begun to improve by 1797. A contractor at Plymouth had been fined £300 and sent to jail for six months for supplying rotten food to the hulks there and this example procured an improvement in the supplies to other prisoners. More important, funds were wrung from a reluctant Treasury to build a large depot for prisoners at Norman Cross and the first batch of inmates was admitted to it on April 1st, 1797. At about the same time the French agreed to regular exchanges of prisoners and it was decided that each country should station a resident commissioner, responsible for the feeding of the prisoners, in the country of the other. This brought about a considerable change in the feeding of those in British hands. Before 1797 the daily ration for prisoners had consisted of:

¾ lb beef
½ lb bread
1 quart beer

On Wednesdays and Fridays the beef was replaced by cod or herring and there were weekly issues of 4 oz butter, 6 oz cheese, 2 pints pease (or cabbage) and 2 oz soap. Once the French Commissioner took charge the daily ration was changed to:

½ lb beef
26 oz bread
2 oz cheese
½ pint pease
1½ lbs fresh vegetables
1 quart beer

The weekly issues then comprised ½ lb of soap and ¾ lb of tobacco in leaf.

When complete Norman Cross could accommodate more than 6,000 prisoners and life inside the camp was probably as bearable as it can be in that kind of confinement. The regulations laid down for the prisoners are of interest since they are the great-grandfather of the 1929 Geneva Convention, the great charter of the rights of prisoners of war, and were a worthy attempt to deal with an entirely new problem: the security and care of the long-term prisoner of war. It should be explained that, for historical reasons, the care and administration of prisoners were the responsibility of the Admiralty who appointed to each depot an agent, who was usually a naval captain.

1. The Agent's orders are to be strictly obeyed by all the prisoners; it is expressly forbidden that any prisoner should insult, ill-treat and much less strike the turnkeys, or any other person that may be appointed by the Agent to superintend the police of the prison, under pain of losing turn of Exchange, of being closely confined, and deprived of half their ration of provisions, for such time as the Commissioners may direct.
2. All the prisoners are to answer their names when mustered, and to point out to the Agent any errors they may discover on the lists, in order to prevent the confusion which might result from erroneous names; and such prisoners as shall refuse to comply with the regulations shall be put on half allowance.
3. Should any damage be done to the buildings, either in their endeavouring to escape, or otherwise, the expense of repairing the same shall be made good by a reduction of the rations of such as may be concerned; and should the aggressors not be discovered, all the prisoners in that particular building so damaged, shall contribute by a similar reduction of their rations towards the expense of the said repairs.
4. Such prisoners as shall escape from prison and be re-taken, shall be put in the Black Hole [the naval term for solitary confinement], and kept on half allowance, until the expenses occasioned by their escape are made good; and moreover they

177

shall lose their turn of Exchange, and all officers of the navy or army so offending shall, from that time, be considered and treated in all respects as common men.

5. Fighting, quarrelling, or exciting the least disorder is strictly forbidden under pain of a punishment proportionate to the offence.

6. The prisons are to be kept clean by the prisoners in turn, and every person who shall refuse to do that duty in his turn, after receiving notice of the same, shall be deprived of his rations until he shall have complied.

7. The prisoners are from time to time to inform the Agent of the clothing or other articles which they stand in need of, and have money to purchase; and the Agent shall not only permit them to purchase, but also take care that they are not imposed on in the price.

8. The prisoners in each prison are to appoint three or five from among their number, as a committee for examining the quality of the provisions supplied by the contractor; for seeing that their full rations as to weight and measure, are conformable to the scheme of victualling: and if there should be any cause for complaint they are to inform the Agent thereof; and should he find the complaint well-founded, he is immediately to remedy the same. If the Agent should neglect this part of his duty, the prisoners are to give information thereof to the Commissioners, who will not fail to do them justice in every respect.

Considered as a first attempt to answer a new problem, these regulations were a creditable effort. The establishment of a prisoners' committee with the right to appeal over the head of the commandant (Agent) to the Commissioners was a strikingly generous concession and the punishments proposed for misdemeanours were moderate, especially as both the British services used corporal punishment against their own men and did not propose to do so for prisoners. It is not made clear what expenses incurred by an escape (Para 4) would have to be paid by the re-taken escaper. It could hardly be the cost of an extensive manhunt and probably represented only the reward of ten shillings that was paid to those who found prisoners at large. Regulation 3 tried to deal with the recurrent problem of how to recoup the cost of repairing buildings after they had been damaged by escapers. There is little evidence that at Norman Cross it was ever covered by a reduction of rations but at Dartmoor in 1814 all the American prisoners were put on two-thirds rations until the ravages of a large-scale but unsuccessful tunnelling attempt had been repaired. The problem re-emerged as late as 1942 when tunnelling at Colditz resulted in a bill for 12,000 marks, about £800. The camp authorities proposed meeting this by a fine on all the prisoners but they objected that it was contrary to Article 46 of the Geneva Convention – 'Collective punishments for individual acts are prohibited.' The prisoners were supported by O.K.H., the high command in Berlin, and the amount was eventually raised by a levy on the canteen since, under Article 12 of the Convention, 'The profits accruing to the administration of the camp from the canteen shall be used for the benefit of the prisoners.' It was ruled that avoiding the collapse of part of the castle would be to the benefit of the prisoners.

The rule that officers attempting to escape 'shall be from that time considered and treated as common men' appears to be extremely harsh but in fact was not so. The assumption was that all officers would be on parole and would thus have given their word neither to escape nor to assist others to do so. In return each officer was allowed, if he could afford it, to live in lodgings or, if he had quarters in the camp, he could come and go much as he wished. The premise that an officer was a gentleman and that therefore his word could be trusted also worked in reverse. If a commissioned prisoner broke his word, he was not a gentleman and therefore forfeited the right to be treated as an officer. He could expect to be treated as a 'comman man' and a recalcitrant one. Parole breakers were sent to the hulks.

The French Revolutionary Wars saw the first of the great escape sagas. In March 1796 Captain Sir Sidney Smith of H.M.S. *Diamond*(38) was captured in the course of a cutting-out operation near Le Havre. He was a welcome prize to the French since, during the past year, he had created havoc among their coastal shipping. They decided, however, to treat him not as a prisoner of war but as a prisoner of state, accusing him of having set out to burn Le Havre. They may have suspected that he was a spy since his French was faultless and, ten years earlier, he had lived for some time on the coast near Caen. Their real objection to him was that he had done more damage to the French navy than any other single man since the revolution. He had been the officer who commanded the demolition parties when the British evacuated Toulon in 1793 and he had burned nine ships of the line and three frigates, thus depriving the French of more ships than Nelson was to do at either the Nile or Trafalgar.

When they failed to find any evidence of his supposed intentions at Le Havre, they changed their ground and accused him of burning the ships at Toulon at a time when he held no appointment in the Royal Navy. The grounds for this charge were flimsy in the extreme. Smith had served in the American War from which he emerged as a captain at the age of nineteen. He went on half-pay at the Peace of Paris and filled in some of the peace years by serving in the Swedish navy where he had gained his knighthood in the Order of the Sword. He was on a visit to Turkey when the Anglo–French War broke out in 1793 and set off for England only to fall in with the Mediterranean Fleet to whom he offered his services. Lord Hood, knowing his reputation for daring, offered him the command of the demolition parties. The French asserted that, as an officer on half-pay, he was not entitled to take part in active operations, a claim which was barely tenable since it was no business of the French government to decide how much a British officer should be paid. It was enough, however, to have him incarcerated in the Temple prison together with one of his midshipmen, John Wesley Wright, against whom no such accusation could be made although, like his captain, he spoke fluent French.

On May 4th, 1798 British frigates cruising off the mouth of the Seine were hailed by a French fishing boat which was found to contain Sir Sidney, Midshipman Wright and two French royalists, all of whom had succeeded in escaping from the Temple where, since they were locked in their cells, there could be no question of parole. They had, in fact, left the prison with forged documents and there was more than a suspicion that the Directory had connived at their escape, having found the two naval officers a political embarrassment. Sir Sidney went on to become the hero of Acre but Wright was to return to the Temple prison in 1804 and on that occasion he did not emerge.

There is a revealing postscript to the escape of Sir Sidney Smith. In the hope of arranging an exchange for him, the British had sent back to France *Capitaine de Vaisseau* Jacques Bergeret who had been captured, after a gallant defence of his frigate *Virginie*(40), on the same day that Smith was taken. On reaching Paris, Bergeret discovered that his opposite number had made his own arrangements for repatriation. No exchange could thus take place and Bergeret, considering himself still a prisoner, returned to England. The British were so impressed by his close attention to honour that they released him unconditionally.

13

Double-Dealing

The first French republic had started by rejecting the accepted practices in dealing with prisoners of war but, after a few years, agreed to exchanges and other customary arrangements in much the same way that the Bourbons had done. Napoleon Bonaparte never accepted the old conventions. Apart from his massacre of the Jaffa garrison (see p. 158) which was an isolated incident, Bonaparte the field commander showed himself attentive and humane to his prisoners but Napoleon as head of state cynically used them as pawns to further his ends and went far towards wrecking the civilised system which had been built up in the eighteenth century. He was at his harshest when dealing with Spaniards. 'You must,' he wrote in 1811, 'treat the Spanish prisoners very severely' and a year earlier he had ordered that they should be put to any work that was available 'since they cost us nothing'. José Palafox, the defender of Saragossa, was kept for four years in a dungeon at Vincennes on the grounds that he was not a prisoner of war but a rebel against the imposed King of Spain, Joseph Bonaparte. Mariano de Castro Alvarez, captured at Gerona, was sent to France as a prisoner but, on Napoleon's orders, was sent back to Spain. He was found dead, lying on a wheelbarrow, the only furniture in his filthy cell at Figueras.

There was some excuse for Napoleon's ill-treatment of his Spanish prisoners. Not only did the *guerrillas* usually shoot any Frenchman they came across, but the Spanish government had behaved disgracefully over the 17,000 French soldiers who fell into their hands at the Battle of Bailen (1808). By the surrender terms these men should have been repatriated but they were confined on the desolate island of-Cabrera in the Balearics where half of them died from exposure and malnutrition. No such excuse could be made for Napoleon's treatment of his British prisoners over whom he behaved with such duplicity that some 120,000 men of both sides spent years in unnecessary captivity.

The trouble stemmed from the civilians arrested in France when the Peace of Amiens broke down in 1803 (see p. 34) and it is significant that in his letters Napoleon frequently referred to them as *ôtages*, hostages. When they were arrested they were offered the alternative of close confinement or of signing an undertaking not to escape. Naturally they all signed the undertaking and, equally naturally, several of them escaped. The British would not accept that such men were parole-breakers since the basis of parole had always been honour and it applied only to commissioned officers who were not only gentlemen but who were subject to military discipline. The British were quite prepared to discipline any of their officers who broke parole and, as will be seen, they did so. There was nothing they could do about civilians who broke their word, the more so since their promise had been obtained under duress in circumstances which, by all accepted standards, should never have occurred. They were not prepared to take proceedings of doubtful legality against people whom the French government had decided to call gentlemen and had then trusted. If the French wished to accept the pledged word of tradesmen, servants and jockeys that was their own concern. Napoleon did not see it that way and used the escape of some of the *détenus* as a pretext to encourage his captured officers to break their parole.

The official British returns show the scale on which the French were disregarding their undertakings not to escape. Over three years the figures were:

	Number of Officers on Parole	Number breaking Parole	Number re-taken	Number escaped
Year ending June 5th, 1810	1,685	104	47	57
Year ending June 5th, 1811	2,087	118	47	71
Year ending June 5th, 1812	2,147	242	63	179
Total for 3 years		464	157	307

In addition to these regularly commissioned officers, of whose reliability there should have been no question, the Admiralty was in the habit of granting parole to the masters and first mates of privateering ships which mounted fourteen or more guns. Over the same period 218 such officers broke parole, eighty-five were recaptured and 133 succeeded in leaving Britain.

These parole-jumpers had not been living in confinement. Within wide limits they could choose their quarters and were paid, as well as the half-pay of their rank, a lodging allowance of one shilling a day, later increased to one shilling and sixpence. Should they fall sick they were given a special allowance and free medical attention. Those who had private means were permitted to bring money into Britain and many of them lived very comfortably in such social centres as Bath, Tunbridge Wells and London. Others lived as far afield as Bodmin, Brecon and Cupar. Their only obligation was to call monthly on an agent of the Transport Board from whom they collected their allowances.

The most notorious parole-breaker was General Lefebvre-Desnoëttes, an equerry to the emperor, who was captured while commanding the Light Cavalry of the Guard in the Corunna campaign. His wife had joined him in England and they had taken a full part in the gaieties of Cheltenham until, in March 1812, they went to London and, passing as German officers (by some accounts Russians), they took ship for the Continent. The general was immediately re-employed in the Imperial Guard. The British replied by tightening the control on the paroled officers. None were allowed to move more than six miles from their lodgings and those at Norman Cross were restricted to a radius of one mile from the camp.

Even after these restrictions the French officers in Britain were at least as well off as the British officers in France, all of whom were accommodated in the fortress town of Verdun. They were never permitted to leave the town for more than four hours and, according to rank, had to attend roll-calls, once a month for a senior officer, twice a day for midshipmen.

The British took a severe view of their officers on parole. Every officer who escaped and reached England had to face a court of enquiry which had to establish two points: whether the escaper was on parole at the time of his escape and whether he had left debts in France. Close confinement in a cell or *maison de force* was held to cancel parole. Between 1803 and 1814 only four officers, two from each service, were adjudged to have broken parole. One of them, a lieutenant of the Eighty-Ninth Foot, was sent back to France and removed from his regiment. A naval lieutenant named Temple, who left debts of £4,000 in France, was dismissed the service. Some said that he would have been returned to Verdun had he not been a distant relation of Lord Palmerston, then Secretary at War. The second naval officer was put on half-pay and never employed again. The case of the other army officer is obscure. He escaped from a cell but since he had been imprisoned for debt this was not held to cancel his parole. Nevertheless he was not sent back to France and was allowed to continue his military career. The most likely explanation is that he managed to raise enough money in England to clear his French debts.

While Napoleon was encouraging his officers to make a mockery of parole, he was bringing the system of exchange to a standstill. When war broke out in 1803 Hanover had been invaded and its soldiers sent to their homes. The emperor then proposed that they should be sent to England in exchange for the French sailors taken when the Royal Navy reimposed its blockade. When Britain refused this dubious offer, Napoleon suggested another. He would exchange the *détenus* for French officers. This was demonstrably inequitable – Britain was expected to give up trained officers against miscellaneous civilians – and it was refused on the grounds that France had no right to arrest the *détenus* in the first place. Nevertheless 526 French civilians, taken on the high seas, were repatriated in the hope that Napoleon would make a reciprocal gesture. There was no response.

Britain continued her efforts to arrange a cartel and in 1810 went as far as to agree a French proposal that *détenus* should be exchanged as if they had military rank, that peers should count as admirals or generals and baronets or knights as field officers. This concession had the effect of making Napoleon raise his price. Apart from 500 *détenus*, he held 10,526 British prisoners of war while there were 43,774 French prisoners in England, together with 2,609 more from his Danish, Dutch and Russian allies. He suggested a mass exchange regardless of numbers or ranks and a curiously ugly light is thrown on his character when he offered to include the 932 Irish prisoners who had been blackguarded into enlisting in the *Légion Irlandaise*, though he must have known that the British were likely to hang these wretched men for having taken service with the enemy.

Since the numbers were so obviously unequal, Napoleon offered to balance the account by releasing a suitable number of Spaniards but he insisted that Britain would have to undertake the negotiations with the Spanish government and that meanwhile all the prisoners of France and her allies must be sent home on parole. The possibility of Napoleon cheating on such an arrangement and the fact that the text of the French proposal confused Spaniards and Portuguese made the British wary of agreeing. They said they would only deal on a rank-for-rank exchange and recommended the French to make their own agreement with Cadiz. The French then broke off the whole negotiation and, when the war ended, there were 16,000 British and more than 90,000 French and Danish prisoners still in captivity. The breakdown in 1810 was the more unfortunate since it was soon afterwards that Wellington started sending home French prisoners by tens of thousands annually. New prison camps had been built at Dartmoor, Perth and Stapleton, near Bristol, but they could not accommodate the vast influx and more and more men had to be sent to the appalling hulks which should have been reserved for parole-breakers and other *mauvais sujets*.

Individual exchanges were occasionally effected, usually when the French officer concerned had influential friends, but even in these cases the French cheated when they saw the chance. The most glaring case was that of Captain Jaheel Brenton who was taken in July 1803 when his frigate ran ashore off Cherbourg. The British immediately opened talks for his exchange and, believing them to be successfully concluded, sent to France *Capitaine de Vaisseau* Jurien. Brenton was not forthcoming and, in August 1804, a formal protest was sent to Paris. Captain Jurien, finding that his exchange had not been effected, applied for passports to return to captivity in England but Napoleon immediately posted him to a ship and sent him to sea. Brenton was eventually released in 1806, but only when Britain parted with a senior officer, Commodore Louis Infernet, taken at Trafalgar, who had the good fortune to be a cousin to Marshal Massena. Much the same trick was played in the case of Lieutenant Dillon, R.N. for whom the French managed to extort two captains although, as will be seen in Chapter 15, Dillon should never have been considered as a prisoner in the first place. The British complained in 1806 that they had sent back a hundred and fifty French officers but that only eight of their own had been returned.

It was not only Napoleon's honesty that became suspect in Britain. In May 1804 John Wesley Wright, who had been captured with Sir Sidney Smith in 1796 and had escaped with him, was captured again in command of the brig *Vincejo*. Once again he was put into the Temple prison and this time he was accused, probably justly, of having landed dissidents on the French coast. In October 1805 *Le Moniteur*, the French official gazette, announced that he had cut his throat in despair at hearing of the Austrian defeat at Ulm, an unlikely story since it was known that he had also heard the news of the British victory at Trafalgar at about the same time. British opinion immediately assumed that he had been killed on Napoleon's orders. There were demands for reprisals and the First Lord of the Admiralty said, 'If our government could have ascertained the real facts of the case, a French officer would have been similarly treated by us.' Fortunately no action was taken as the French government was almost certainly innocent. As Napoleon remarked at St Helena, Wright was more valuable to him alive than dead since he might have been tricked into giving evidence against those he had landed. In any case there would have been no need to have him murdered. A message could have been sent to London simply saying,

> An officer of yours has been tried for landing brigands and assassins on my territories. I have caused him to be tried by a military commission. He has been condemned to death. The sentence has been carried into execution.

While Napoleon's statement is convincing, there seems little doubt that Wright was murdered. His hand, holding a razor, was found resting beside his thigh and a sheet, unstained with blood, was pulled up to his severed windpipe. The probability is that he was murdered for his money and valuables by one of his jailers at the Temple.

Although no general cartel of exchange was agreed, the British, between 1803 and 1814, repatriated 17,607 or fourteen per cent of French and allied prisoners. Apart from the rare individual exchanges, most of these men had lost at least a limb and would not have been able to fight again. Occasionally prisoners would be sent back as a reward for acts of courage or humanity. A master's mate was set free for his share in putting out a serious fire at Lichfield and a naval lieutenant for 'saving a child's life at Oswestry'. The captain and clerk of a privateer were repatriated when it became known that they had succeeded in saving the lives of seventy-nine British seamen wrecked on the French coast. A surgeon earned his passage home 'in consequence to his attention to the British sick on board the *Spence* transport, as represented by Lieutenant T. W. Lloyd of the Eighth King's Regiment'. From the French side twenty-one British prisoners were released for their part in containing a fire which swept through the town of Auxonne. Fourteen seamen earned the same reward for repairing a pontoon bridge swept away in a flash flood and thus enabling Napoleon to cross the river at Givet where they were imprisoned.

The best chance of a speedy return home lay in arranging an exchange as soon as possible after capture. This might be possible if the enemy commander was a humane man. Major Charles Napier, later the conqueror of Scinde, had been wounded at Corunna and was still there recovering when, three months later, a

186

British frigate arrived off the harbour and sent in a flag of truce. His mother, Lady Sarah, daughter of the Duke of Richmond and once the girl that George III had wished to marry, had refused to believe the reports of Charles's death published in the *London Gazette* and pestered the Admiralty until the First Lord agreed to ask the French for his body. The message from the frigate came to Baron Clouet, chief of staff to Ney, who took it to the marshal.

'Let him see his friends and tell them that he is well and well treated', was the marshal's immediate response. Clouet looked earnestly but moved not and Ney, smiling, asked him why he waited? 'He had an old mother, a widow and blind.' 'Let him go then and tell her himself that he is alive.' He also released twenty-five badly wounded English soldiers, jocosely adding, 'Provided they take all the Englishwomen with them, as they make our French soldiers quarrelsome.'

Napier was immediately released and sent home in the frigate, having given a written undertaking that he would take no further part in the war until a formal exchange had been arranged between London and Paris. This was soon done, two *enseignes de vaisseau* being repatriated, and on Napier's return to the army in the Peninsula he sent a note across the lines to Ney thanking him for his kindness.

However willing the French commander on the spot might be to allow exchanges, they had to be arranged quickly or peremptory orders would arrive from Paris insisting that all prisoners must be sent to France. Marshal Mortier, who found himself with 1,500 severely wounded British soldiers after the Battle of Talavera (July 1809), was most anxious to help and Wellington wrote to him,

I am most obliged for the undertaking you give me to take care of the wounded of the British army who have fallen into your hands. I am sending you Colonel Waters to whom I have given 139 *onces d'Espagne* or £500 sterling; and I shall be much obliged to you if you will allow this sum to be given to the senior British officer, for distribution among the officers and surgeons who are prisoners. I would be obliged to you if you would allow any officer who is sufficiently recovered to return on his parole; and if you would wish to establish an exchange, I undertake to send to France as many of the same rank, both officers and soldiers, as you send me, and you shall nominate those who shall return to France.

The marshal was willing to cooperate and it is probably at this time that the two sides agreed a table of equivalents which is to be found, undated, among the Wellington papers.

Captain General, Field Marshal, General commanding	= 60 men
General or General of Division	= 40 men
Lieutenant General or General of Brigade	= 30 men
Major General or inferior to above	= 20 men
Brigadier General or Colonel or Adjutant General	= 15 men
Lieutenant Colonel or Major or *Chef de Battalion*	= 8 men
Captain	= 6 men
Lieutenant	= 4 men
Ensign	= 3 men
Non-commissoned officer down to corporal	= 2 men

That this draft cartel was never implemented was largely the fault of the Spaniards who insisted on interfering with the French officers who carried Mortier's messages and, on several occasions, imprisoning them, despite their flags of truce. This so delayed agreement that only two British officers were recovered in exchange for two French lieutenants, one each from the army and navy, nominated by the marshal, who were sent back to France. Then Mortier was directly ordered to send all his prisoners back to France and dared not disobey. Even then he did his best for them. Captain Robert Boothby, R.E., who had lost a leg at Talavera, wrote,

> The marshal, not content with his efforts to procure me my liberty, has recommended me to his friends in Paris, supplied me with cash at Madrid to prepare my journey, and given me besides a letter of credit to Paris to an unlimited amount.

Dealing with Marshal Massena was a very different business to making arrangements with Mortier or Ney. *L'enfant gâté de la victoire*, as Napoleon called him, was a tricky character whether he was dealing with friends or enemies. In Wellington's opinion there was little point in trying to arrange a cartel with him.

> He excuted with so little good faith the only agreement for an exchange that I ever made with him, that it is impossible to propose another to get out of his hands the few prisoners he may

have. Upon that occasion having, as he stated, 120 British soldiers and Captain Percy, Lieutenant Carden and a midshipman of the Navy as prisoners, he detained the three officers and sixty of the soldiers, and sent instead of them Portuguese militia and *ordenanza* to be exchanged for French soldiers.

There can be little doubt that Massena's action in this case accurately reflected his master's wishes, for Napoleon was pursuing a deliberate policy in respect of British prisoners and one which resulted, almost for the first time, in long-term prisoners of war. It was a policy which affected only Britain. Napoleon counted on quick victories and, when he had achieved one, the captives were sent home. His great Continental adversaries fought only for short periods and soon got their prisoners back. Prussia fought the French Empire in two wars, one of ten months and one of thirteen. Russia also fought twice, on each occasion for about two years; Austria for three short periods of five, three and nine months. By contrast, Britain was continually at war for only a month short of eleven years.

Publicly Napoleon declared that there was no exchange of prisoners because, 'The King of England has shown that he wants none, by persisting in making arbitrary conditions [i.e. by refusing to exchange civilians and Hanoverians] and quite contrary to established custom.'

In reality the aim was to wear Britain down. While France lost the services of many soldiers and sailors, Napoleon calculated that she could afford to do so while Britain could not. The French Empire had a population of more than thirty million and could draw on her satrapies of Italy, Naples, Switzerland, Warsaw and the Rhine. Great Britain and Ireland had only fourteen millions and her forces depended on voluntary recruitment which was known to be difficult. Mathematics made it plain that it was to France's advantage to keep as many of Britain's few fighting men for as long as possible. It was not until 1812, when Wellington's great victories began to bring in prisoners in large numbers, that the balance of advantage swung to Britain. By the time that the *Grande Armée* was destroyed in Russia Napoleon would have been glad to be able to reclaim the 70,000 Frenchmen who languished in British camps and hulks. By that time Britain had so little trust in his good faith that they would not have agreed a general exchange with him.

If the duration of captivity was extended greatly, the worst feature of being a prisoner, the shock of capture, remained unaltered. It

189

was almost always followed by plunder. A British non-combatant officer who was taken in 1813 wrote home,

In a moment my two horses and cloak, pistols, sword, telescope, handkerchief, were all gone. I had about fifteen doubloons about me; one half they found instantly, and were so pleased that they scarcely searched more, except to take my knife, comb, &c.

This experience was much the same whichever side you were fighting for. At almost the same time that Judge Advocate Larpent was having his knife and comb filched above the Bidassoa, Colonel St Chamans, *7ᵐᵉ Chasseurs-à-Cheval*, was lying wounded in an inn at Leipzig with several of his brother officers.

The waiter carefully led to the door of our room a squad of Prussian grenadiers. They came in with bayonets at the ready as if they were going to make an attack and one of them, who seemed to be their leader, asked in German, 'Are there any French here?'

The doctor went to him and said, 'We are all French.'

The grenadier, in bad French, said, 'Money?'

The doctor gave him a purse as we had arranged; he looked inside it and seemed satisfied, putting it in his pocket, and saying in French, 'Watch?' The doctor gave him his, which he had forgotten to hide, and my cousin having made a sign that he had none, they seemed satisfied with their booty and went away without searching our bags. Nor did they take our weapons . . . Hearing that a senior Russian general was going to be billeted at our inn, our doctor went to him to ask for a safe-conduct.

'Don't worry,' said the general, 'nothing will happen. I have given the strictest orders on the subject. The prisoners will be well treated.'

'But,' said the doctor, 'we have just been robbed.' 'Imposs-ible,' said the general. 'We have made such an offence punish-able by death. There is no need to worry.'

'But . . .' said the doctor as they pushed him out of the door.

For six hours we tried not to worry and my three companions were going to bed when there was a rough knock at the door and a drunken Cossack officer stumbled into the room. The follow-ing dialogue took place between him and the doctor, both of whom spoke very bad German, while the Cossack spoke a little French.

'Give me money. I must have money.'

'We have none. The Prussians took it all this morning.'

'The Prussians! Those dreadful robbers! Give me your watches. I must have your watches.'

'The Prussians took them this morning. They have left us with nothing.'

'The Prussians! Those brigands! Have you nothing at all left for me?'

'Alas, no, and there is my wounded colonel who is very sick and has lost everything.'

'Those rascally Prussians! There must be something left!'

'Look at us! We have only the clothes we wear.'

'Thieving Prussians! But . . .' seeing the knot of my sabre, 'there is gold there!'

'That is the colonel's sabre.'

'The colonel is a prisoner and has no further use for a sabre. It is a good one and I need it. I shall take it. Have you nothing else?'

'Nothing at all.'

The Cossack opened the door and left muttering, 'Oh those thieving Prussians, the thieves, the thieves. They shall pay for this.'

Few prisoners have ever escaped with all their personal possessions intact and, if the enemy is poorly equipped, they are likely to lose at least their boots. The Spanish army in the Peninsular War habitually shod themselves at the expense of their captives and so did the *goumiers* in Tunisia in 1943. When Napoleon's armies were in desperate straits in 1814 he gave orders for shakos and greatcoats (*capotes*) from the prisoners to be taken '*pour les donner aux soldats et gardes nationaux qui en manquent*'. Occasionally there was some physical violence at the moment of capture. Charles Napier, already wounded, was struck over the head by an Italian soldier using a sabre before being rescued by a French drummer. Lieutenant William Brooke, taken at Albuera, was maltreated by a Polish lancer whom he believed to be drunk. He was also unfortunate since, when he and the other officer prisoners had marched back to Seville, Marshal Soult, in a fit of bad temper, shut them all up in the cells of the Inquisition. Then things began to improve when,

The Grand Master of the French Freemasons' lodge discovered that Captain Allman and I were fellow masons. He waited on me and took me to his own quarters. He introduced me to his lady and her sister, who gave me cake, wine and French liqueurs. He requested his wife to bring me half a dozen of his own shirts and as many pairs of stockings, which he wished me to accept as a

191

brother mason. I refused them with thanks, but accepted half a dozen bottles of choice wines, which he sent to the room of our confinement. A few days later he called, in company with a deputation from his lodge, on Captain Allman and myself, to ask whether they could serve us in any way: he assured us that even if we wanted a thousand dollars the masons would get it for us. Being already provided with money, we did not accept this kind offer.

At sea the fellow feeling between sailors usually ensured a kind reception from the captors. When the crew of the frigate *Hussar*, wrecked off the Saintes in February 1804, had to surrender they were, according to Midshipman John Hopkinson,

> Uncommonly well treated on board. One of the mids made me change my clothes, and they gave us every refreshment in their power, after which I fell asleep till 3 a.m. when I was called to go on board *Foudroyant*. Here the French captain behaved to us in a more handsome manner than we had any right to expect, furnishing us with linen and every delicacy he had to offer, and giving up his cabin for our use.

Whatever his reception on capture, the prisoner had eventually to move to a permanent prison camp. French prisoners in Britain were almost always moved by water, by coastal shipping and, where possible, by inland barge. Even those bound for the inland camp at Norman Cross had only a six-mile march since barges could take them as far as Peterborough. The longest unavoidable march was the fourteen-mile uphill pull from Plymouth to Dartmoor. No doubt the discomforts of the troop transports were considerable but they were certainly less prolonged than the interminable marches which British prisoners had to make to their camps in the fortified towns on the Belgian frontier where the French kept most of them, or to the two isolated depots of Briançon and Montdauphin in *Hautes Alpes*. Sailors captured off Brest or Rochefort would have to march five hundred miles to reach their depots and soldiers taken on the Portuguese frontier with Spain had 1,100 miles to go before they reached Verdun.

Officers who could afford to do so were allowed to hire carriages for themselves and Captain Boothby, with Mortier's money behind him, had a very enjoyable journey from Madrid, despite his amputated leg.

192

We found everybody amiable and agreeable on our entrance into France, where people seemed to consider us with a sort of friendly distinction. We found no difficulties, were immediately left in the full enjoyment of our liberty, have put ourselves at our ease, consider ourselves travellers in France, and prepare to trace with a sort of triumph our considerable routes on the map of Europe.

For the great majority of officers and all the other ranks conditions were very different. They had to trudge across Europe for months on end. During the day those whose parole could not be accepted were frequently chained together and at night parties of prisoners were often lodged in the common jail. One of them complained that, 'We were placed among criminals and malefactors of every description, where we found ourselves covered with vermin in spight [sic] of every effort to avoid it.'

On the rare occasions when transport was provided there was little more comfort. When a group of seventy-nine midshipmen and merchant navy officers were being sent to Givet in the Ardennes no chances were taken about their security.

We were placed, two by two, under bundles of straw in five waggons: four horse-gendarmes formed the van and four the rearguard: one on each side of each waggon, and twenty-four foot soldiers in files, with others in each carriage, made up the escort, the commander bringing up the rear on his black charger. Whenever the road passed a wood, which frequently occurred, we halted to give the infantry time to occupy its skirts; two gendarmes on each side were posted midway, whilst the rest occasionally displayed their pistols ostentatiously.

That writer, who was on the look-out for a chance to abscond, thought that the guard was excessive and remarked that 'In England twice the number of prisoners might safely be entrusted to the care of a sergeant's guard.' He was right to some extent since the standing orders of the Peninsular army called for batches of 250 or 300 prisoners to be in the charge of an officer, a sergeant and twelve men. 'The principal object of this guard is to prevent the prisoners of war being maltreated by the natives which, without this precaution, might be expected.' On the other hand American privateersmen, taken in the war of 1812, were held to require very heavy escorts. A detachment of forty-six U.S. sailors was marched from Plymouth to Dartmoor with a guard of sixty-three soldiers and when a batch of 200 privateersmen was marched from

193

Plymouth to Stapleton, an exceptional journey, a guard of 250 was provided.

In the end the prisoners reached their permanent camp, fortress, hulk or depot. Some were bad, some were as tolerable as any place of incarceration can be. To a great degree conditions depended on the men in charge. Some were detestable and none more so than General Wirion whose peculations and extortions at the expense of the prisoners and *détenus* at Verdun were so gross that, rather than face a French enquiry into them, he committed suicide. There were others who did all in their power to make life tolerable for those in their charge. When Commandant Le Doux was posted away from the depot of prisoners at Besançon, he was presented with a gold medal and chain which cost 430 *livres*. The medal was inscribed *Justice et Sagesse s'unissent* and its cost must have been a severe strain on the financial resources of the prisoners who gave it, few of whom were officers. Another such man is commemorated by a tablet in the parish church of Yaxley, Huntingdonshire, which reads,

> Inscribed at the desire and the sole expense of the French prisoners of war at Norman Cross to the memory of Captain John Draper, who for the last eighteen months of his life was Agent to the Depot, in testimony of their esteem and gratitude for his humane attention to their comfort during that all too short period. He died February 23rd, 1813, aged 53 years.

No doubt Le Doux and Draper were exceptional commandants but there were probably more such men than most prisoners' memoirs would have us believe. Few men can feel much sympathy or understanding of those whose task it is to confine them for years in, usually, the dreariest kind of barracks. The medical officer at Dartmoor in 1813 when 9,000 French and American prisoners were held there described the prison as,

> This great tomb of the living, embosomed as it is in a desert and desolate waste of wild and, in the wintertime, desolate scenery, exhibiting a sublimity and grandeur, occasionally elemental strife, but never partaking of the beautiful of nature, its climate too cheerless and hyperborean.

In the opinion of the prisoners the doctor was a good one and he was proud of the medical state of Dartmoor where the death rate, 1.7 per cent annually, compared well with other depots. He attributed this healthiness not, as other medical men might have done, to the superabundance of fresh air but to 'the density of congregated numbers creating an artificial atmosphere'.

There can be no doubt that even hyperborean Dartmoor was preferable to the conditions endured by Midshipman Worth and a merchant navy captain called Brine who were put into the lowest *souterrain* at Bitche, a punishment camp reserved for persistent escapers and recalcitrant prisoners. There was no daylight in their cell and, since it was hewed from solid rock, the walls dripped continuously. The two men spent their time 'on a door which they had managed to unhinge and lay as a platform to keep them out of the excrement and wet which was more than ancle [sic] deep: they had a little straw and a blanket'.

Such conditions were very exceptional but, even in the better depots and camps, on both sides of the Channel,

The greater part, by endless grinding *ennui*, were reduced to such a state of apathy that they were worn down into mere brute existence; while those who had any energy left magnified the most trifling occurrence into an important event.

It is a description that will wake memories from any prisoner of war but few of them will realise that, by his rejection of exchange, that 'endless grinding *ennui*' was Napoleon's special legacy to the prisoners of his time and of the future.

14

Rules and Regulations

Napoleon's rejection of the customary practices for dealing with prisoners of war meant that, sooner or later, a more formal code would have to be evolved and agreed. In fact the first formal agreement on the subject had been made in 1785, the year in which Bonaparte had been commissioned as a second lieutenant of artillery, and it was part of a treaty of friendship between the United States of America and Prussia. This treaty laid down that there should be 'firm, inviolable universal peace' between the two countries but it also included some realistic agreements about what should happen if the peace turned out less firm and inviolable than had been hoped. The provisions about prisoners of war included one that the rations and accommodation of prisoners should be the same as those in the capturing army, another that they should not be kept in unhealthy or intemperate climates and a third that they should be permitted to receive letters and parcels from their own countries. To ensure that these arrangements were carried out, each country would station a resident commissioner in the enemy country.

The next step towards codification of existing practices also came from the United States. Dr Lieber's paragraphs about prisoners in *General Order Nᵒ 100* of 1863 could reasonably be considered as the first draft of the Geneva Convention of 1929. In particular he laid down that basic guarantee of a prisoner's rights, the fact that he was a prisoner of the enemy state and not of any individual. 'A prisoner of war, being a public enemy, is the prisoner of the government, and not of his captor. No ransom can be paid by a prisoner of war to his individual captor, or to any officer in command.'

The Geneva Convention, and intermediately The Hague Rules, worded this as, 'Prisoners of war are in the power of the hostile government but not of the individual or corps who capture them.'

Lieber aimed at regulating every phase of captivity, starting by trying to stop the pilfering of personal property which is almost inevitable at the moment of capture.

Money and other valuables on the person of a prisoner, such as watches or jewelry, as well as extra clothing, are regarded by the

American army as the personal property of the prisoner, and the appropriation of such valuables or money is considered as dishonorable and is prohibited.

At Geneva this wording was found not to go far enough and was amplified.

All personal effects and articles in personal use – except arms, horses, military equipment and military papers – shall remain in the possession of prisoners of war, as well as their metal helmets and gas-masks. Sums of money carried by prisoners may only be taken from them on the order of an officer and after the amount has been recorded. A receipt shall be given for them. Sums thus impounded shall be placed to the account of each prisoner.

Their identity tokens, badges of rank, decorations and articles of value may not be taken from prisoners.

The weakness of this regulation lies in the absence of any definition of military equipment. The *Manual of Military Law* (1914) suggests that a prisoner should be allowed to keep his binoculars if he could prove that they were his own property although they fail to suggest how such possession could be proved in the circumstances. Is, for example, a watch military equipment? Lieber believed that it was personal property and the Canadian prisoners at Dieppe were left with their watches, although their cigarette lighters were taken. In Italy in 1944 the author complained to a German general that his watch had been taken only to be told that watches were military stores. The same general, however, went to considerable trouble to restore a personal photograph which had also been abstracted.

As soon as a prisoner has been searched (or plundered) his captors will interrogate him. Since any newly-taken prisoner will be in more or less a state of shock there is always a temptation to excess in this process. In particular the interrogator may use threats in the hope that a badly-shaken prisoner might reveal information that, in normal circumstances, he would keep to himself. Usually the threats are no more than threats but the prisoner can never be quite certain. In 1803 Midshipman Edward Boys was threatened with being treated as a pirate and pirates were always hanged.

Our refusal to answer questions put to us respecting the strength and situation of Lord Nelson was construed into contempt and so excited the rage of the captain of the *Rhin* that he told us we were pirates. This novel information did not in the least discompose us, for we suspected the ignorance of the man. When, however, it was explained to him that midshipmen in the British Navy never had commissions, he resumed his composure; and on my producing my written orders from Captain Capel, I was dismissed.

Clearly Boys was not seriously intimidated. It was inconceivable to him that the French captain would hang him. The same tactics would have been far more frightening to the crew of a U.S. bomber shot down over Japan.

After having been subjected to all the standard forms of torture they were taken, one at a time, marched blindfolded for a considerable distance and then halted. The victim then heard voices and marching feet, the sound of a squad halting and loading their rifles as a firing party would.

A Japanese officer then approached the American pilot and said, 'We are the Knights of Bushido, of the order of the Rising Sun. We do not execute at sunset, but at sunrise.' The pilot was then marched back to his cell, and told that unless he talked before dawn he would be executed.

General Order N° 100 does not forbid threats or mental pressure but suggests that their use would be unsporting.

Honorable men when captured will abstain from giving to the enemy information concerning their own army, and the modern law of war no longer permits the use of any violence against prisoners, in order to extort the desired information, or to punish them for having given false information.

The Hague Rules were content to ignore the question of threats but laid down that the prisoner need only give his name and rank (giving his number also was added at Geneva in 1929) but the British *Manual of Military Law* of 1914 felt that that needed amplification.

The right of interrogation is not limited to name and rank, yet a prisoner is not bound to reply to other questions. It is permissible to employ every means, provided they are humane and not compulsive, to obtain all the information possible from prisoners with regard to the numbers, movements and location of the enemy. A prisoner cannot be punished for giving false information about his own army.

The German *Kriegsbrauch* took the same line but added that to shoot a prisoner for giving false information would be 'cowardly murder' although it ruled that it would be in order to execute a requisitioned civilian guide who misled the troops.

The Geneva Convention of 1929 was more restrictive than either the German or the British view.

No pressure shall be exerted on prisoners to obtain information regarding the situation of their armed forces or their country. Prisoners who refuse to reply may not be threatened, insulted, or exposed to unpleasantness or disadvantages of any kind whatever.

The least satisfactory part of Dr Lieber's prescriptions for dealing with prisoners in 1863 was the one about feeding them. He says merely, 'Prisoners shall be fed upon plain and wholesome food whenever practicable.'

Apart from his qualifying phrase, 'whenever practicable', which might relieve an unscrupulous captor of any duties in that direction, it is surprising that he lays down no scale of rations, the more so since the treaty of 1785 between Prussia and the U.S.A., his native and adopted countries, had stipulated that the prisoners should receive the same rations as the captor's soldiers. Even Napoleon had laid down scales, although he divided his prisoners into two classes. The first class was reserved for British prisoners, pehaps because Britain was the only country which held more French prisoners than the French held of theirs.

The English prisoners of war belong, without exception to the first class, and are to be allowed daily, 1lb of bread, one ration of vegetables and salt, with 7½ centimes in cash [i.e. the same basic allowance as the French private soldier]. Prisoners of all other nations belong to the second class and are to receive only one half of the pay of privates of the French army, and one ration of bread each.

The Hague Rules followed the precedent of Napoleon's first class, agreeing that all prisoners 'shall be treated as regards board, lodging and clothing as the troops of the government which captured them'. The British modified this by ruling,

The scale of rations need only be that authorised for peace, without extras reserved for soldiers in the field. Prisoners are only entitled to what is customarily used in the country, but due allowance should, if possible, be made for differences of habits, and captured supplies should be used if they are available.

The first part of this formulation was adopted at Geneva in 1929. 'The food ration of prisoners of war shall be the equivalent in quantity and quality to that of the depot troops [of the captor's army].'

It was unfortunate that the Geneva article did not pick up the British reference to 'difference of habit' probably because the framers failed to envisage wars taking place between countries with a widely differing conception of what constituted an adequate ration for their own troops. The problem was highlighted when, in 1941–42, the Japanese captured a very large number of British, Commonwealth and United States troops. It was the Japanese claim that, once the initial chaos was over, their prisoners did receive the same rations as their depot troops. What is certain is that the food provided was inadequate and unsuitable for Western prisoners, particularly when, unlike depot troops, they had no chance of supplementing it from other sources. As a result most of them suffered from severe vitamin deficiencies, resulting in a death rate of twenty-seven per cent, as compared to the four per cent of deaths among prisoners in German and Italian hands. Another example was the fate of the prisoners taken by the Turks at Kut-al-Amara in 1916. On that occasion the death rate among British prisoners was above sixty per cent while among the Indians, used to a different standard of living, it was only sixteen per cent.

Cultural differences also affected another of Lieber's *dicta,* that prisoners should be treated with humanity, a phrase repeated in The Hague Rules and amplified at Geneva into, 'They shall at all times be humanely treated and protected, particularly against acts of violence, from insults and from public curiosity.'

After the early Japanese victories of the Second World War savage brutalities were practised against many of the allied prisoners but thereafter they were usually treated as if they were junior, and recalcitrant, members of the Japanese armed forces.

At all times the rank of a prisoner is an insoluble problem. As the *Kriegsbrauch* had said, 'Officers who are prisoners are never the superiors of the soldiers of the capturing state but become the subordinates of those responsible for guarding them.'

While captured officers are usually treated with the formal courtesy due to their rank, it cannot be denied that a captured general is bound to obey the reasonable orders of a private soldier guarding him, with the proviso, inserted for the first time at Geneva, that such orders 'shall be communicated to him in a language he understands'. The Japanese chose to consider that, since all prisoners had to obey the guards, they ranked lower even than a 'first-year private'. First-year privates were the lowest form of life in the Japanese army and led a brutish life, being required to salute and bow to every senior soldier, to run errands and perform all kinds of services for them and to accept blows from them. Blows of all kinds were the commonest form of discipline in their army and were frequently passed down from sergeant to corporal and from there down through the intricately-graded private soldiers until they reached the lowest class of all, the first-year private. It was a scheme of military life abhorrent to the West but it was the Japanese scheme and it had turned their soldiers into magnificent fighting machines. It was thus natural that the first-year privates should pass on the blows and abuse they received to an even lower form of life, their prisoners. To those from the West it was unquestionably a form of violence. To the Japanese soldier it was a part of everyday life and in this case the tendency was reinforced by the teaching he had received that those who surrendered rather than fighting to the death were dishonoured men and unworthy of any special treatment.

With these beliefs it is not surprising that the Japanese did not hesitate to use officers on working parties. Often they were only required to work in the camp vegetable gardens, sometimes they were ordered to supervise the work of other ranks but on many occasions, notably on the Burma–Siam railway, they were forced to undertake heavy manual work. According to the Japanese, all such officers had 'volunteered' to work and no doubt there was an element of volunteering when the Soviet authorities put their Polish officer prisoners to manual work in 1939–40.

Genuine volunteering, without compulsion, would have fallen within the Geneva rules which, while excluding 'officers and persons of equivalent status' from the obligation to work, add that if they should 'ask for suitable work, this shall be found for them as far as possible'.

Another difficult problem is the type of work which a prisoner may be required to do. Lieber wrote that prisoners may be required to work for the benefit of the captor's government, according to their rank and status, but set no limit to the kind of work they might do. In The Hague Rules work which has 'any connection with the operations of war' was excluded but this was too vague a phrase to be useful. In the First World War the Germans did employ some prisoners on the making of munitions and this was generally regarded as stretching the definition too far. More questionable was the employment of 2,000 German prisoners on the harbour works at Le Havre, an important supply port for the B.E.F. The Germans protested and, getting no satisfaction, sent a similar number of British soldiers to work on the port installations of Libau [Liepaja] in Latvia. The British, however, refused to withdraw the prisoners from Le Havre.

At Geneva, the definition was drawn much closer and added to The Hague wording, 'In particular, it is forbidden to employ prisoners in the manufacture of arms or munitions of any kind, or in the transport of material destined for combat units.'

This would seem to rule out the use of prisoners in military supply ports and, incidentally, the Japanese use of prisoners for building a strategic railway line. It must, however, be increasingly doubtful whether, by the middle of the twentieth century, there was any work to which prisoners could be put which would not have 'any connection with the operations of war'. In the past the most usual tasks given to prisoners have been agriculture, forestry, mining and the reclaiming of marshy land. In the age of blockade and total war all these operations could be held to assist the war effort, even if only by relieving the strain on a country's resources of manpower.

The killing of prisoners is one of those points where the 'laws of war' part company with reality. Dr Lieber took a realistic view when he laid down that,

> It is against the usage of modern warfare to resolve, *in hatred or revenge*, to give no quarter. No body of troops has the right to declare that it will not give, and therefore will not expect, quarter; but a commander is permitted to direct his troops to give no quarter, in great straits, when his own salvation makes it *impossible* to give quarter.

The Hague Rules would not face up to this possibility and said that, 'It is especially forbidden . . . to kill or wound an enemy who, having laid down his arms, or having no longer means of defence, has surrendered at discretion.'

The great powers felt this was going too far, although the British hoped that the situation would not occur.

> A commander may not put his prisoners to death because their presence retards his movements or diminishes his means of resistance by necessitating a large guard, or by reason of their consuming his supplies, or because it appears certain that they

will regain their liberty through an impending success of their own army. Whether nowadays such extreme necessity can ever arise as will compel a commander on grounds of self-preservation to kill his prisoners may well be doubted.

That did leave the door barely ajar to the demands of military necessity. In the *Kriegsbrauch*, the Germans were more definite.

> Prisoners can be killed . . . in cases of extreme necessity when other means of security are not available and the presence of prisoners is a danger to one's own existence . . . Exigencies of war and the safety of the State come first and not the consideration that prisoners of war must at any cost remain unmolested.

This is a harsh ruling but it was not in accordance with this that Hitler sent out his special order of October 18th, 1942 after the bodies of Germans, pinioned and then shot, had been found after British raids on Dieppe and the Channel Islands.

> From now on all enemies on so-called Commando missions in Europe and Africa challenged by German troops, even if they are to all appearances soldiers in uniform or demolition troops, whether armed or unarmed, in battle or in flight, are to be slaughtered to the last man. It makes no difference whether they are landed from ships and aeroplanes for their actions, or whether they are dropped by parachute. Even if these individuals, when found, should appear to be ready to give themselves up, no pardon is to be granted to them on principle.

Fortunately the *Wehrmacht* decided that this was not an order that ought to be obeyed. According to General Siegfried Westphal,

> [Rommel] received it in the desert near Sidi Barrani. The Marshal and I read it standing beside our truck. I immediately proposed that we should not publish it. We burned it at once where we stood . . . We did not wish this order to reach our troops, for that would have led to an aggravation of the war of which it was impossible to see the consequences.

Although the regular German forces would have nothing to do with an order so clearly contrary to the usages of war, the Nazis' political troops acknowledged no such restraint. During the invasion of North-West Europe a hundred members of the Special

Air Service Regiment fell into German hands. Only eleven of them survived, four by escaping and one, most unusually, by exchange. Thirty were shot near Poitiers by an S.S. execution squad and more than forty were murdered in the concentration camp at Belsen. At Sachsenhausen the S.S. murdered Sub-Lieutenant John Goodwin, R.N.V.R., and six naval ratings who had destroyed several German ships in Norwegian waters with limpet mines.

The murders of Goodwin's party and of the S.A.S. men were not reprisals but were committed as deterrents *pour décourager les autres*. A similar deterrent was proposed by Göbbels in February 1945 when he heard of the devastating air raid on Dresden. He suggested that Germany should renounce the Geneva Convention and shoot all allied pilots in their hands. Hitler momentarily supported this plan, seeing it not only as a way of preventing further air raids but of stopping his own people from surrendering, since he assumed that the allies would kill prisoners in their turn. As he said,

> If I make it clear that I show no consideration for prisoners but treat them without any consideration for their rights, regardless of reprisals, then quite a few [Germans] will think twice before they desert.

Göbbels's plan was not carried out, largely because it would have created an open breach between Hitler and his regular armed forces. The largest killing of prisoners remains therefore the Soviet slaughter of 14,000 Poles, mostly officers, in Katyn Wood and elsewhere, a butchery that would have sickened Sultan Bajazet.

The Hague Rules are silent about using reprisals against prisoners of war. Lieber was unexpectedly ungenerous. 'All prisoners of war are liable to the infliction of retaliatory measures.'

He does not, however, specify what measures should be taken against them and for what actions reprisals could be taken. It is to be presumed that he meant reprisals for action taken against the prisoners held by the enemy. It must be remembered that, only two years before *General Order Nº 100* had been issued, the courts of the Union had been finding privateersmen guilty of piracy (see p. 79). President Jefferson Davis's reaction to this had been to order into 'cells appropriated to felons' fourteen senior prisoners, one to represent William Smith, who had already been sentenced to death in Philadelphia, and the others to represent named prisoners whose fate had yet to be decided. Accordingly Colonel Corcoran of the 69th New York State Militia was drawn by lot to suffer whatever fate was in store for William Smith and six colonels, two lieutenant-colonels, three majors and two captains, were held against the sentences of the other prisoners. Since President Lincoln soon released the privateersmen to prison camps, Davis's threat did not have to be implemented but it is interesting to observe that the command of the Union army appeared, as evidenced by the General Order, to believe that the Confederate president would have been within his rights to execute the hostage prisoners.

A somewhat similar situation arose in 1915 when, on Churchill's orders, prisoners taken from U-boats were treated not as prisoners of war but as criminals. Since at that time the German submarines were doing their best to obey 'cruiser rules', their government felt justifiably aggrieved and took thirty-nine British officers and put them into cells in military jails. There they remained until Balfour succeeded Churchill at the Admiralty and sent the U-boat men to normal prison camps.

The Geneva Convention of 1929 outlawed all such retaliation, saying forthrightly that 'Measures of reprisal against [prisoners] are forbidden'. Apart from minor incidents, this injunction was obeyed by the signatories (which did not include Japan and the Soviet Union) during the Second World War with one conspicuous exception. After the ill-fated raid on Dieppe, Hitler learned that, on raiding operations, the British had orders to bind the hands of their prisoners. This roused him to order that all the Dieppe prisoners, who were for the most part Canadians, should be shackled in their prison camps. The British and Canadian governments retaliated by manacling an equal number of German prisoners but, in face of protests from the military and an outcry in the press, desisted after a few weeks. The German orders, however, were not withdrawn for thirteen months. The inconvenience to the prisoners was, at first, considerable but it soon became clear that the *Wehrmacht* disapproved of such treatment and did what it could to minimise its effects, insisting only that the manacles be worn at roll-calls. At the camp at Eichstätt, 'the Kommandant requested the officers to be kind enough, for appearances sake, to slip the handcuffs on (the locks had been ruined) should he send word of a visit by a general or other senior German officer'.

The problem of the escaping prisoner was one which the nineteenth century had to tackle as a new one since, before Napoleon broke down the customs of parole and exchange, it had not been worth a prisoner's trouble to escape except in a few unusual circumstances. Even in Napoleon's day it had become accepted that, while an escaper was liable to be shot when he was actually making his break for freedom, he should not be severely punished while at liberty unless he was unwise enough to attempt to resist arrest. As Lieber codified this practice,

> A prisoner who escapes may be shot, or otherwise killed, in his flight; but neither death or any other punishment shall be inflicted upon him simply for his attempt to escape, which the law of war does not consider a crime. Stricter means of security [i.e. a period of close confinement] shall be used after an unsuccessful attempt to escape.

The Hague Rules agreed with this prescription and merely said that re-captured escapers should be 'liable to disciplinary measures', a phrase which was found too imprecise in the 1914–18 war, when some German prison camps awarded no more than two weeks in the cells while at others, notably at Magdeburg, sentences of a year were given. The Geneva Convention sought to regularise such treatment by making the maximum punishment for any military offence (including escaping) thirty days' confinement and urging 'the competent authorities to exercise the greatest leniency . . . in appraising facts in connection with escape or attempted escape'.

Unfortunately Lieber had added another paragraph about escapers to the sensible and humane one quoted above. This read, 'If, however, a conspiracy is discovered, the purpose of which is a united or general escape, the conspirators may be rigorously punished, even with death . . .'

This was very dangerous ground. It is clear that the guards have the right to fire at any attempt at mass escape, particularly where violence is used. There were two serious cases of this in the Second World War, both of which concerned Japanese prisoners. Forty-six prisoners were killed when they tried to break out of a camp in New Zealand and at Cowrah in New South Wales the dead included four guards and 251 prisoners. In both cases the number of casualties suggests that the attempt was deliberately suicidal, a belated assertion of the Japanese belief that a soldier should die before he surrenders.

Shooting prisoners who try in concerted rushes to overpower their guards is, however, a different matter from punishing conspiracy to escape as a capital crime. Most successful escapes are the result of teamwork and it could be held that the prisoner who forges identity documents, those who keep watch on the movement of the sentries and those who conceal absences at roll-calls would all be members of the conspiracy and liable to the death penalty. The *Kriegsbrauch* of 1902 seemed to support this view,

Attempts to escape on the part of individuals who have not pledged their word of honour might be regarded as the expression of a natural impulse for liberty, and not as a crime. They are therefore punished by restriction of the privileges granted and by a sharper supervision but not with death. But the latter punishment will follow as a matter of course in the case of plots to escape, if only because of the danger of them.

It should be added that none of the regular German forces ever put the thinking behind the final sentence into practice but it might have been that which influenced the German government when it instigated the mass execution which was carried out against the escapers from *Stalag Luft III* at Sagan in 1944. In March of that year seventy-nine R.A.F. officers got away from the camp through a tunnel and three of them regained their freedom. Fifty of the remainder were shot by the S.S. on Hitler's personal orders. The rest were fortunate enough to fall into the hands of the regular forces or of other authorities not closely connected with the more evil manifestations of the Nazi party and managed to return safely to prison camps.

In both world wars the *Wehrmacht* behaved with conspicuous tolerance towards the escaping proclivities of their Western prisoners. This is the more remarkable when it is considered how much of their scarce manpower was consumed in hunting escapers. To take only a single example, 50,000 Germans – soldiers, police and *Hitler–Jugend* – were employed to recapture the sixty-five British officers who got away from Eichstätt through a tunnel in March 1943. All were returned unharmed to their camps.

Colditz, encrusted though it is becoming by a verdant mythology, is a fine example of German tolerance. Recognising that some prisoners were going to try to escape whatever happened, the *Wehrmacht* collected the most persistent escapers into a *Sonderlager*, a camp with 'a special regime of surveillance' such as was permitted by Article 48 of the Geneva Convention for 'prisoners who have been punished as a result of an attempt to escape'. The Convention insisted that confinement in such a camp should not 'involve the suppression of any of the safeguards accorded to prisoners by the present Convention' and one of the safeguards was that the capturing government should encourage 'as far as possible . . . sporting pursuits of the prisoners'. The courtyard of Colditz castle measured only forty-five yards by thirty-five and the view of the camp staff was that, although this space was clearly inadequate, it would have to suffice if security was to be maintained. They were firmly overruled from Berlin which insisted that prisoners must have regular access to the nearby park, a concession which greatly increased the difficulties of the guards. There can be no doubt that the way Colditz was run was a recognition by the Germans that they were prepared to indulge, without rancour, in a duel of wits with their prisoners, an elaborate game in which the unwritten rules were acknowledged by both sides and which was played by guards and prisoners alike in a way that reflects as much credit on the humanity of the Germans as it does on the ingenuity and persistence of the prisoners.

The Japanese had little trouble with Western prisoners escaping. The problems were too great to make the attempt worthwhile although a handful got away from Hong Kong to Chinese-held territory. The fate of those re-taken was usually harsh. Three men who escaped from a camp in Java were arrested, taken back to their camp, stripped naked and tied to the barbed wire. Then their comrades were paraded to watch while they were bayoneted slowly to death.

Escape was not the only crime for which prisoners could be punished. Both The Hague Rules and the Geneva Convention made it clear that they were subject to the laws of the country in which they were. This was no new idea. Two French inmates of Norman Cross in the Napoleonic Wars were sentenced to death for forging English bank notes and although their sentences were commuted to life imprisonment, they spent the rest of the war in Huntingdon jail. In 1914 the French put a particularly severe interpretation upon this liability. During their first drive on Paris a German cavalry patrol led by two officers, Captain von Schierstädt and Lieutenant Count Schwerin, penetrated into the Forest of Fontainebleau, south of the capital, where they were cut off from their own troops. For some days they tried to find a way back and during that time they requisitioned some food, an old coat and a small waggon on which to transport a wounded trooper. Eventually they were captured and brought before a court-martial charged with pillage. The two officers were sentenced to be degraded from their ranks (a penalty not mentioned in The Hague Rules and subsequently forbidden at Geneva) and the whole detachment was condemned to transportation to Cayenne – Devil's Island. The intervention of the U.S. ambassador secured the remission of the transportation but all the prisoners were treated as convicts. There was great indignation in Germany which mounted when it became known that von Schierstädt had gone out of his mind in captivity. Reprisals against French prisoners were threatened.

By this time the French were greatly embarrassed by the incident and were anxious to find a way out without conceding the principle which they conceived to be at stake. It was the Americans, as Protecting Power, who suggested a solution. Their formula was that if it was assumed that von Schierstädt's mental breakdown had preceded his capture, it could be held that he was not responsible for his actions and his subordinates, who acted under his orders, could not be held culpable. The French were glad to grasp at this escape route. They repatriated the unfortunate captain, who subsequently recovered, and transferred the rest of his patrol to prison camps.

American intervention in this case marks one of the earliest emergences of the idea of a Protecting Power. Whatever rules are made for securing the proper treatment of prisoners, they will not be seen to be effective unless there is some body to which complaints can be made in the assurance that they will be considered. In the eighteenth century each side had appointed a Commissioner to reside in the other country but Napoleon would allow no British official to approach the prison camps, permitting them only to pay occasional visits to the Breton port of Morlaix, some five hundred miles from the nearest depot. The last known resident Commissioner was Reuben C. Beasley who looked after the American prisoners in England during the war of 1812. He seems to have been a well-meaning functionary who suffered from a reluctance to answer letters or to visit the depots and from a total lack of support from his government. His reward was to be hanged in effigy by the Americans in Dartmoor who accused him, unjustly, of misappropriating the money sent for their clothing.

The Hague Rules made no mention of independent inspection and the outbreak of war in 1914 saw a rash of complaints from both sides about the treatment of their prisoners. Since the United States was looking after the diplomatic interests of both Germany and Britain it was suggested that it should undertake the protection of prisoners. The German Foreign Office immediately agreed but the War Ministry, in whose charge the prisoners were, answered no letters on the subject. The deadlock was broken by the American ambassador, James W. Gerrard, who presented himself at the War Ministry and said, 'If I cannot get an answer to my propositions about prisoners, I will take a chair and sit in front of your palace until I do get an answer.' These tactics resulted in a meeting with the generals and,

In twenty minutes we managed to reach an agreement, the substance of which, as between England and Germany, was that the American Ambassador and his representatives in Great

Britain should have the right to visit the prison camps on giving reasonable notice, which should be twenty-four hours where possible, and should have the right to converse with prisoners within sight but out of hearing of the camp officials; that an endeavour should be made to adjust matters complained of before bringing them to the notice of higher officials; that ten representatives should be named by our Ambassador and that these should receive passes enabling them to visit camps.

This and a parallel agreement permitting American inspection of British prisoners in Germany were signed by Britain in January 1915, the Germans signing eight weeks later and soon afterwards the Germans agreed, on British insistence, to allow unannounced visits by the Protecting Power.

It was a very necessary precaution since every belligerent had underestimated both the length of the war and the number of prisoners that would be taken. In no country was the situation satisfactory, though it was probably worst in Germany where, by mid-1916, there were, apart from 45,000 interned civilians, 1,646,233 prisoners of war, of whom 1.2 million were Russians and 355,000 were French. It was a problem which pre-war planning had failed to take into account and, as one of Ambassador Gerrard's representatives wrote,

No forethought or provision had been made for it; like other military operations it could not have been part of military manoeuvres or military practice. To provide for and guard one and a half million men, at a time when all the forces of the nation were centred on the destruction of the opposing army, will be admitted to be rather a large problem.

The German management of this influx of prisoners could well have been worse although those prisoners who received no food parcels, notably the Russians and the 23,000 Serbs, fared badly, if better than the German prisoners in Russia who had to subsist almost wholly on food provided by the American Red Cross. Deaths among allied prisoners in the first two years of the war totalled 29,297 even including 6,270 who died as a result of wounds sustained on the battlefield. This was an annual death rate of less than one per cent, better than that of which the medical officer at 'hyperborean Dartmoor' had been so proud a century earlier, and this despite 6,000 deaths due to tuberculosis and 4,201 from typhus, a disease which was endemic in the Russian army and which spread to other nationalities.

In the two world wars neutral inspection of prisoners of war worked very well, although the Soviet Union permitted no inspection and Japan was not above concealing the existence of small and unsatisfactory camps from the Protecting Powers. In 1939 Germany refused to allow her Polish prisoners to have this protection since the Polish state had, in the Russo–German phrase, 'disintegrated' and the former Polish nationals could thus have no right to neutral inspection. They were, in time, induced to allow the International Red Cross to watch over the interests of the Poles and, certainly in Europe, the I.R.C. acted most effectively as a supernumerary Protecting Power for prisoners of all nationalities.

Neutral inspection, where it was properly conducted and had the cooperation of both sides, provided a most efficient safeguard for all the prisoners. Much, of course, depended on the character of the individual neutral representatives. Little could have been looked for from the American representative who visited Colditz in May 1941. 'His idea of helping to ameliorate our lot was expressed in the momentous enquiry: "Have you any difficulty here in getting married by proxy?"'

PART FIVE

DIALOGUE

When you have to kill a man, it costs nothing to be polite.
Winston S. Churchill, *The Second World War,* vol III

15

The Courtesies of War

If armies or navies at war wish to make arrangements for 'general convenience' they must have some means of communicating with each other. Five hundred years ago this communication was the business of the herald, a court official of considerable seniority and influence, whose job in wartime was more than carrying messages, since he was expected to perform the functions, if not of a referee, at least of a second in a duel. In 1339 Edward III assembled an army in the Low Countries and, having given due notice to King Philip VI (on this occasion through the intermediary of a bishop rather than a herald), invaded France by way of Cambrai. Philip, an indeterminate character, sent a herald to the English king accepting his challenge and, according to some accounts, inviting him to choose a suitable site for a battle. Edward then sent his own herald, undertaking to fight and asking the French king to suggest a convenient day for the contest. The English herald was greeted with joy in the French camp and was presented with a number of rich fur mantles. It being a Wednesday, he returned with a message arranging the fixture for the following Saturday and on that day Edward's army was deployed in its chosen position but, although the French army came within sight, nothing happened. There were some who pointed out that nothing had been agreed about who was to do the attacking but the real reason for the cancellation was that the naturally nervous King Philip had received a letter from the King of Sicily, an astrologer of some note, pointing out that the auguries for a battle were not good. The French army consequently withdrew, leaving the English to make their way to Boulogne grumbling at the lack of proper feeling among the French.

The French herald, Mountjoye, made famous by Shakespeare in *Henry V*, was in reality a conflation of the three heralds who were sent to the English king to ask him his intentions after he had crossed the Somme. They wanted to know which road he would take so that the French army could 'meet thee to fight with thee, and to be revenged for thy conduct'. Henry's reply was,

Straight to Calais, and if our enemies try to disturb us in our journey, it will not be without the utmost peril. We do not intend to seek them out, but neither shall we in fear of them move more slowly or more quickly than we wish to do. We advise them not to interrupt our journey, nor to seek what would be its consequence – a great shedding of Christian blood.

Before sending them back with this message he gave each of the heralds a purse containing a hundred gold crowns. Mountjoye was probably one of these heralds for it was he, described as the Herald of France, for whom Henry sent five days later to enquire whether the French formally conceded to him the victory of Agincourt.

As well as arranging battles, heralds conducted all the exchanges of messages between the opposing nations. The Duc de Berri, best known as the patron of *Les Très Riches Heures*, was also a dog-lover and he heard that a rare breed of greyhound was only to be found in Scotland. Since France and England were at war, the sea passage was hazardous so the duke sent a herald to Richard II of England asking for a safe-conduct for four of his courtiers to go to Scotland and collect the dogs. Richard agreed without hesitation.

The war functions of heralds disappeared when mercenaries became the principal type of combatants but in their place appeared the officer with a white flag. It seems impossible to date the emergence of the custom of considering the white flag as an acknowledged sign that a truce was being proposed, nor does any authority refer to the difficulties that must have arisen because, until the revolution, the national flag of France was white. Certainly by the late seventeenth century it was accepted that an officer accompanied by a white flag and a trumpeter (or drummer) was inviolate on the battlefield.

The messages they brought were not necessarily important. In June 1810 an engineer officer noted in his diary,

A flag of truce, by a colonel, has just come in on Carpio [near the Spanish–Portuguese frontier]; and gave in Marshal Ney's compliments to General Crauford, hoping he is well; also a message to Captain Krauchenberg, saying his dog is safe and shall be returned at the first opportunity. The dog followed a party of French when skirmishing with Krauchenberg some days back.

A few months later a British flag of truce was crossing the lines and the instructions from the adjutant general to the bearer read,

I send herewith a sword, which you will deliver to Monsieur le Doux, with my compliments to *M.le Général de Division*

Fririon, *Chef de l'État Major*. He will be pleased to explain that the sword was taken with Adjutant Oberlet, of the *22me Régiment d'Infanterie*. The Adjutant declares it was lent him by the Captain of his Company, and under such circumstances I have much pleasure in returning the captain his sword.

Occasionally flags of truce were used for more private matters. When the French were facing the Lines of Torres Vedras and were isolated from all news from the outside world, one of their generals, Maximilien Foy, regularly sent flags in to a Dutch officer on the British staff, Captain Jonkheer Tripp van Zoutland, requesting the loan of the latest English newspapers. When Wellington heard of this,

> I put a stop to it, and desired Baron Tripp to ask [Foy] what he wanted them for. He said he was speculating in the English funds and only wanted to know the price of the three per cents. I desired that he might be informed of the price of the three per cents as often as he pleased, but he should not see the papers.

There were occasional misunderstandings. Believing that Napoleon's troops had put themselves outside the normal practices of civilised armies, the Spaniards were apt to detain French officers with white flags. When they imprisoned one sent to Wellington he felt he must make a strong official protest to his ally.

> The pretences for detaining him are as idle as the detention of him is improper and ungracious towards myself. It is said that he crossed the river by swimming; upon which I have to observe that he was sent with a letter to me and the Spanish troops being on one side of the river and the French on the other, he could deliver the letter only by crossing the river, and it is probable that at that place he would have to swim. But if his passage was irregular, he might have been sent back, and might have been ordered to bring his letter where the Spanish Commander in Chief chose to receive it; or if there had been anything irregular in his conduct, it might and ought to have been mentioned when he first arrived.

Wellington was so angry at this Spanish impropriety that he sent a copy of his protest to his French opponent, Marshal Mortier, whose messenger had been detained.

The French were not always blameless. For at least a century it had been acknowledged that, when Britain and France were at war, ships carrying messages could be received at certain 'cartel ports' – Calais, St Malo, Le Havre and Morlaix on the French side; Dover, Poole and Falmouth on the British. Equally well understood was the custom whereby the cartel ships must be unarmed and unladen, flying the national flag of their destination at the fore-top-gallant and their own flag on the ensign staff. In July 1803 Napoleon changed the rules, laying down that cartels could only be received at Morlaix. This was most unfortunate for Lieutenant W. H. Dillon of H.M.S. *Africaine* who, on the day after the First Consul's notification had been despatched, before it could have reached England, was sent in a ship's boat to deliver a message to Helvoesluis, the usual Dutch cartel port. His business was entirely a Dutch matter since he was returning some money which had become owing to a Dutch officer during the Peace of Amiens. Since he was expecting to return to his ship before dark, Dillon,

> had provided myself with something like a sandwich and a volume of Shakespeare's plays, expecting to be away about four hours. Over the foresail I spread the Dutch flag and over the mainsail the English. My boat sailed inshore in capital style with a fine breeze, and I got well inside the anchorage before there appeared to be any notice taken of me by the Dutch frigates.

A Dutch boat put out to meet him and,

> Having lowered my sails, I handed my package over to a Dutch officer, who invited me into his boat, and by him I was conveyed to his chief. By him I was courteously invited into his cabin where he opened the despatch and remarked that it was not of much consequence but that he should send it to The Hague, and I was to wait for an answer. He ordered some lunch for me.

It was eight days before word came from The Hague but after that time the Dutch told him he could return to the fleet. As he was setting sail,

> I was boarded by a large French launch full of armed men, the officer of which ordered me to lower my sail and surrender. When he saw me hesitate, he ordered his crew, some of them soldiers, to point their muskets at me; then he said he should fire if I attempted any resistance. Under such circumstances, my seamen not being armed, and seeing no chance of getting away, I was obliged to yield.

The Royal Navy were greatly affronted by this detention of a flag of truce, nor could they send in another flag to remonstrate lest the same fate overtake it. The senior officer off the coast, Commodore Sir Sidney Smith, therefore sent in some Dutch fishermen with a letter demanding Dillon's release 'according to the laws of war and the usages of civilized nations'. He added acidly that, if a reply was sent, 'I will not follow the example of detaining a Flag of Truce.' The Dutch admiral at Helvoesluis immediately replied in some embarrassment,

> I flatter myself that your Honour will be perfectly sensible that Lieutenant Dillon's detaining can by no means be ascribed to the Batavian [Dutch] Government, but that, to the contrary, every method has been tried to effect his free departure; and I can moreover assure your Honour that the most energical [sic] remonstrances are still made to the French Government in behalf of his case, which, I am confident, will not remain ineffectual.

Sadly the Dutchman's confidence was misplaced and Dillon spent four and a half years as a prisoner before the French consented to exchange him at the extortionate rate of two post captains. The reason given for their obduracy, that Dillon should have gone to Morlaix rather than Helvoesluis, was absurd since, even had he wished to communicate with the French, there was no way he could have known that Morlaix was the only cartel port.

The Royal Navy can be accused of one piece of sharp practice although it was far from being on the scale of that practised by the French over Dillon. In 1799 the French Admiral Bruix, with twenty-five ships of the line, sailed from Brest for the Mediterranean, evading the blockading squadrons. At Gibraltar Lord St Vincent, commanding the British Mediterranean Fleet, was ashore in poor health, but his ships, fifteen of the line, were off Cadiz. St Vincent saw the French sail through the Straits but, with a strong westerly wind blowing, he could not send a despatch vessel to them with orders to pursue. However, there was on the Rock Captain Isaac Coffin, R.N., who was on his way from Minorca to take up a shore appointment at Halifax, Nova Scotia. A flag of truce was sent to the Spaniards investing Gibraltar with a request for a safe conduct which would enable Coffin to travel overland to Lisbon from where he could take ship to his new post. This was immediately granted and the captain set off without delay. On his way he suborned a Spanish fisherman who took a letter out to the fleet off Cadiz which sent them hurrying after Bruix.

219

The regular use of flags of truce continued into the nineteenth century. In 1861 when President Jefferson Davis wished to remonstrate with President Lincoln about the treatment of the captured privateersman (see p. 78) he sent his letter by the hand of Colonel Thomas H. Taylor of the Confederate Army. With a small escort the colonel rode out from Fairfax in the direction of Arlington and, about seven miles from the Potomac, he met a detachment of Union cavalry whose commander, Colonel Porter, greeted him civilly, enquiring after the health of *Colonel* Lee, with whom he had served. Taylor replied that he knew no Colonel Lee and Porter rephrased his question and asked after *General* Lee who, he was assured, was in excellent health. The two colonels rode amicably together to the headquarters of the Army of the Potomac only to find that General McDowell was away in Washington. A messenger was sent to him but in reply arrived a carriage containing Colonel Van Rensselar, first A.D.C. to General Winfield Scott, the veteran commander of the Union army, who invited Taylor to accompany him to the capital. It was ten o'clock at night when they arrived there but Scott was waiting to greet the emissary in full uniform. He accepted the letter for the president and forwarded it by a staff officer. According to the New Orleans paper, the *True Delta*,

> During the absence of the messenger, the general ordered in wine, introduced Colonel Taylor to his staff, and invited the party to join him in a glass of champagne, a request to which those present responded with an alacrity altogether characteristic of the profession. After the lapse of half an hour, spent in the interchange of civilities, the messenger returned and reported that the president had retired and could not therefore be seen that night. General Scott, promising that a reply should be returned at an early hour, if not on the morrow, and that he would take care that it should be entrusted to an officer who would return it to the [Confederate] Government in person, dismissed Colonel Taylor, recommending him to the hospitality of General McDowell, with whom he returned to Arlington. There he spent the rest of the night and on Thursday morning, after partaking breakfast at the quarters of General McDowell and being kindly supplied with files of the eastern newspapers, he bade adieu to his courteous hosts.

Probably General Scott's offer of champagne was a gesture of pure hospitality and not made in the hope of extracting military information from Taylor when his tongue was loosened by drink. When Colonel Garnet Wolseley published his *Soldier's Pocket*

Book in 1869, this was a point on which he laid much stress. He recommended that when a flag of truce came in,

> The officer and his trumpeter should be separately conducted, so as to be unable to converse together. The latter should be given plenty to drink if he likes to have it, in the hope of being able to extract news from him when liquor has untied his tongue: note the regiment to which he belongs.

To ensure that the enemy did not attempt the same trick, Wolseley gave detailed guidance about the men who should be sent on such missions and on the way in which they were to be conducted.

> Select a fine soldierlike-looking officer, having a good address, and possessing great tact, to carry your message. He should be a good horseman, very well mounted, and thoroughly conversant with the enemy's language. The trumpeter to accompany him should be selected for somewhat similar characteristics, and for his sobriety. He should be warned on no account to accept any wine or intoxicating drink whilst in the enemy lines.
> The officer should be provided with a large white flag, and should approach the enemy's lines in the most open manner, selecting the most open ground in doing so, taking care that his white flag is clearly visible, and making his trumpeter sound frequently to attract attention . . . If the enemy is determined not to receive it, the party will be fired upon – a chivalrous enemy will content himself by firing over their heads. The officer with the flag should not, however, take a few shots fired at him as a positive No; for private soldiers are often very ignorant of the conventionalities of war.

It was to be hoped that the enemy private soldier's markmanship was as abysmal as his ignorance.

The Hague Rules codified the traditional use of the white flag, laying down that the bearer,

> Has the right of inviolability, as well as the trumpeter, bugler or drummer, the flag-bearer and interpreter who may accompany him.
> The commander to whom a *parlementaire* is sent is not in all circumstances obliged to receive him. He may take all the necessary steps to prevent the *parlementaire* taking advantage of his mission to obtain information. In case of abuse, he has the right to detain the *parlementaire* temporarily.

221

As so often happened with The Hague Rules, this one looks backwards rather than to the war that was soon to come. It is hard to imagine an officer with a white flag, accompanied by a trumpeter (far less a drummer), picking his way across no-man's land on the Western front in 1916. In practice the use of wireless enabled commanders to pass messages to their opposite numbers. Increasingly the white flag became regarded as a token of surrender, although there were occasional incidents in which it was used to establish a temporary local truce to collect the wounded or bury the dead. In Tunisia in 1943 there was an incident which recalled earlier practices. A German brigadier found that his casualty clearing station was frequently shelled by British artillery. Believing this to be inadvertent, he sent a patrol through the British lines to post a letter, correctly addressed with rank, decorations and appointment, to the opposing brigadier, telling him what was happening. No more shells fell on the clearing station.

The American *General Order N° 100* included a clause that, 'Outposts, sentinels, or pickets are not to be fired upon, except to drive them in, or when a positive order, special or general, has been issued to that effect.'

Garnet Wolseley echoed this sentiment in the *Soldier's Pocket Book*. 'If you fall in with an enemy's patrol in advance of the chain of sentries, retire without exchanging shots, as firing between patrols only tends to harass and to uselessly disturb the troops in rear.'

This was an expression of the classic doctrine that war should be made as tolerable as possible to those taking part. Nobody stood to gain if sentries were shot solely because they happened to be on duty at a time when neither army was contemplating offensive action. Wellington said that, in the Peninsula,

> The advanced posts always gave notice to each other when they were in danger. On one occasion, when the French army was advancing suddenly and in force, the French outposts cried out to ours, '*Courez vite! courez vite! On va vous attaquer!*' I always encouraged this; the killing of a poor fellow of a vidette or carrying off a post could not influence the battle, and I always, when I was going to attack, sent to tell them to get out of the way.

How this worked out in practice was described by a young officer who was on duty at the outposts on December 10th, 1813, the morning of Soult's great attack at the Battle of the Nive.

The French . . . called out to our sentinels in French and
Spanish. At half past nine a.m., the enemy's skirmishers came
forward in a careless fashion, talking to each other, and good-
naturedly allowed our sentinels to retire without firing at them.

According to another account some of the French helped a British
sentry to put his knapsack on before allowing him to retire.

Special care was taken to ensure that mistakes should not occur
at night. On the evening after the incident last described, a British
brigade major,

Was posting the night's sentries when I saw a French officer doing
the same. We civilly greeted each other. I said I wished to speak
to him and he came up with the greatest confidence and good
humour. I showed him my vidette and then remarked that his
was too far in advance and might create an alarm while relieving.
He said he did not see that, but to please me, if I would point out
where I wished he should be, he would immediately move
him – which he did.

With things arranged in such a friendly fashion between the
officers, it is hardly surprising that after the Battle of Fuentes de
Oñoro (May 1811), when the outposts were separated only by a
narrow stream, the French sentry should cross over for a light for
his pipe.

All civilised armies and navies had a common interest in avoiding needless casualties. When the French approached Coimbra on
their advance towards Lisbon in 1810 they found at the gates one of
Wellington's staff officers. He explained that the allies did not
intend to defend the city and that, since there were many seriously
wounded men of both sides inside it, it seemed best to hand it over
without disturbance. He and a French officer then made a circuit of
the gates, relieving British sentries with French. Four years earlier,
Rear Admiral Sir Sidney Smith, with a small squadron, sailed into
the Bay of Naples intending to attack shipping in the harbour.

The city was illuminated on account of Joseph Bonaparte proc-
laiming himself King of the Two Sicilies. It would have been easy
for the fire of the ships to have interrupted this ceremony and
show of festivity: but I considered that the unfortunate inhabitants had evil enough on them; that the restoration of the city to
its lawful Sovereign and fugitive inhabitants would be no gratifi-
cation, if it should be found a heap of ruins, ashes and bones; and
that as I had no force to land and keep order, in case of the

French army retiring to the fortresses, I should leave an opulent city prey to the licentious part of the community who would not fail to profit by the confusion the flames would occasion: not a gun fired.

Since they always faced a greater enemy than their terrestrial opponents – the sea – navies have always had a strong fellow feeling for each other. In 1780, at the height of the Franco–British fighting during the American revolution, the West Indies were ravaged by a hurricane and several British warships were driven ashore on the French island of Martinique. The governor, the Marquis de Bouillésant, sent the survivors back in a cartel ship, writing that he could not look on such unfortunates as enemies. The greatest misfortune suffered by the French in that war was the result of an act of French generosity. While France and Britain were still at peace, Admiral Sir George Rodney had gone to Paris to evade his creditors but, as war became inevitable, he was anxious to go home. Unfortunately he then owed money widely in Paris and it was intimated to him that he would be arrested for debt if he tried to leave the city. A loan of a thousand *louis d'or* from his friend the Maréchal de Biron, given with the consent of the French Admiralty, enabled him to make his escape. He returned to England, was given a command and proceeded to defeat first the Spaniards off Cape St Vincent, a victory which ensured the survival of Gibraltar, and then the French at the Battle of the Saints, thus saving Jamaica.

Rescuing shipwrecked sailors, irrespective of nationality, was a time-honoured custom. One of the most striking examples occurred in January 1797 when the French battleship *Droits de l'Homme* was driven ashore by two British frigates. She had earlier captured two British merchantmen off the coast of Ireland and their crews were still aboard when she struck a sandbank in the Bay of Audierne. The prisoners were immediately brought on deck, to discouraging cries of *'Montez vite, nous sommes tous perdus'*, and found the ship dismasted and with great seas breaking over her. She lay there four days before the last of the survivors reached the shore but four hundred of her complement had drowned and more would have done so had it not been for her involuntary passengers. According to a French source,

The British prisoners on board *Droits de l'Homme* behaved very well during the shipwreck. Two merchant captains set an example of courage and devotion. The first dived into the water fourteen times to bring to the shore men on the point of drowning. The second, with the help of his seamen, made rafts on which some of the [French] soldiers were able to reach the shore. The government set all the prisoners free, repatriating them under a white flag. The two captains also received a sum of money.

The man chiefly responsible for driving *Droits de l'Homme* ashore was Sir Edward Pellew, a magnificent frigate captain and a man who showed every courtesy to his enemies. In command of *Nymphe* in one of the earliest actions in the war of 1793, he and the captain of his opponent, the frigate *Cléopatre*, had ceremoniously raised their hats to each other before action was joined and, after the French ship had been taken, he heard that her captain's widow was in reduced circumstances and sent her a sum of money. Three years later, when in command of *Révolutionaire*, he captured the French frigate *Unité* and found on board the wife of the Governor of Rochefort with her children and servants. Pellew at once sent them into Brest, including in the party her eldest son who had been an officer in *Unité*.

Such civilities were not confined to the navies of the two sides. Lieutenant-Colonel Felton Hervey had lost his right arm in 1809 but this did not stop him charging with the 14th Light Dragoons at Fuentes de Oñoro two years later.

He was ridden at by a French officer of the *13me Chasseurs à Cheval*, who raised his sword to cut him down; when, perceiving that his enemy had but one arm, he dropped his sword to the salute and passed on.

At Waterloo an artillery officer came to Wellington and asked permission to fire since he had his guns trained on Napoleon. The Duke replied, 'No, no. I will not allow it. It is not the business of commanders to be firing on each other.' This was presumably a survival of the eighteenth-century reluctance to kill foreign heads of state and other prominent persons (see p. 102) and seems to have been widely held in the British army. In 1810 Charles Napier wrote that Marshal Ney had ridden down to a ford over the River Coa which was guarded by the company commanded by his brother, George Napier.

The men fired at him without George's orders, wounding one person of his suite. Had Ney been hit it would not have been creditable; it is not right to fire at people without necessity. Our firing was stopped by George immediately.

Later in the same year, when Massena pressed his first re-connaissance of the lines of Torres Vedras too close, 'A shot was fired at the party from Redoubt N° 120, which striking a wall whereon the Marshal was resting his telescope, he acknowledged the warning by taking off his hat and moving on.'

The French do not seem to have been so scrupulous in their shooting. As early as 1743 they were believed to have aimed deliberately at George II during the Battle of Dettingen. Accord-ing to an English eye-witness, 'The French fired at his Majesty from a battery of twelve cannon, but levelled too high. I saw the balls go within half a yard of his head.'

Similarly Napoleon was popularly supposed to have laid the gun which mortally wounded his old comrade and rival Jean Victor Moreau at the Battle of Dresden (1813).

It was an axiom that unnecessary suffering and discomfort should be avoided. In the American war, when Gibraltar was under Franco–Spanish siege, the garrison was suffering from scurvy and the enemy commander, the Duc de Crillon, sent in a cartload of carrots. In 1855 Admiral Sir Edmund Lyons sent to the Russian commander of besieged Sebastopol a present of a fat buck. Not to be outdone, Admiral Nachinoff repaid the gift with a hard Dutch cheese. Lower down on the scale when, in 1812, the French and British armies were facing each other across the River Douro, a doctor noticed that,

> It is not uncommon to see five hundred of the enemy, and as many of our own men bathing together in the river in the most perfect good humour possible, at the same time that the cavalry of the two armies come down on their respective sides of the river to water, it being perfectly understood that neither party shall ever approach the river armed.

Another eye-witness at that time wrote that 'If we wanted wood for the construction of huts, our men were allowed to pass without molestation to the French side to cut it.' As a Guards officer put it, 'We are wonderfully polite at the outposts; and, in short, are cutting each others' throats in quite a friendly way.'

Such friendly conduct could go on even in the middle of a great battle. When one of the French attacks at Talavera (1809) had been beaten off, there was a long unofficial truce while the soldiers of both sides refilled their water-bottles in the muddy waters of the Portina brook, the officers exchanged news and newspapers, and the stretcher-bearers mingled to carry off the wounded of their own armies. Nor was this only an Anglo–French form of civility.

226

Three years later, when the French armies were advancing on Moscow, a Polish officer in the French service described an incident in the battle for Smolensk.

After a time the Russians stopped firing, posted their skirmishers at fifteen or twenty paces intervals, and sheathed their swords as a sign that they did not wish to continue to fight. We followed their example and stationed our *tirailleurs* in the same way, at a range of a hundred yards, with orders to hold their ground and not to fire.

Soon an officer of Russian dragoons rode forward a short distance, called to us and made signs with a bottle. I went in front of the *tirailleurs* and eventually we came to within thirty paces of each other, whereupon the Russian called out in French, '*Mon camerade!* It is useless to wear out our horses and kill our men for nothing. Let us drink together. There will be plenty of time for fighting later.' We went closer, though there was still firing in the distance. Some more Russian officers came up and I made to retire but the dragoon said, 'I give you my word of honour that they will do you no harm.' I therefore stayed and we talked in a most friendly fashion. I found his rum good but I could give him none in return until some of my brother officers arrived bringing our sutler, Frau Ehmke, who always rode among our light troops and had two little casks of brandy on her horse. She gave the Russians a free drink although usually she charged highly. An officer of Russian Uhlans, Polish by birth, asked about some of his compatriots and, hearing that some Polish lancers were in our rear, rode confidently over to them as fast as his horse would go . . .

Meanwhile General Bruyère, who was some way away, saw what was going on and sent an A.D.C. to order the officers back to their posts and to tell the Russians to retire behind their skirmishers. He also ordered the Polish Uhlan to be arrested but his A.D.C. rode so slowly, probably on purpose, that the Pole was warned and got away. We remained opposite each other until the evening and did not fire a shot.

The most famous unofficial truce was that of Christmas 1914. It was not as widespread as is sometimes represented. The French and Belgians took no part and even on the British front it was far from complete, being largely confined to sectors where the German line was held by Bavarians and Saxons. It began on Christmas Eve when, in some sectors, coloured lanterns appeared on the German parapet and, in at least one place, a Christmas tree was erected.

Carols were sung on both sides and the firing stopped. A sergeant of the Royal Warwicks went, by invitation, to the German trenches and exchanged cigarettes and a tin of Maconochie's 'Meat and Vegetables' for cigars.

On Christmas Day itself the truce became widespread. From both sides soldiers of all ranks swarmed out of the trenches and fraternised, exchanging souvenirs and rations. The Bedfordshire Regiment played a fifty-a-side football match with a German battalion. No result was achieved since the ball was punctured on the barbed wire. From both lines burial parties dealt with the corpses that littered no-man's land. Frank Richards, the creator of Billy Bunter, who was serving in the Queen's Westminsters, remembered that the Germans opposite them sent over two barrels of local beer for his company. He commented, 'If it was possible for a man to have drunk the two barrels himself, he would have bursted before he had got drunk. French beer was rotten stuff.'

A private of the Warwicks searching a ruined cottage for coal found a German on the same errand and they helped each other fill their sacks. Bruce Bairnsfather, whose 'Old Bill' cartoons are one of the more bearable souvenirs of trench warfare, wrote that,

> The last I saw of this little affair was a vision of one of my machine gunners, who was a bit of a hair-dresser in civil life, cutting the unnaturally long hair of a docile Bosche, who was patiently kneeling on the ground whilst the automatic clippers crept up the back of his neck.

War was resumed next day in most sectors but in places the truce prolonged itself. On Hogmanay a private of the Cameron Highlanders, a regiment that had fired as usual on Christmas Day, staggered drunkenly but unmolested between the lines before finally falling into his own trench to sleep it off. On the same day the London Rifle Brigade hauled a drunken German out of the wire and pointed him back to his own trench.

The Christmas truce of 1914, with scenes that might well have been enacted in the Peninsula a century earlier, was the last occurrence of its kind. Generals, and even more civilians, deprecated such temporary friendliness and orders were issued against a repetition. The growing bitterness of total war ensured that such orders were obeyed, but as late as Christmas 1943, on at least one part of the Italian front, the guns were silent all day and, after dark, the strains of *'Stille Nacht, Heilige Nacht'* could be heard coming from the German bank of the Garigliano.

16

Making Terms

August 13, 1704

I have not time to say more but beg you will give my duty to the Queen, and let her know her army has had a glorious victory. Monsieur Tallard and two other Generals are in my coach and I am following the rest. The bearer, my aide-de-camp Colonel Parke, will give her an account of what has passed. I shall do it in a day or two by another more at large.

At Blenheim the Duke of Marlborough and Prince Eugene had killed, wounded or captured two-thirds of the enemy army, captured his commander in chief and taken most of his artillery. It was an overwhelming victory but it settled only the immediate course of that year's campaign. Marshal Marsin rallied the remnants of the Franco–Bavarian army and led them away to recruit, reorganise and fight another day. Three years later much the same happened when Galway's Anglo–Portuguese army was smashed at Almanza in Spain. In the eighteenth-century context it was most unusual for an army in the field to be forced to surrender. Defeated troops could always move faster than their victorious opponents. 'It is obvious,' observed Wellington,

> that if an army throws away all its cannon, equipments, and everything that could strengthen it, and can enable it to act together as a body . . . it must be able to march by roads through which it cannot be followed with any prospect of being overtaken by an army which has not made the same sacrifices.

Fortresses could be forced to capitulate but field armies, in one shape or another, escaped to reform.

In 1777 there were few precedents to guide either side when John Burgoyne, with the remnant of his army, found himself stranded at Saratoga. Abandoned by his colleagues to the southward, surrounded by a greatly superior force and with supplies and ammunition running low, Burgoyne sent a flag to General Horatio Gates, asking permission for one of his staff officers to visit American headquarters. This was agreed and Gates sent an A.D.C. down to the stream which separated the two armies.

At the hour appointed, I repaired to the advanced posts. The bridge over the Fishkill had been destroyed, but the sleepers remained. We did not wait many minutes before the *chamade* [the drum-call to denote a parley] was beat at the advanced guard of the enemy and an officer descending the hill, stepped across the creek on one of the sleepers; he called out it was 'Major Kingston with a message from Lieutenant General Burgoyne to Major General Gates.' I named myself to him 'Colonel Wilkinson, on the part of General Gates, to receive the message.' He paused for a moment, pulled out a paper, looked at it and said, 'My orders direct me to Major General Gates.'

'It is to save you time and trouble that I am authorised to receive the message you bear.'

He then took General Gates's note to General Burgoyne from his pocket and said, 'General Gates has agreed to receive this message and I am not authorised to deliver it to any other person.'

'Well then, Sir, you must submit to being hoodwinked.'

He affected to start at the proposition and objected on the grounds of it being an indignity. I could but smile and observed that I had understood that there was nothing more common than to blindfold military messengers when they were admitted within the guards of a camp. He replied, 'Well, sir, I will submit to it but under the express stipulation that no indignity is intended to the British arms.'

I then carefully bound up his eyes with his own handkerchief; he took my arm and in this way we walked upwards of a mile to headquarters . . . When I introduced into General Gates's tent and named him, the gentlemen saluted each other with, 'General Gates, your servant,' and 'Ah, Kingston, how do you do,' and a shake of the head.

Gates and Kingston had been 'old acquaintances formerly' and they spent a few minutes in general conversation before the Englishman put forward Burgoyne's proposals for an armistice 'during the time necessary to communicate the preliminary terms'. Gates, however,

put his hand in his side pocket, pulled out a paper and presented it to Kingston, observing, 'There, sir, are the terms on which General Burgoyne must surrender.' The major appeared thunderstruck but read the paper whilst the old chief surveyed him attentively through his spectacles.

Having finished his perusals . . . Major Kingston said, 'I must beg leave to decline delivering this paper to General Burgoyne because, although I cannot speak for him, I think the propositions it contains cannot be submitted to.'

The general observed that he might be mistaken, and there could be no impropriety in his delivering them.

Gates's demands amounted to unconditional surrender as prisoners of war but Kingston eventually agreed to take them to Burgoyne, who found them unacceptable. Eventually he persuaded the American to modify them and grant terms so generous that Congress refused to ratify them (see p. 173). Nevertheless there was no alternative to reaching an agreement and, on the morning of October 17th, 1777, the small Anglo–German army marched out of its camp and laid down its arms. That done, their general and his staff rode to the American camp where the whole of Gates's army, more than 17,000 men, were paraded to receive them. The American general rode forward to meet Burgoyne and,

> They had approached nearly within sword's length when they reined up and halted. General Burgoyne, raising his hat, said, 'The fortune of war, General Gates, has made me your prisoner,' to which the conqueror replied, 'I shall always be ready to bear testimony that it has not been any fault of your Excellency.'

Cornwallis at Yorktown and Mack at Ulm surrendered beleaguered fortresses rather than field armies and it was almost a century before another complete army surrendered *en rase campagne*. Once again the scene was the United States. On April 7th, 1865 Ulysses S. Grant wrote to Robert E. Lee, 'General, The result of the last week must convince you of the hopelessness of further resistance on the part of the Army of North Virginia.'

The reply came back,

> Though not entertaining the opinion you express of the hopelessness of further resistance . . . I reciprocate your desire to avoid useless effusion of blood and therefore, before considering your proposition, ask the terms you will offer on condition of surrender.

At Appomatox on April 9th, the surrender was conducted with every possible courtesy and striking generosity on the part of Grant who even allowed the Confederate troops to keep their horses since 'They will need them for the spring plowing.'

Five years later another flag of truce was received with great ceremony outside the town of Sedan. According to the Crown Prince of Prussia,

> The Cavalry Guard of the Staff was drawn up behind the King; before these all present formed a wide half-circle with His Majesty and myself at his side standing out alone in front of it. Prince Karl, Prince Luitpold of Bavaria, the Grand Duke of Saxe-Weimar, the Duke of Saxe-Coburg, the Hereditary Grand Dukes of Saxe-Weimar, Mecklenburg-Schwerin and Mecklenburg-Strelitz, Prince Wilhelm of Württemberg, the Hereditary Prince zu Hohenzollern, Duke Frederich zu Schleswig-Holstein-Augustenburg, together with Count Bismarck, General von Moltke and the War Minister von Roon stood close behind us.
>
> Then appeared Comte Reille, accompanied by Captain von Winterfeld of the General Staff and a Prussian trumpet. Directly he came in sight of the King, Reille dismounted, quickly adjusted something about his riding-breeches, and then took off his red cap and strode up to the King, a heavy stick in his hand, eyes downcast . . . and with a few words presented Napoleon's letter.
>
> The King opened it and read the brief holograph message it contained. *'Monsieur mon frère, n'ayant pu mourir au milieu de mes troupes, il ne reste qu'a remettre mon epée entre les mains de Votre Majesté. Je suis de Votre Majesté, le bon frère, Napoleon. Sedan 1 Sept.*

While the King of Prussia insisted that the French troops should lay down their arms before negotiations started, he was willing enough to accept the personal surrender of his *bon frère* and decided to write to him in his own hand. This taxed to the limit the resources of the Prussian General Staff, a body which had shown itself notably competent in the campaign up to that point.

> It was not easy to see where we were to find the necessary writing materials. No table was to be found nearby but a couple of straw-bottomed chairs fetched from a peasant's cottage were put together to form a kind of stand and my Orderly Officer, Lieutenant von Gustedt, laid his sabre-tache across them for a table-top. I produced my writing paper and eagle signet from my holster, the Grand Duke of Saxe-Weimar supplied pen and ink, and thus our victorious King wrote his reply.

It is impossible not to feel sympathy for the pain-racked emperor as he interviewed the King of Prussia, with 'copious tears running

down his cheeks, which he kept wiping away with his hand'.
Almost more pathetic is the appeal of Captain Niu-chang-ping of
the Chinese warship *Kuang-ping* who, in February 1896, found
himself involved in the surrender at Wei-hai-wei of the Northern
Chinese squadron. To the Japanese Admiral Ito, he wrote,

Excellency, I have the honour to point out that the *Kuang-ping*
belongs to the Canton squadron. In the spring of last year, at the
usual inspection, the *Kuang-chia*, the *Kuang-yi* and the *Kuang-
ping* came to attend the review of the Northern Squadron and,
for various reasons, remained temporarily with them. The
Kuang-chia and the *Kuang-yi* have both been sunk, and of the
three Canton ships only the *Kuang-ping* remains. Canton has
nothing to do with the present war, and if it loses all three ships
we shall have no excuses to offer the Commander in Chief at
Canton. Should Your Excellency sympathise with us, restore the
Kuang-ping and I promise that she shall take no further part in
the war. If you cannot consent to this, perhaps you will agree
that the armament be taken from the ship, and that her hull
alone be restored, in which case I shall not be disgraced, but will
have some apology to offer to my commanding officer. Trusting
that Your Excellency will appreciate my situation.

The Japanese admiral was not moved by this plea and the *Kuang-
ping* remained in captivity although he did release a somewhat
larger Chinese warship to take home the body of the Chinese
admiral who had committed suicide rather than sign the surrender.

Such courtesy found little echo forty-six years later when the
Japanese attacked Singapore. The preliminaries, however, were
conducted in terms of the greatest politeness. As soon as they had
established bridgeheads on Singapore Island, a letter was dropped
by an aircraft on British headquarters.

To the High Command of the British Army,
You Excellency, I, the High Command of the Nippon Army,
based on the spirit of Japanese chivalry, having the honour of
presenting this note to Your Excellency advising you to surrender the whole force in Malaya.

My sincere respect is due to your army which, true to the
traditional spirit of Great Britain, is bravely defending Singapore which now stands isolated and unaided. Many fierce and
gallant fights have been fought by your gallant officers and men,
to the honour of British warriorship. But the developments of
the general war situation have already sealed the fate of Singa-

pore, and the continuation of futile resistance would only serve
to inflict direct harm and injuries to thousands of non-
combatants living in the city, throwing them into further mis-
eries and horrors of war, but also would not add anything to the
honour of your army. I expect that Your Excellency, accepting
my advice will give up this meaningless and desperate resistance
and promptly order the entire front to cease fire and will
despatch at the same time your *parlementaire* according to the
procedure shown at the end of this note. If on the contrary
Your Excellency should neglect my advice and the present
resistance be continued, I shall be obliged, although reluctantly
from humanitarian considerations, to order my army to make
annihilating attacks on Singapore. In closing this note of advice,
I pay again my sincere respects to Your Excellency,

      Tomoyuki Yamashita.

1. The *parlementaire* should proceed to the Bulit Timah Road.
2. The *parlementaire* should bear a large white flag and the
Union Jack.

That was the end of the courtesies. When General Perceval was
finally driven to surrender he found that Yamashita would not deal
with intermediaries but insisted on Perceval in person coming to
his headquarters on foot and carrying the same flags. There he was
hectored until he had signed an immediate and unconditional
surrender, after which he was forced to march into captivity at the
head of his troops.

Not all surrenders in the Second World War were conducted
with the same ruthlessness. When General Cunningham was on
the point of capturing Addis Ababa, he sent aircraft to drop letters
to the Italian authorities urging them to surrender so that the safety
of the Italian women and children in the capital could be ensured.
He required an answer to be dropped at Diredawa on the following
day, specifying a precise time so that the Italian aircraft might not
be fired on. A Savoia bomber appeared neatly on cue but the note
it dropped only said that it would be back at the same time on the
following day. It duly returned and landed to enable some staff
officers to receive Cunningham's surrender terms before taking off
again. On the third day it landed once more and negotiations went
forward. On this occasion the Italian pilot brought a case of wine
for the South African airmen who had entertained him on the
previous day.

When Colonel General Jürgen von Arnim surrendered to 1st/
2nd Gurkhas near Tunis on May 12th, 1943, he was quickly

forwarded to the headquarters of General Sir Harold Alexander, who gave him supper and a tent for the night. 'I felt,' wrote Alexander,

> He was expecting me to say what a splendid fight he and his men had put up, but I'm afraid I disappointed him. However, looking back, I think it would have been a little more generous if I had been a little more chivalrous.

Quite different was the reaction of Alexander's superior, General Eisenhower,

> When von Arnim was brought through Algiers on his way to captivity, some members of my staff felt that I should observe the custom of bygone days and allow him to call on me. The custom had its origin in the fact that mercenary soldiers of old had no real enmity towards their opponents. Both sides fought for the love of a fight, out of a sense of duty or, more probably, for money . . . For me World War II was far too personal a thing to entertain such feelings . . . None would be allowed to call on me.

On this point the future President of the United States was not wholly sound in his history. The practice of entertaining a defeated enemy pre-dates the heyday of the mercenary. When the Black Prince captured the King of France at Poitiers in 1356, he provided a great dinner for him, the food and wine coming mostly from supplies captured in the French camp.

> The Prince also invited the greater part of the counts and barons who had been taken prisoner. The King of France and his son Prince Philip were put at a well-laid table, set on a dais [and] the Prince himself served the King at table with every mark of humility, refusing to sit in spite of numerous entreaties, saying that he was not yet worthy of such an honour . . . He knelt before the King and added, 'Sir, do not dine miserably because God has not granted your wishes: the King my father will certainly treat you with all honour and friendship.'

Similarly Marlborough received Marshal Tallard with every courtesy, dined with him and sent a white flag to the French army to collected his coach and baggage. His words of greeting to him were, 'I am very sorry that such a cruel misfortune should have fallen upon a soldier for whom I have the highest regard.' Following the custom of the time, he allowed Tallard to send his own aide-de-camp to Louis XIV with his own account of his defeat.

Forty-three years after Blenheim, it was a general in the British army who fell into French hands and it was a general in an anomalous position. Sir John Ligonier had been born a French subject but had gone into exile as a boy with the rest of the Huguenots after the revocation of the Edict of Nantes. He might therefore be regarded by the French as a traitor.

> They led me off to the King [Louis XV], who was quite close, being in the thick of the fight. On the way some of the Household Provost Guards, whom I recognised from their uniforms, pressed in on me and I thought, seeing my situation, they were going to kill me. But when I came to the King, he greatly reassured me, saying with a charming smile, 'Well, general, we shall have the pleasure of your company at supper tonight.' . . . The King was very gracious and paid me every attention at table, which set an example to others.

General Eisenhower can scarcely have believed the Black Prince and King John II, Marshal Tallard and the Duke of Marlborough, Louis XV and Sir John Ligonier to have been mercenary soldiers. It is more probable that his decision not to meet von Arnim was dictated more by the probable reaction of the American press if he had dined with him. There was an ugly precedent in the case of General Sir Charles Townshend, the unfortunate defender of Kut-al-Amara in 1915. He was pilloried in the British press for having dined with Khalil Pasha, his Turkish captor. The same thoughts may have been in the minds of the French generals whom Rommel met at St Valéry in the débâcle of 1940.

> One corps commander and four divisional commanders presented themselves to me in the market place, having been forced by my division to surrender . . . The generals were invited to an open-air lunch at a German field kitchen, but they refused with thanks, saying they had supplies of their own.

Stopping a complete war is a very different matter from bringing a campaign to an end. Historically it was a leisurely process with plenipotentiaries endlessly debating difficult points and eventually reaching compromises. Six months of negotiations preceded the Peace of Amiens in 1801 which ended the war of the French revolution. For three months there was a series of conferences to end the Napoleonic War and the diplomatic haggling was only settled when the allies entered Paris. Even at the end of the Franco–Prussian War some small scope was left for the defeated French to dispute points proposed by the victors.

All this changed in 1918. By mid-August the German authorities knew that they were beaten. The Kaiser declared that 'The war must be ended', and even von Ludendorff admitted that, since the army could no longer hope to win, the diplomats must bring the fighting to an end. Nevertheless more than six weeks elapsed before, early in October, the Swiss minister in Berlin was asked to pass a message to President Wilson, requesting him to 'take in hand the restoration of peace' on the basis of his Fourteen Points. 'With a view to avoiding further bloodshed, the German Government requests the immediate conclusion of an armistice on land, sea and in the air.'

This was easier said than done. America's associates (she formed no alliances in 1917–18) were far from accepting the Fourteen Points as a basis for peace or anything else and it was not until November 6th that the Germans were told that the Western powers were prepared to make peace on the basis of the Points but subject to certain reservations by the European allies.

Marshal Foch has been authorised by the Government of the United States, and the Allied Governments to receive properly accredited representatives of the German Government and to communicate to them the terms of an armistice.

When, in consequence, the German delegates went to Compiègne at seven o'clock in the morning of November 8th, they knew that they would have to accept harsh terms. However bad their military situation was in Belgium, they felt that they had some good cards to play and might be able to ameliorate the Western conditions. They were soon disillusioned. No mention was made of the Fourteen Points. Foch held an overwhelming hand and he laid it down for a grand slam.

Marshal Foch asked the German delegates the purpose of their visit.

Herr Erzberger [Minister without Portfolio] replied that they had come to receive the proposals of the Allied Powers looking to an armistice on land, on sea and in the air, on all fronts and in the colonies. Marshal Foch replied that he had no proposals to make.

Count Oberndorff [representing the Foreign Office] asked the

237

Marshal in what form he desired that they should express themselves. He did not stand on form; he was ready to say that the German delegation asked the conditions for an armistice.

Marshal Foch replied that he had no conditions to offer.

Herr Erzberger read the text of President Wilson's last note, stating that Marshal Foch is authorized to make known the armistice conditions.

Marshal Foch replied that he was authorized to make these known if the German delegates asked for an armistice.

'Do you ask for an armistice? If you do, I can inform you of the conditions subject to which it can be obtained.'

Herr Erzberger and Count Oberndorff declared that they asked for an armistice.

Marshal Foch then announced that the armistice conditions would be read.

There were no negotiations. Once the Germans had asked for a cessation of hostilities they were told what would be required to achieve one. They were not permitted to argue. All they could do was sign.

Germany bitterly resented the way in which the war of 1914–18 was ended. It was a trick. They had agreed to peace on the basis of one set of terms and were forced to accept it on another. In 1945 there could be no such complaint. The allied demand for unconditional surrender by the Axis Powers probably extended the war against all three of them but it left no room for argument.

In practice it was only against Germany that unconditional surrender was enforced. The Japanese succeeded in making one stipulation, the preservation of the 'imperial institution'. In the case of Italy the demand for unconditional surrender led to endless complications and a very untidy result. Mussolini was dismissed and arrested on July 25th, 1943 and it was immediately clear to both sides that the new government of Marshal Badoglio, for all its declaration that 'The war goes on', was intent on making peace. The Western allies had not at that stage considered what peace terms might be offered to a non-fascist Italy and were unable immediately to agree a suitable formula. The United States wanted to insist on unconditional surrender while the British favoured a list of strict armistice conditions. Before this difference could be resolved, the two governments authorised allied headquarters in Algiers to make repeated broadcasts to Italy which seemed to be a formal peace offer.

You can have peace immediately and peace on honourable terms that our governments have already offered you. We are coming to you as liberators. Your part is to cease immediately any assistance to the German military forces in your country. If you do this, we will rid you of the Germans and deliver you from the horrors of war.

Although it was untrue that the allies had already offered terms, since none had been formulated, the fact that terms were mentioned left no doubt that this was an offer of something other than unconditional surrender.

Meanwhile Badoglio was taking up with Hitler the unrewarding task of suggesting that both Germany and Italy should initiate peace talks with the allies. Simultaneously members of his government were trying to make contacts with the West, an undertaking made more difficult because the only Western diplomats within reach, the missions to the Vatican, could only communicate with their governments with codes that the Germans had broken long before. A number of emissaries, some from the army, some from the Foreign Office, were therefore despatched on seemingly innocent missions to Madrid, Tangier and Lisbon to propose peace to Britain and America. Due largely to the intense need for secrecy, some of these emissaries had little or no idea of what the others were doing.

Eventually the Western allies succeeded in hammering out a peace formula which, in effect, stated, 'We insist on unconditional surrender but we do not intend to enforce it.' With this the Italians reluctantly agreed. The problem was the timing of the announcement. The allied view was that the Italians should broadcast their surrender before the main landing was made but, for security reasons, they could not divulge the place or the time of the landings. To the new Italian government such a course seemed suicidal. Their home army, dispirited, ill-equipped and almost without transport, was already outnumbered by Germans in Italy. With more Germans steadily streaming over the Brenner, there were nineteen divisions of them already in the country and the Italian government tried to stipulate that their surrender should not be announced until the allies had landed at least fifteen divisions north of Rome. They were not to know that the most that could be contemplated was a landing by five divisions, to be increased to eight over two weeks, south of Naples.

In practice the Badoglio government was in no position to make stipulations. The allies could compromise both the cabinet and the *Commando Supremo* with the Germans at the flick of a switch.

They insisted that they were going to announce the Italian surrender six hours before they landed and they required Badoglio publicly to confirm their announcement as soon as he could get to the radio station. At the last moment, realising that Rome could not be secured, the government begged for a postponement of both announcement and landing. The allies could not agree. With the troops due to go ashore at Salerno in the small hours of September 9th, Eisenhower broadcast the news of the surrender from Algiers at six-thirty p.m. on the previous evening. When no response was forthcoming from Rome, the prearranged text of the Italian announcement was also put on the air from Algiers. After agonising hesitations, Badoglio finally went on the air at eight-thirty p.m. and then, gathering up King Victor Emmanuel – 'pathetic, very old and rather gaga' – he fled for the sanctuary of the allies without having given any orders to the Italian army, navy or air force. Italy was not easily delivered from the Germans, nor was she spared the horrors of war.

Untidy as the Italian surrender had been, it was at least conducted with more dignity than that of France three years earlier. Just before midnight on June 16th, 1940 the new cabinet headed by Marshal Pétain held its first meeting which lasted less than half an hour. Before one a.m. on June 17th, the Foreign Minister, Paul Baudouin, sent for Señor Lequerica, the Spanish ambassador, and handed him a note:

> The French government of Marshal Pétain requests the Spanish government to act as rapidly as possible as intermediary with the German government with a view to the cessation of hostilities and the settlement of conditions of peace. The French government hopes that the German government, as soon as it takes notice of this request, will give orders to its Air Force to stop the bombing of the cities.

This was a sufficiently precipitate way for a great nation to beg for peace and Lequerica, who was expecting something of the kind, had made his arrangements in advance. Since the cables across the Franco–Spanish frontier were disconnected, he telephoned Baudouin's message to the Spanish consulate in Hendaye, from where a messenger took it across the Bidassoa into Spain and telephoned it to Madrid from Irun. The Spanish Foreign Ministry then sent it to the German embassy who forwarded it to Berlin. In the circumstances it can scarcely have reached the Wilhelmstrasse when, half an hour after noon, Marshal Pétain broadcast to the French people the ominous message, 'It is necessary to stop the fighting.' The remaining resistance of the French forces thereupon evaporated.

It was two days later, at six-thirty in the morning, that Lequerica woke Baudouin to give him the German reply which led the French delegates to the clearing in the forest at Compiègne where, twenty-two years earlier, Foch had humiliated Erzberger and Oberndorff. General Hunzinger and his colleagues fared no better than they had done.

Epilogue

Excess and Indiscriminate Violence

One must exterminate; exterminate to the bitter end.

Lazare Carnot, 1793

In 1947 Henry L. Stimson, who had been Secretary of War under Presidents Roosevelt and Truman, expressed the opinion that 'War in the twentieth century has grown steadily more barbarous, more destructive, more debased in all its aspects.'

Secretary Stimson was in a position to know. Apart from the important office he had held, he had been the president's adviser on the military employment of atomic energy and had coordinated the four years of work that went to construct the atomic bomb. The final decision to use the bomb rested with President Truman but Stimson had had a considerable say in deciding where it should be dropped.

The attack on Hiroshima was not the most destructive air raid in the history of war. Five months earlier, on March 9th, 1945, a force of three hundred and thirty B-29 bombers struck at Tokyo, killing 83,793 of the inhabitants and destroying 267,171 buildings. At Hiroshima 71,379 were dead or missing, 40,653 buildings were destroyed and 8,793 were damaged. Whereas the Tokyo raid had cost U.S.A.A.F. fourteen aircraft and about a hundred men, the plane that carried the atomic bomb to Hiroshima flew unopposed and returned safely to its base.

Did the Hiroshima bomb transgress any of the recognised laws of war? It was certainly contrary to The Hague Declarations of 1899 and 1907 which prohibited 'the discharge of projectiles and explosives from balloons or any other new method of a similar nature' but, in view of events between 1939 and 1945, it is difficult to regard this prohibition as valid. There remains Article 23 of The Hague Rules under which it might have been 'especially prohibited' as coming under the heading of 'arms, projectiles, or materials calculated to cause unnecessary suffering'. It is an insuperable task to decide on the relative suffering caused by various means of killing people, to rule between napalm, 'conventional' explosives or atomic explosion. It is equally impossible to judge the relative necessity of attacking Rotterdam, Coventry, Hamburg or Tokyo. The level of necessary suffering cannot be defined.

There is, however, no reasonable doubt that the decision to use the atomic bomb was taken in the honest belief that it was necessary. It was used in the hope that it would make it superfluous for the U.S. army to invade Japan, an operation which, it was believed, the Japanese armed forces would oppose with all the suicidal fanaticism of which they had shown themselves capable. According to President Truman, 'General Marshall told me that it might cost half a million American lives to force the enemy's surrender on his home ground.'

George C. Marshall, Chief of Staff, U.S. Army, and thus the president's principal military adviser, was not a man given to exaggeration and his troops had recently fought their way through the bloodiest campaign of the war, that on Okinawa. On the other hand, the Americans knew, from their interception of diplomatic messages, that certain members of the Japanese government were anxious to surrender and that it was 'the emperor's heart's desire to see the swift termination of the war'. They also knew, from the same source, that the military leaders were prepared to see Japan destroyed rather than agree to an inglorious peace. There was no way in which Washington could divine which of these factions would prevail and the fact that, after atomic bombs had been dropped, a military coup was staged in an endeavour to prevent surrender suggests that it would have been unwise to assume the success of the ministers urging peace. If the Japanese decided to fight on, and they were only deterred from doing so by the emperor acting in a manner totally contrary to constitutional tradition, the preparations they had made for a last-ditch defence suggest that Marshall's estimate of American casualties was realistic.

It was Truman's unenviable task to weigh the necessity of using a bomb of which the potentiality was largely conjectural but which would probably destroy a medium-sized town and annihilate its population. On the other side of the scale he had to set the lives of half a million Americans and the lives of those Japanese who would die resisting them. That figure could not be calculated but, from experience of the desperation of Japanese defensive tactics, it could scarcely be less than a quarter of a million and might well equal the estimated American losses. To this huge total of deaths among servicemen he had to add the number of Japanese non-combatants who would inevitably be killed not only in the invasion but in the continuing American bombing campaign which, according to General Arnold, Commanding General U.S.A.A.F., would have obliterated every major Japanese city by the end of October 1945. Truman's choice was, therefore, between dropping the bomb or risking a number of American and Japanese deaths which would be ten or fifteen times the total population of Hiroshima. It is scarcely possible to dispute the president's decision that the Hiroshima bomb was 'necessary', however difficult it is to justify the dropping of a second bomb on Nagasaki a few days later.

The atomic bomb was the first primarily civilian weapon in the history of warfare. It was devised by civilians (who belatedly developed qualms about the morality of what they had done) for use against civilians and its employment was resolved upon by a civilian (except to the extent that the president of the United States is *ex-officio* commander in chief of the armed forces). Only its delivery was a military responsibility and, among the senior ranks of the U.S. services, there was a conspicuous lack of enthusiasm for the assignment. General Carl Spaatz, commanding the Strategic Air Forces, contented himself with saying, 'The dropping of the bomb was done by military men under military orders. We're supposed to carry out orders and not question them.' General Marshall 'looked to the civilians to make the decision . . . and didn't presume to exercise any discretion over it'. General Eisenhower, when told of the testing of the bomb in New Mexico,

> expressed the hope that we should never have to use such a thing against any enemy because I disliked seeing the United States take the lead in introducing into war something as horrible and destructive as this weapon was described to be.

The president's chief of staff, Admiral William D. Leahy, wrote in his memoirs, 'In being the first to use it, we had adopted the ethical standards common to barbarians in the dark ages. I was not taught to make war in that fashion.'

These were the natural reactions of professional combatants. The bomb was an excessive and indiscriminate weapon and pointed the way to 'excess and indiscriminate violence' which has always been anathema to any disciplined body. It is fair to add that none of the officers quoted were on record as raising objections to the strategic bombing of German and Japanese towns using 'conventional' weapons and it is hard to understand why a single attack on Tokyo killing 83,793 people should be more acceptable than a single attack on Hiroshima killing 71,379. Moderation in war had vanished many months before August 1945 and the fireball over Hiroshima was no more than the pall at the funeral.

Three days after the dropping of the first atomic bomb the American, British and Soviet governments formally agreed to set up an international tribunal for the trial of those accused of war crimes. Such trials had been discussed in 1918 but, although the

Germans had held some ineffective enquiries into the alleged misdeeds of some of their own nationals, the victorious allies had brought no charges against their former enemies. It would have been difficult for them to have done so since, with the single exception of the German emperor, the accused would have had little difficulty in securing acquittals on the grounds that they were acting on superior orders. Both the American and British codes held this to be a complete defence. The British *Manual of Military Law* laid down that,

> Members of the armed forces who commit violations of the recognized rules of warfare as are ordered by their Governments or their commanders are not war criminals and cannot, therefore, be punished by the enemy. He may punish the officials or commanders responsible for such orders if they fall into his hands but otherwise he may only resort to other means of obtaining redress.

It was not until 1944 that this form of words was hastily changed to the effect that 'members of the armed forces are bound to obey lawful orders only' and adding that,

> The fact that a rule of warfare has been violated in pursuance of an order of the belligerent Government or of an individual belligerent commander does not deprive the act in question of its character as a war crime; neither does it, in principle, confer upon the perpetrator immunity from punishment by the injured belligerent.

This brought the ruling into line with that which had obtained in Germany since the beginning of the century and it was consequently in order to bring enemy war criminals to trial. No allied personnel were similarly indicted since 'the injured belligerents', having been defeated, were in no position to prefer charges.

What constitutes a war crime is another matter. It could be argued that the total destruction of a large and populous town, even if it contains some installations connected with the prosecution of the war, might be such an offence, even if carried out by the winning side, if the act did not substantially contribute to a military decision. The onslaught on Dresden in February 1945, an attack of dubious military value, might be held to constitute such a crime but, in the climate of opinion in 1945, it is inconceivable that the aircrew who carried out the raid and the higher officials responsible, such as the C in C Bomber Command, the Secretary of State for Air and the Prime Minister, together with their American counterparts, could have been brought to trial for it. Nevertheless if tens of thousands of non-combatants can be slaughtered for no better reason than that they live within five miles (see p. 148) of a military target, it is difficult to decide what acts of violence may be considered legitimate. Few would deny that there is a moral difference between attempting to massacre large numbers of people because they happen to live in Dresden or Tokyo and attempting to massacre large numbers of people because they happen to be Jews. Even fewer would care to have to define the line between the two acts.

It is ironic that the first international trials of war criminals should have started at the period when the rule of law in war had collapsed, leaving only vestigial remains. The strategic bombing campaigns which culminated in the destruction of Hiroshima and Nagasaki showed clearly that 'excess and indiscriminate violence' were in the ascendant but it was not only in the use of weapons of gigantic power that the collapse was apparent. Quite as disastrous was the abolition of the distinction between non-combatants and belligerents on which The Hague Conventions were based. The extent of the Axis conquests and the repression with which they were sustained drove men, women and, in some cases, children to take up arms against the invaders and the victorious allies did everything they could to encourage this trend. The desirability, even the urgent necessity, of forming and supporting resistance movements cannot be questioned but it is equally unquestionable that to do so was contrary to the agreed laws of war and undermined the foundation on which they were built.

The Hague Rules and all similar agreements rested on the assumption that mankind could be divided into two categories, belligerents and non-combatants. Belligerents, by which was meant men in uniform, were within their rights to kill or disable all armed enemies also in uniform. Non-combatants must be left unharmed unless they took up arms or acted as spies, in which case they could look to instant execution. The rise of guerrilla movements in the Second World War made nonsense of this assumption. Great numbers of un-uniformed civilians took up arms and acted against uniformed troops who were left with no alternative to treating all 'non-combatants' as potentially hostile. The fact that both Germans and Japanese frequently acted with unnecessary and pointless brutality towards occupied populations made the situation worse but did not affect the basic situation. The Soviet government called out its partisans before the German atrocities could have become apparent. Equally, it was not the excesses of the Gestapo which raised the resistance movement in France and the rest of occupied Europe although it undoubtedly swelled the ranks of those who fought against the occupation.

Unfortunately those who drew up the laws of war at the turn of the twentieth century were looking backwards, largely to the eighteenth century, to wars that were fought on a limited scale with weapons of limited range. To take a single example. The arrangements for protecting hospitals and cultural monuments by agreed markings were valid only so long as bombardment took place at visual range. If a gunner could see his target he could also see the Red Cross and could take precautions which would enable him to avoid hitting the hospital. Once he started shooting at an invisible target with the aid of a map, the Red Cross might as well not have been painted and it is obvious that such markings were useless when the bombardment came from aircraft operating in darkness with a navigational system which made it doubtful whether a substantial city could be identified with certainty.

In much of their work the negotiators at The Hague can be forgiven for failing to appreciate the changes that were to affect war in the twentieth century. Like Dr Lieber, they based their work on the Napoleonic Wars. The greatest campaign they could conceive was the invasion of Russia in 1812 when half a million men, armed with no weapon with a range greater than a mile, took fifty-eight days to trudge from the Niemen to Smolensk. By 1941 Hitler could send three million men, whose armament included bombers which could strike five hundred miles behind the lines, into Russia. Against comparatively stronger opposition, it took them twenty-three days to reach Smolensk. Since while they were working, a one-way trip by air across the Straits of Dover was still a novelty, it could not be expected that The Hague Conference could have anticipated strategic bombers with an operational radius of a thousand miles any more than they could have foreseen intercontinental rockets and nuclear weapons.

The real fault with The Hague Rules was the decision to confine war to 'legitimate belligerents'. This was not, as in the case of weapons, a lack of prevision but a deliberate ignoring of the past. The Napoleonic and Franco–Prussian Wars had shown that, if large areas of territory were overrun by invading armies, guerrilla or *franc-tireur* movements would inevitably arise. The fact had been debated, exhaustively and inconclusively, at the Brussels Conference of 1874 but, since it appeared to raise an insoluble problem, it had been shelved. At The Hague it was ignored and the entire system of regulations was based on the clear distinction between belligerents and non-combatants. The relative stability of

248

the battle fronts in the war of 1914–18 obscured this fault for some time but, when mobility returned to the battlefield in 1939 the question was bound to be reopened. Deep penetration inevitably stirred up armed intervention by non-combatants and the laws of war could only collapse. While the motives which drove oppressed people to take the war into their own hands are comprehensible and, in most cases, admirable, the fact remains that their actions destroyed the laws of war as they were agreed up to 1945.

If there are to be laws of war in the future it is unlikely that they can follow The Hague formulation. It is inconceivable that the nations of the world would agree to renounce the possibility of employing irregulars without uniform as active combatants. One of the Additional Protocols signed at Geneva in 1977 showed the strength of the trend away from the distinction between belligerents and non-combatants by conferring combatant rights on all peoples,

> Fighting against colonial domination and alien occupation and against alien régimes in the exercise of their rights of self-determination as enshrined in the Charter of the United Nations.

Given the contributions made to the history, and in some cases the mythology, of many nations by guerrillas, partisans, *francs-tireurs*, freedom fighters and other designations of irregulars, it was inevitable that they should be formally legitimised but the corollary must be faced. Either civilians are non-combatants and entitled to immunity from deliberately hostile acts or they are combatants and must suffer the consequences. If civilians are to take an active part in the war they must be prepared to be exposed to the full severity which it entails, a severity which must inevitably entail the deaths of many who are innocent of direct participation. There is seldom time in war to examine the credentials of those who seem likely to commit a hostile act. If a nine-year-old child has, in the name of freedom from oppression, the right to throw a grenade at enemy soldiers, it must follow that every nine-year-old child must run the risk of retaliation.

Sir Garnet Wolseley commented that 'private soldiers are often very ignorant of the conventionalities of war'. He might have added that civilians are at least as ignorant and frequently fail to see any valid reason for such conventionalities to be observed. Nor are civilian irregulars under a discipline which can seek to enforce the rules. The observed fact that guerrilla campaigns are more brutal than those waged between regular combatants cannot be blamed wholly or even principally on the soldiery. Such operations lead directly to the 'excess and indiscriminate violence' that regular combatants abhor.

What then can be salvaged from the wreck of the laws of war? With weapons of intercontinental range and unexampled power and with the privileges, and pains, of combatant status conferred on every civilian regardless of age and sex, little remains of the rules so confidently agreed before the First World War. Nor can there be much hope for the plethora of conventions subsequently negotiated. The most that can be looked for is that in limited operations in which all the participants are professionals in uniform and under discipline the customs of war will be observed so long as the fighting takes place in sparsely populated areas. Under such conditions it is in everyone's interest that moderation should prevail and the experience of the campaigns in Sinai, on the Golan Heights, around the Schott-el-Arab and on the Falkland Islands suggests that this will be the case. Even in the Korean War, also fought by professionals, a measure of moderation was observed on the battlefield, though this was not the case in the prisoner-of-war camps. Experience over the same period equally suggests that the laws of war will break down when combatants are indistinguishable from the local population. In Vietnam both the French and the Americans were confronted by opponents able to merge with their surroundings but dependent for many of their supplies on the indigenous population and determined to extract what they needed by fair means or foul. In such circumstances the distinction between combatant and non-combatant, between friend and foe becomes irretrievably blurred. If a peasant furnishes an enemy with food or information how can it be established whether he did so willingly or under irresistible duress? Mistakes, if nothing worse, become inevitable and breed reprisals. A long war exacerbates the problem. Bitterness intensifies as reports, true or false, circulate of enemy atrocities and the level of professionalism falls as discipline becomes dependent on officers with less and less experience. The greatest American atrocity in the Vietnam war, the massacre of My-lai, was not evidence of United States barbarism but a reflection of the level to which their system for officer training and selection had sunk. In Afghanistan, where Soviet regulars are opposed to an armed and embittered populace, there is no evidence that any respect is being paid to the customs of war by either side. This, like the long French operation in Algeria during the nineteen fifties, is a classic example of a situation in which, since there is no distinction between combatant and non-combatant, the laws of war are as irrelevant as they would be in a nuclear war.

If nuclear weapons are not used in future wars, there can be some hope that the Red Cross will continue to be respected on the comparatively rare occasions on which it can be seen but it will continue to be violated when it is invisible to those who pull the trigger. Rigid blockade and unrestricted submarine warfare have already destroyed the laws of war at sea and it has never been possible to agree any rules for war in the air. The protection agreed for prisoners of war survived reasonably well on the Western fronts between 1939 and 1945 but elsewhere was largely disregarded. Soviet Russia has never admitted Red Cross inspection of prisoners of war and, since 1945, China, North Korea and North Vietnam have followed this example. To the other hazards to which prisoners have traditionally been exposed has been added political indoctrination. There seems little hope that this practice can be halted and it is probable that the methods employed will, in time, become more effective.

It may be that new laws of war will be agreed and that these may include the prohibition of the more indiscriminate weapons but it must remain doubtful whether any of the great powers will accept them implicitly. None of them have much cause to put great trust in the loyalty of the potential adversary. Without such trust there can be neither effective laws of war nor any great confidence in the avoidance of war. The best hope for the defence of the world in the future would appear to be a very ancient one, 'Give peace in our time, O Lord.'

Select Bibliography

Abell, Francis, *Prisoners of War in Britain, 1756–1815,* Oxford University Press, 1914

Adams, E. D., *Great Britain and the American Civil War* (2 vols), Longmans Green, London, 1925

Atwood, Rodney, *The Hessians,* Cambridge University Press, 1980

Baker, A. J., *Townshend of Kut,* Cassell, London, 1967

Barber, Noel, *Sinister Twilight,* Collins, London, 1968

Bell, A. C., *A History of the Blockade of the Central Powers, 1914–18,* H.M.S.O., London, 1937

Best, Geoffrey, *Humanity in War,* Weidenfeld & Nicolson, London, 1980

Bethell, Nicholas, *The War Hitler Won,* Allen Lane; Penguin Books, London, 1972

Bonet, Honoré, *The Tree of Battles* (ed. & tr. G. W. Coopland), Liverpool University Press, 1949

Boothby, Charles, *A Prisoner of the French,* A. & C. Black, London, 1898

Boyle, Andrew, *Trenchard,* Collins, London, 1962

Boys, Edward, *Narratives of a Captivity, Escape and Adventures in France,* Newby, London, 1863

Bulloch, John, *Akin to Treason,* Arthur Barker, London, 1966

Burne, Alfred H., *The Noble Duke of York,* Staples Press, London, 1949

Byam Martin, Admiral of the Fleet Sir Thomas, *Letters and Papers* (2 vols) (ed. R. V. Harrison), Navy Records Society, London, 1898

Churchill, Winston S., *The World Crisis* (6 vols), Thornton Butterworth, London, 1923–29

—— *Marlborough: His Life and Times,* Harrap, London, 1933–38

—— *The Second World War,* (6 vols), Cassell, London, 1948–54

Ciano, Count, *The Ciano Diaries* (ed. Malcolm Muggeridge), Heinemann, London, 1947

Corbett, Julian, and Newbolt, Henry, *History of the Great War: Naval Operations* (5 vols), Longmans Green, London, 1920–31

Corbett, P. E., *Law and Society in the Relations of States*, Harcourt Brace, New York (nd), 1951

Crosskill, W. E., *The Two Thousand Miles War*, Robert Hale, London, 1980

Dean, Maurice, *The R.A.F. in Two World Wars*, Cassell, London, 1979

Dillon, W. H., *A Narrative of My Professional Adventures, 1790–1839* (Ed. Michael Lewis), Navy Records Society, London, 1956

Edmonds, J. E., and Wynne, G. C., *Military Operations: France and Belgium, 1915*, vol i, Macmillan, London, 1927

Egger, Reinhold, *Colditz: The German Story* (ed. & tr. Howard Gee), Robert Hale, London, 1961

Eisenhower, Dwight D., *Crusade in Europe*, Doubleday, New York, 1948

Farrer, J. A., *Military Manners and Customs*, Chatto & Windus, London, 1885

Fleming, Peter, *Invasion 1940*, Rupert Hart Davis, London, 1957

Fletcher Cook, J., *The Emperor's Guest, 1942–45*, Hutchinson, London, 1971

Foot, M. R. D., and Langley, J. M., *MI9*, Bodley Head, London, 1979

Frederick III, Emperor, *War Diary, 1870–71* (ed. & tr. A. R. Allindon), Stanley Paul, London, 1927

Froissart, Jean, *Chronicles* (ed. & tr. John Joliffe), Harvill Press, London, 1967

Fuller, F. F. C., *The Conduct of War 1789–1961*, Eyre & Spottiswood, London, 1961

Garland, A. N., and Smyth, H. McG., *U.S. Army in World War II: Sicily and the Surrender of Italy*, Dept. of the Army, Washington, 1965

Garner, J. W., *International Law and the World War* (2 vols), Longmans Green, London, 1920

Gerard, James W., *My Four Years in Germany*, Doran, New York, 1917

Giovanitti, L., and Freed, F., *The Decision to Drop the Bomb*, Methuen, London, 1967

Gooch, G. P., and Temperly, *British Documents on the Origins of the War, 1898–1914* (vol xi), H.M.S.O., London, 1926

Graves, Charles, *The Home Guard of Britain*, Hutchinson, London, 1943

Grew, Joseph C., *Ten Years in Japan*, Simon & Schuster, New York, 1944

Grotius, Hugo, *De Jure Belli et Pacis* (tr. W. Whewell), Cambridge University Press, 1853

Haber, L. F., *Gas Warfare* 1914–15, Stevenson Lecture, Bedford College, University of London, 1976

Hart-Davis, Duff, *Peter Fleming: a Biography*, Jonathan Cape, London, 1974

Hastings, Max, *Bomber Offensive*, Michael Joseph, London, 1979

Henderson, Neville, *Failure of a Mission*, Hodder & Stoughton, London, 1940

Hibbert, Christopher, *Agincourt*, Batsford, London, 1964

Higgins, A. Pierce, and Colombo, C. J., *The International Law of the Sea*, Longmans Green, London, 1943

Holland, T. E., *The Laws of War on Land (Written and Unwritten)*, Clarendon Press, Oxford, 1908

Holls, F. W., *The Peace Conference at The Hague*, Macmillan, New York, 1900

Howard, Michael, *The Franco–Prussian War*, Rupert Hart-Davis, London, 1961

—— *War in European History*, Oxford University Press, 1976

Howard, Michael (ed.), *Restraints on War*, Oxford University Press, 1979

Hyde, H. Montgomery, *British Air Policy Between the Wars, 1918–1939*, Heinemann, London, 1976

Jones, Neville, *The Origins of Strategic Bombing*, William Kimber, London, 1973

Kriegesbrauch im Landkriege: The German Warbook (ed. & tr. J. H. Morgan), John Murray, London, 1915

Kumanyev, G. A., 'The Soviet People's Partisan Movement, 1941–44', *Revue Internationale d'Histoire Militaire*, N° 47, 1980

Larpent, G. (ed), *Private Journal of Judge Advocate Larpent*, Bentley, London, 1853

Lewis, Michael, *Napoleon and his British Captives*, George Allen & Unwin, London, 1962

Lieber, Francis, *Contributions to Political Science* (vol ii), J. Lippincott, New York, 1881

McCarthy, Daniel J., *The Prisoner of War in Germany* (3rd edn), Skeffington, London, 1918

Macintyre, Donald, *The Privateers*, Paul Elek, London, 1975

—— *Admiral Rodney*, Peter Davies, London, 1962

Mackenzie, F., *The Diary of Frederick Mackenzie, 1775–81*, Harvard University Press, 1930

Maclay, E. S., *A History of American Privateers*, Sampson Low, London, 1900

Mansell, Captain John, *The Diaries of Captain John Mansell, 1940–45* (ed. E. G. C. Beckwith), Privately printed, 1977

Manual of Military Law, H.M.S.O., London, 1914

Marsden, R. G. (ed.), *Documents relating the Laws and Customs of the Sea* (2 vols), Navy Records Society, London, 1915–16

Martens, G. F., *The Law of Nations* (tr. William Cobbett), London, 1803

Mockler, Anthony, *The Mercenaries,* Macdonald, London, 1969

Napier, William (ed.), *Life and Opinions of Sir Charles Napier* (vol i), John Murray, London, 1857

Napoleon Ier, *Correspondence* (32 vols), Plon, Paris, 1854–69

Lettres Inédites de Napoleon Ier (ed. L. Lecestre), Plon, Paris, 1897

Nicolson, Nigel, *Alex: The Life of Field Marshal Alexander of Tunis,* Weidenfeld & Nicolson, London, 1973

Nott, G. H. (ed.), *The Trial of Roger Casement* (2nd edn), Hodge, London, 1926

Oman, Charles, *The Art of War in the Middle Ages* (2 vols), Methuen, London, 1932

Origines Diplomatiques de la Guerre de 1870–71 (vol xxix), Paris, 1932

Parmiter, G. de C., *Roger Casement,* Arthur Barker, London, 1936

Perry, W. C., *On the Employment of Mercenaries in Ancient and Modern Times, Nineteenth Century* (vol lxi), 1907

Piggott, Francis, *The Declaration of Paris, 1856,* University of London Press, 1919

Platt, J. Ellison, *Padre in Colditz* (ed. Margaret Duggan), Hodder & Stoughton, 1978

Poyntz, Sydenham, *The Relation of Sydenham Poyntz, 1634–36,* (ed. A. T. S. Gooderich), Camden 3rd Series xiv, 1908

Robinson, W. M., *The Confederate Privateers,* Yale University Press, 1928

Rommel, Field Marshal Erwin, *The Rommel Papers* (ed. B. H. Liddell Hart), Collins, London, 1953

Roskill, S. W., *The Navy at War 1939–45,* Collins, London, 1960

Runciman, Steven, *The History of the Crusades* (3 vols), Cambridge University Press, 1951–54

Russell of Liverpool, Lord, *The Knights of Bushido,* Cassell, London, 1958

—— *The French Corsairs,* Robert Hale, London, 1970

St Chamans, A. A. R. de, *Mémoires,* Plon, Paris, 1898

Satow, Ernest, *A Guide to Diplomatic Practice* (3rd edn), Longmans Green, 1932

Savory, Reginald, *His Britannic Majesty's Army in Germany,* Oxford University Press, 1966

Scott, J. B., *The Hague Conventions and Declarations of 1899 and 1907,* Oxford University Press, 1918

Shirer, William L., *Berlin Diary,* Hamish Hamilton, London, 1941
—— *The Collapse of the Third Republic,* Heinemann, London, 1970
Simpson, Colin, *Lusitania,* Longmans Green, London, 1972
Smith, Sir Sidney, *Memoirs of Admiral Sir Sidney Smith* (2 vols) (ed. E. G. C. Howard), Richard Bentley, London, 1839
Spaight, J. M., *War Rights on Land,* Macmillan, London, 1911
—— *Aircraft in War,* Macmillan, London, 1914
—— *Air Power and War Rights,* Longmans Green, London, 1924
Stark, F. R., *The Abolition of Privateering and the Declaration of Paris,* Columbia University, New York, 1897
Taylor, A. J. P., *English History, 1914–1945,* Oxford University Press, 1965
Terraine, John, *To Win a War,* Sidgwick & Jackson, London, 1978
Thomson, Basil, *The Story of Dartmoor Prison,* Heinemann, London, 1907
Trevor Roper, H. R. (ed.), *Hitler's War Directives, 1939–45,* Sidgwick & Jackson, London, 1964
Trumpener, Ulrich, 'The Road to Ypres: Beginnings of Gas Warfare in World War I', *Journal of Modern History,* 1975
Tuchmann, Barbara W., *A Distant Mirror: The Calamitous Fourteenth Century,* Macmillan, London, 1978
Vattel, Eméric de, *The Law of Nations* (4th English edn), 1811
'Vladimir', *The China–Japan War,* Sampson Low, London, 1896
Walker, T. J., *The Depot for Prisoners of War at Norman Cross, 1796–1816,* Constable, 1913
Warner, Oliver, *The Sea and the Sword: The Baltic 1630–1945,* Jonathan Cape, London, 1965
Webster, Charles, and Frankland, N., *The Strategic Air Offensive against Germany, 1939–45* (4 vols), H.M.S.O., London, 1961–64
Wedgwood, C. V., *The Thirty Years War,* Jonathan Cape, London, 1938
Wellington, Duke of, *The Despatches of Field Marshal the Duke of Wellington* (12 vols) (ed. J. Gurwood), John Murray, London, 1834–39
—— *Supplementary Despatches and Memoranda of Field Marshal the Duke of Wellington* (14 vols) (ed. 2nd Duke of Wellington), John Murray, London, 1858–72
West, Rebecca, *The Meaning of Treason,* Macmillan, London, 1949
Whitlock, Brand, *Belgium under German Occupation: A Personal Narrative* (2 vols), Heinemann, London, 1919
Whitworth, Rex, *Lord Ligonier,* Oxford University Press, 1958

Wilkinson, James, *Memoirs of My Own Time,* Philadelphia, 1816
Wood, E. F., *Notebook of an Attaché,* Century, New York, 1915
Wright, J. W., 'Sieges and Customs of War at the Opening of the Eighteenth Century', *American Historical Review,* xxxix, 1936
Young, Desmond, *Rommel,* Collins, London, 1950

Index

Abbé, General, 51
Aboukir (armoured cruiser), 122
Acre, 158, 180
Adda, river, 132
Addis Ababa, 234
Afghanistan, 250
Africaine, H.M.S., 218
Agincourt, Battle of, 159, 160, 170, 216
Ahlers, Nicholas Emil, 38
Aircraft in War, 138
air offensives, 138–53
   and civilians, 141–2, 143, 144–5, 148–50, 151–3, 247
   atomic bomb, 153, 243, 244–5
   history of, 138–40
   precision bombing, 141–3
   strategic bombing, 144–53
Alabama, 79
Albuera, 191
Alexander, General Sir Harold, 235
Alexandria, 104
Algeria, 250
Algiers, 238, 240
Aljubarotta, Battle of, 159
Allman, Captain Francis, 191–2
Almanza, 229
American Civil War, 13, 47, 57
   and scorched earth policy, 115–16
   blockades during, 120–1
   privateering during, 76–7
   sieges during, 131–2
American War of Independence, 86, 163, 172–3, 180, 229–31
Amery, John, 165, 166
Amiens, Peace of, 88, 163, 181, 218
   negotiations for, 236–7
Anjou, Duke of, 170
Anne, Queen, 90
Ansbach-Bayreuth, 86
Ansbach-Zerbst, 86
Antwerp, 63
Ardennes, 193
Arlington, 220
Armée de Portugal, 113
armies, 47–8, 56, 168
   and Commando missions, 203–4

   uniforms of, 59, 60–2
   see also under individual headings
Arnold, General Henry H., 153, 244
Asturias (hospital ship), 109
Athenia (liner), 126
atomic bomb, 153, 243, 244–5
Audierne, 36, 224
Austria, 22, 75, 104, 105, 119, 185, 189
   and First World War, 31, 38, 121
   and use of mercenaries, 87
Auxonne, 186
Azores, 118

Badajoz, 134, 135
Badoglio, Marshal Pietro, 238, 239, 240
Bailen, Battle of, 181
Bairnsfather, Bruce, 228
Bajazet, Sultan, 158, 160, 204
Baker, T. Harrison, 77, 78
Baldwin, Stanley, 143
Balfour, Arthur, 205
Baltic Sea, 74, 93
Banks, John Cleaver, 34
Barfleur, 73
Barralong, H.M.S., 125
Barrés, Colonel, 140
Bart, Jean, 71
Bath, 183
Baudouin, Paul, 240, 241
Baygorry, 53
Bayonne, 69
Bazeilles, 57
Beasley, Reuben C., 209
Beauregard, Brigadier General P. G. T., 76
Belgium, 65, 105, 237
   German violation of neutrality, 26–7
   guerrilla action in, 62–4
Belgrade, 31
Bellisle, Marshal Charles, 30
Belsen concentration camp, 204
Bergeret, Captain Jacques, 180
Berlin, 28, 40, 240
   air bombardment of, 146
   British embassy in, 26, 31, 32, 33
   French embassy in, 22, 27, 31, 32–3

259

INDEX